The Most Revolutionary Act:
Memoir of an American Refugee

By Dr. Stuart Jeanne Bramhall

Eloquent Books

Copyright © 2010
All rights reserved – Dr. Stuart Jeanne Bramhall

No part of this book may be reproduced or transmitted in any form or by any means, graphic, electronic, or mechanical, including photocopying, recording, taping, or by any information storage retrieval system, without the permission, in writing, from the publisher.

"The low road", from THE MOON IS ALWAYS FEMALE by Marge Piercy, copyright ©1980 by Marge Piercy. Used by permission of Alfred A. Knopft, a division of Random House, Inc.

Eloquent Books
An imprint of Strategic Book Group
P.O. Box 333
Durham CT 06422
www.StrategicBookGroup.com

ISBN 978-1-60911-858-7

Printed in the United States of America

Dedication

To my late parents: my father, who taught me never to let a cop in without a warrant; and my mother, who taught me to see the world as it really is.

Acknowledgements

Rosa Luxemburg, *Die Rote Fahne*, 1919.

"The low road", from THE MOON IS ALWAYS FEMALE by Marge Piercy, copyright ©1980 by Marge Piercy. Used by permission of Alfred A. Knopft, a division of Random House, Inc.

TABLE OF CONTENTS

Preface xi
Part I – My Long Harrowing Journey to Ward 6 1
Part II – The Murder of Oscar Manassa 103
Part III – Revelation, Enlightenment and Despair 167
Part IV – Our Enemies Are All Around Us 231
Part V – The End of a Friendship 297

THE MOST REVOLUTIONARY ACT: MEMOIR OF A U.S. REFUGEE

"*The most revolutionary act is a clear view of the world as it really is.*"
—Rosa Luxemburg (1871-1919)

Preface

Human memory is fallible and events may have occurred in a different order than I recall them. All the people I write about are real. For confidentiality and liability reasons, I give patients and undercover operatives fictitious names and identities. I use real names for friends, family, comrades, and historical figures. In doing so, I run the risk that they have a different recollection or perception of what occurred, what was said, or what was intended. Any discrepancies are unintentional.

Part I –
My Long Harrowing Journey to Ward 6

What can they do
to you? Whatever they want.
They can set you up, they can
bust you, they can break
your fingers, they can
burn your brain with electricity,
blur you with drugs till you
can't walk, can't remember, they can
take your child, wall up
your lover.
from *The Low Road* by Marge Piercy

CHAPTER 1

"Excuse me, madam. Could you come this way, please? We must ask you to undergo a full body search. You have the right to refuse, but you will not be allowed to board the aircraft unless you consent to a search."

The Air New Zealand security guard who detained me at the boarding gate was a tall, pretty woman in her early twenties. She wore tiny pearl earrings with pale blue uniform trousers, a plain white short-sleeved blouse, and a matching blue ribbon attached under her collar. Her accent sounded English to my untrained ear, but this was unlikely. The New Zealand dialect is closer to Australian than British English.

I listened to a number of alternative news broadcasts and was aware the FBI had a no-fly list. Its alleged purpose was to prevent potential terrorists from boarding commercial aircraft. Yet to the best of my knowledge, as of October 2002, only anti-war and environmental activists had been barred from flights they had reserved and paid for. In any case, I assumed the airlines informed passengers they were potential terrorists when they checked in at the ticket counter. After months of nerve-wracking preparations—

the legal and financial complications of closing my practice and selling my home—the last thing I expected was to be pulled out of line once boarding started.

Thanks to the Patriot Act enacted shortly after 9-11, I had no legal recourse if the government banned me from flying. For a split second I identified with the helplessness and shame young Palestinians must feel when they exhaust all other alternatives and strap explosives to their chest.

Too frightened to object, I followed the security guard to a dimly lit alcove at the back of the waiting area. It was furnished with an office desk and two plain wooden chairs. "You need to take your coat off, love." The woman's tone was apologetic as she helped me out of my gray velveteen jacket. I have white hair now, and my boarding pass designated clearly the fact that I was a doctor. She folded the jacket in half over the back of one of the chairs. "And your belt and shoes."

She placed my belt and black oxfords on the desk while she passed an electronic wand over my entire body and patted down my breasts, buttocks, and groin. When she finished, she helped me into my jacket and sat me down on one of the chairs. She put my shoes on for me and would have tied them if I let her. Then she handed back my boarding pass and hurried me down the ramp to the waiting plane.

As a fifty four-year-old board-certified psychiatrist, I was fortunate to have options other than blowing myself up. In October 2002 I made the agonizing decision to leave my home, family, and twenty-five-year psychiatric practice to begin a new life in a small Pacific nation at the bottom of the world. Despite being named on the FBI's no-fly list, I am not and have never been a terrorist. I am not a criminal, either, and have broken no laws. Yet in 1986, for some unknown reason, some faceless higher-up in one of the eleven federal agencies that spy on American citizens decided I posed a threat to national security. Prior to the enactment of the Patriot Act, it was illegal to target US citizens for their political beliefs or activities. Nevertheless, any leftist over fifty can tell you it was a common occurrence as far back as the 1920s for the FBI to target political dissidents for phone harassment and wire-taps, mail intercepts, break-ins, malicious rumor campaigns, false arrest and imprisonment, summary deportation and even extrajudicial murder.

After twenty-three years I am still at a total loss why the government selected me as a target. Although I consider myself a leftist, I am at best a lukewarm radical. I am a physical coward and will go to any extreme to avoid conflict or confrontation. I prefer following to leading. Likewise, wherever possible, I go with the flow and take the path of least resistance.

■

This was my second attempt to emigrate. When I first graduated from medical school in June 1973, I joined the mass migration to Europe by artists and activists disillusioned with the Vietnam War and the Watergate scandal—which ultimately forced Nixon to resign the presidency. At the time I was reacting less to large-scale political corruption than to a deep sense of loneliness and alienation. Already at twenty-four, I knew my future life, at least in the US, would be vastly different from that of my parents and grandparents. I saw a rampant consumerism taking over a culture that previously placed great store in human values, such as community and emotional intimacy. The young people around me were totally taken in by the mass marketing of sex and sex appeal in TV programming and advertising. For young men this meant acquiring all the latest status symbols—via bank loans or time payments, as only the department stores offered "charge" cards—that were supposed to make them irresistible to women. This included the latest-model, fastest car on the market, as well as the latest eight track car stereo and other car accessories to go with it, and the latest color TV and stereo hi-fi. While young women felt compelled to diet compulsively, to spend thousands of dollars a year on the newest fashions and hair-dos and hundreds more on make-up, hair, skin, and nail products—or be doomed to spinsterhood.

After eighteen months in England, I decided I was incapable of working the thirty six-hour shifts the National Health Service required of first year house officers. In November 1974, with a profound sense of failure, I returned to the U.S. At twenty-seven, my highest priority was to complete the specialty training I needed to start a practice while I was still young enough to have children. Finding my native country no less alien or devoid of humanistic values than when I left, I fully intended to either return to the U.K. or emigrate to Canada, Australia, or New Zealand once I completed my psychiatric residency. I never dreamed I would wait twenty-eight years.

∎

I was a very late bloomer politically. Despite my early disenchantment with the "establishment," as we called it in the sixties and seventies, it never occurred to me to blame political factors for my chronic sense of loneliness, alienation, and unmet emotional and social needs. At thirty-five, I fell into Marxism almost by accident when Marti, a fellow doctor and feminist in Chico, California, invited me to join the Committee in Solidarity with the People of El Salvador. CISPES was a national grassroots organization formed in 1981 to protest Ronald Reagan's covert war against El Salvador. Marti, who also turned thirty-five that year, was drawn to Marx for exactly the same reason I was—he helped us make sense for the first time of a political system riddled with contradictions. We had just lived through one of the most turbulent decades in U.S. history. Despite living in a so-called democracy, we had watched powerful defense contractors strong-arm Congress into an unpopular, undeclared war in Vietnam. The result was a massive political and military disaster that cost taxpayers billions of dollars and resulted in massive loss of human life.

Despite embracing most Marxist values and principles, I have never accepted the need for violent revolution to overthrow capitalism. In 1983, after moving to Seattle with my two-year-old daughter Naomi, I joined International Socialists Organization. But only after other members assured me workers would bring down capitalism by uniting and refusing to work—that it was only the counter-revolution that was violent. In fact the only virtues I can claim as an activist are single mindedness (my mother called it stubbornness) and my inability to push my knowledge of government crimes and atrocities to the back of my mind.

Although most Americans saw the 2004 photos of U.S. soldiers torturing Iraqi prisoners at Abu Ghraib, for the most part the images of naked Iraqi prisoners receiving electric shocks, being attacked by dogs, and having water poured down their throats have slipped from conscious awareness. The American public is worn down by the pressures of putting food on the table, keeping up with mortgage and credit-card debt, and finding some way to pay for medical care for themselves and their children. It's much easier not to think about a horrific act for which they share responsibility, as U.S. citizens and taxpayers, but over which they have no control. In other words to move on.

I can't move on. The images linger and fester in my head until there is no room for anything else.

■

I still have no idea which of the eleven spy agencies—CIA, FBI, army, naval, air force intelligence, National Security Agency, or five others whose names are classified—targeted me for harassment. The shadowy figures who spy on and harass American leftists rarely keep a written record of their activities. Moreover they maintain complex links with law enforcement that permit them to commit unthinkable crimes with no fear of arrest or prosecution. The Patriot Act makes it legal for the federal government to tap Americans' phones, read their letters and emails, break into their homes, imprison them without criminal charge and interrogate them under torture. However where it suited their interests, the government has engaged in all these activities from the moment they developed the technological wherewithal to do so—even in the face of federal laws and Constitutional provisions prohibiting them. American nuns who were tortured in El Salvador in the 1980s all reported the presence of blue Anglos in the room who spoke perfect North American English.

Our government comes down hard on dissidents, as ruthlessly as the former Soviet Union or any Third World country. I knew none of this when I became a leftist. I obtained my political education in the most brutal way possible, a process that shattered my oldest and most deeply held beliefs.

■

To the best of my recollection, the frequent hang-ups and prank calls began in November 1986—shortly after I placed a classified ad in an African American weekly called the *Facts*. The ad offered free treatment—based on a "grant"—for African Americans suffering from depression or attention deficit disorder. There was no grant. After three years my Seattle practice was still quite small. As Freud did, I filled the empty slots with low-income patients unable to afford my full fee.

At the time I placed the ad I was extremely disenchanted with my initial foray into leftist politics. Both Seattle CISPES and the Seattle chapter of ISO disbanded in 1985. For a long time I blamed the collapse of both groups on the mostly male academics and professionals who dominated them with their constant moralizing about political correctness. It left me determined to connect with other organizers with working-class backgrounds. Therefore, in late 1985

I began a systematic appraisal of women's, gay, and African American groups for activists whose values coincided more closely with my own. It was easy to connect with women's and gay liberation organizations through friends I had met in CISPES. However, I had no African American friends—or patients—which I hoped to remedy by placing my ad.

Six months later, in May 1987, the harassment escalated after I became involved with two former Black Panthers who were illegally occupying an empty school building to transform it into an African American Museum. Unlike the activists I worked with in CISPES and ISO, who were all strictly law-abiding and provided their own security during demonstrations to ensure no one blocked traffic or damaged parked cars or shop windows.

■

My involvement with Jabari Sisulu started as a result of an ad he ran in the May 5, 1987 *Facts*. It was common for Central Area groups to use the weekly to advertise upcoming meetings. It was in this way that I became involved in a prison reform group that met at the Central Area Chamber of Commerce, and the small anti-apartheid group that met at the Nation of Islam office on East Cherry.

I first met the African American activist in 1984, after CISPES joined the city-wide coalition to change Empire Way to Martin Luther King Way. Unlike Mohammed Ali and Kareem Abdul-Jabar, who took Muslim names when they converted to Islam, Jabari was an atheist and took a Swahili name. It meant *fearless*. He had a reputation for being intelligent, well-read, and prone to angry rants about gentrification and other malicious schemes to undermine the economic and cultural integrity of the African American community. In December 1985 he achieved front-page notoriety after he and five friends broke down the front door of the old Coleman School and renamed it the Seattle African American

Museum. In May 1987 they were in their eighteenth month of occupation.

Jabari actually ran two three-column display ads in the May 5 edition of the *Facts*. The first was a call for black males between eighteen and twenty-five to volunteer as mercenary soldiers to defend Mozambique's communist-led government against CIA-sponsored rebels. This would have rung warning bells for a more experienced activist. The obvious question of who would pay these mercenaries never occurred to me. The second ad was directed at activists frustrated with the "sham" demonstrations at the South African Consulate and who wished to engage in more "militant" activity. In early 1985, I accompanied a friend from ISO and one of his friends from International Workers of the World to some of these anti-apartheid protests. After a month Joe and Mike decided they were a waste of time. They claimed the organizers weren't serious about shutting the consulate down. My friends' ability to deliver this verdict mystified me, as neither of them knew anyone in the leadership of the Coalition to Abolish Apartheid.

Yet their predictions proved impressively accurate. Nearly two and a half years later, the South African émigré who served as Seattle's official representative of the South African government continued to conduct business from his palatial Madison Valley home. Every Sunday the same thirty or forty mostly white activists marched in circles, carried signs, and sang protest songs in the middle of Thirty-second Avenue. After about twenty minutes, a steering-committee member made a speech, and two volunteers mounted the two-tiered stairway leading up the steep hill to the Consul's front door. There were always two uniformed police officers waiting at the top of the stairs. After cuffing them, the cops led them back down the stairs to a waiting patrol car.

Jabari's ad directed us to meet in front of the consulate on Sunday May 13, after the demonstration. Arriving at 11:45 a.m., just as the protest was breaking up, I sat down on the curb to wait for him. It took me several moments to realize there were others waiting with me. Across the street a willowy, almond-skinned African American woman was leaning over to talk to two slightly darker men in work clothes in a Convenient Plumbing work van. The woman, who introduced herself as Debra, made a point of informing me she was a lesbian. The men, who I later learned were new converts to Shiite Islam, got out of the van and introduced themselves as Amen Ptah and Anita. Although Jabari and Earl always referred to them as the Shiite brothers, they were "brothers" only in the sense they were both African American. Unlike Arab Shiites, they were both clean-shaven. Ahmen Ptah was a well-proportioned six feet and had shoulder-length hair that he wore in a coarse hair net. Anita was only an inch taller than me at five-foot-four, and about fifty pounds overweight. He was more outgoing than Ahmen Ptah, who seemed to let Anita talk for him. The latter kept us entertained while we waited with wry quips about corrupt cops and politicians that made them sound like mischievous children.

"This is all very comical." Anita gestured with his head at the patrol car as it pulled away. Like Jabari, he spoke perfect grammatical English and had the same clipped north Pacific accent as my white friends. "It seems the Coalition has worked a deal with someone in Mike Lowry's office." Lowry was Seattle's most "liberal" Congressman and represented the Sixth District. "They agree to stage manage the protests so they don't interfere with consular business in any way. And in return the cops take off the handcuffs and let them go. They don't even take them downtown anymore."

After about twenty minutes Jabari arrived. In his early forties in 1987, he was about five-foot-nine and had the lanky build of a runner. His physical resemblance to Malcolm X, with his short-cropped hair, square gold-framed glasses, and short goatee, seemed deliberate. He began by giving each of us a copy of his FBI file with a cover sheet from the FBI Freedom of Information Officer. To the front of the file he had stapled an undated, unsigned FBI memo directing field agents to cooperate with local law enforcement in "targeting" potential black liberation leaders. The memo didn't specify what was meant by "targeting." It was well publicized that black males were convicted more often and received harsher sentences than white men for the same crimes. I also knew from my prison reform work that it was common for the Seattle police to harass black men. This ran the gamut—from keeping their photos on file and monitoring their activities, stopping them on the street and detaining them for petty or non-existent crimes, fabricating evidence against them, beating them up and charging them with resisting arrest—to shooting unarmed African Americans in the process of apprehending them.

The FBI file was two pages of fine print with all the names other than Jabari's blacked out. It consisted mostly of entries by an unidentified Seattle field agent regarding the activist's attendance at rallies in the mid- and late-seventies that were organized by the Seattle Black Panthers and Students for a Democratic Society. There was also a brief psychological profile, obtained by interviewing one of Jabari's former high school teachers. He spoke highly of the black youth's performance as quarterback for the Garfield High School football team. He also expressed concern over Steve's—in high school Jabari still used his European name Steve Williams—lack of close friendships.

"The FBI has always collaborated with the PO-lice." Although Jabari grew up in Seattle, he put the stress on the first syllable like African Americans I worked with from the South or the big-city ghettos. Jabari loved to dazzle new acquaintances with his incisive logic and instantaneous recall of facts and dates. "It is well known there is a historic government conspiracy to strip the ghetto of its competent male role models. It's nothing but an extension of four hundred years of violent European settler colonialism, as well as the determination of the white ruling class to deprive African American youth of their authentic identity and culture." He finished by reminding us about the unarmed mentally ill black man the Seattle police shot and killed in 1984.

Jabari's claims struck me as credible. It was well known on the left that the FBI spied on and harassed Martin Luther King. I had also heard widespread rumors of FBI involvement in his and Malcolm X's assassinations.

"What about you, Jabari? Don't you ever worry about getting shot?"

Locking his gaze on mine, he pointed his index finger at my breast bone. "White professionals who fraternize with black radicals are at much greater risk than I am."

CHAPTER 2

Jabari held the second meeting of our new group in the home of a white gay radical named Patrick, who helped care for the activist's nine-year-old son, Mosi. In addition to Patrick and the group that assembled in front of the consulate, there was a second new member, a heavy-set friend of Jabari's named Earl Debnam. Earl didn't crave the spotlight the way his long-term friend did. In fact I had no idea prior to that night the two men had co-led the Museum occupation.

Only a few inches taller than Anita, Earl had a full afro and threw his chest out in a way that gave him an illusion of height. He was much darker and better dressed than the other men, in a hand-knit white pullover. He didn't speak at all during the meeting, spending most of it rifling through a briefcase full of papers. My initial, mistaken impression was that he was a bookish intellectual who felt out of his comfort zone in discussing militant political activity.

Jabari had also invited a matronly black woman in her late thirties named Dawn Mason. Unlike the rest of us, who were dressed casually in jeans and overalls, Dawn wore stockings, heels, and a light beige linen suit. Jabari introduced her as president of the African American Parents Association at Meany Middle School.

She, in turn, spent about five minutes describing the Association's outrage about Meany receiving an Excellence in Education Award from the state Superintendent of Instruction. This occurred despite at least six documented and well-publicized incidents of bullying and "racial abuse" by several of Meany's white teachers.

Dawn excused herself to attend another meeting, and Jabari took the floor. "I propose we make Meany the focus of our first action. That we shut it down until they do something about their racist teachers."

After five minutes of discussion it was agreed we would meet at Meany Middle School at eight o'clock on the morning of Monday May 21. As one of two white people in a room full of African Americans, it seemed wrong to question the process the others had agreed upon. Nonetheless, I was extremely uneasy about the group's total lack of planning for a major criminal act. There was no mention at all of how we would go about blockading the school, how we would approach teachers or students who were already inside the building, or what we planned to do after we barricaded the entrances. Nor was there any consideration that some of us might be arrested and would need to post bail and hire attorneys.

The meeting ended and Earl stood up and asked for a ride. He had an accent I couldn't place. I knew he wasn't from Seattle. Although he didn't speak the dialect I associated with a ghetto background, he lingered over his vowels in a way that would have identified him as African American on the phone. I volunteered to take him home. It was only when he gave me directions to the African American Museum on Thirty-third and Massachusetts that I realized he was one of the activists who had assisted Jabari in the takeover of the old Coleman School. A year and a half later, Earl, the last of the six to remain in the building, continued the occupation entirely on his own.

When I asked how he became involved in the Museum

occupation, he became more talkative. "The African American Museum grew out of a 1981 action Jabari and I organized to block the installation of a new police precinct at Twenty-third and Yesler." Earl explained that about twenty protestors occupied the old fire station on Twenty-third and Yesler until Mayor Royer agreed to move the new police station to Capitol Hill. "In fact, an African American Museum was one of our demands. We pointed out that the police weren't reducing crime by locking up more and more black men. It seemed pretty obvious. Genuine crime prevention has to offer black teenagers positive alternatives, such as an African American Museum to help them appreciate their history and culture."

One of the first things I noticed about Earl was that his political analysis was more thoughtful and tolerant than Jabari's. The latter always expressed his radical views in vehemently bitter and angry terms. Earl went on to express grave concern about the increasing level of psychological unrest he observed in Seattle's African American community. "It's a timber box ready to explode if something isn't done soon." Earl, whose family moved from Baltimore to South Central Los Angeles when he was a teenager, had lived through the nightmare of the 1968 Watts riots and the economic devastation that resulted—the small businesses and livelihoods that were destroyed in a neighborhood that had yet to fully recover.

"Routing Interstate 90 through Rainier Valley has decimated our community," he said. "It's shut down enough small businesses to wipe out our whole economic base. On top of that, the whole Central Area has been flooded with this crack cocaine stuff." I knew, based on comments by patients, that before 1984, the preferred drug in Seattle's Central Area was marijuana. Prior to the mid-eighties, cocaine was an extremely expensive habit, reserved for white professional males and a few highly placed African American dealers. Then came the discovery that baking soda could be used to transform cocaine into a solid crystal that could be smoked. Crack cocaine sold for as little as three dollars a cigarette. This put it in easy reach of teenagers and desperate welfare moms.

"Jabari and I mainly see the Museum as a powerful alternative to drugs. It will make this whole area inaccessible to dealers, for one thing." We had arrived at the empty school, which fronted on Twenty-third Avenue. Earl had me turn at Massachusetts and drive three blocks to Martin Luther King Way. We made a left on Martin Luther King to access the gravel driveway that led through the Department of Transportation portables to the entrance at the back of the school building.

"A few years ago this was a thriving business district. Thanks to our city fathers it has been totally ghettoized." The three blocks immediately adjacent to the school grounds looked like a bomb site, with boarded up, partially demolished buildings alternating with vacant lots covered with old timber, shattered glass, broken concrete slabs and knee-high weeds. The school district had closed Coleman School to make way for an I-90 access road. However, the occupation abruptly halted further construction. Earl didn't need to tell me this was a prime location for illicit drug sales. I had lived in East Harlem briefly during medical school.

"After we redevelop the Museum, we will also have a basketball court and a cultural center where children will have art lessons. The result will be a whole island of legitimate commercial activity. Forcing the drug dealers to take their bargain-basement happiness someplace else."

■

On Monday morning I arrived at Eighteenth and Union across from Meany School to find Hussayn, a black Muslim I met at one of the first anti-apartheid demonstrations, waiting for me. I had asked him to bring his video camera to discourage the police from beating up or shooting any of the protesters. I knew older CISPES activists who participated in civil rights and anti-Vietnam protests in which police clubbed and kicked non-violent protestors and then tried to cover up their misconduct by charging them with resisting arrest. I also phoned several white activist friends, as well as Dawn Mason. As I suspected, Jabari never informed the African American Parents Association of our plans to barricade and occupy the school. She said their group would support the blockade but not participate.

Jabari joined us at 8:25 a.m. Without waiting for anyone else, he led us into the school building, where he demanded a meeting with the principal. With Hussayn videotaping, the vice principal, a tall African American in his mid-forties in a short-sleeved shirt and bow tie, escorted us into his office. The administrator responded calmly to Jabari's lengthy tirade about the school's racist teachers and their abusive treatment of black students. Handing us a letter from the state Superintendent of Instruction praising Meany for its low expulsion rate, he gave us a brief explanation of what he called "the Meany Middle School non-suspension policy."

"As you know," he began, "physical punishment by school staff is illegal under state law. However, there is no law against a parent administering corporal punishment." I was already irritated by his smug tone, more so when he gave the two men a knowing smile. He was obviously very pleased with himself. "When one of our students is sent out of class, we summon one of the parents and let them know the anteroom at the back is at their disposal."

In other words because he was forbidden to beat his students, he invited the parents to come and do it with his blessing. Horrified by the sadistic cruelty of this approach to discipline, I couldn't contain myself. "Don't you see what you're doing?" I was about to expound on twenty years of research into the cycle of violence perpetuated by harsh physical punishment. Jabari cut me off. He and Hussayn seemed to have no problem with Meany's "non-suspension" policy.

Again, I felt I had no right to object to what seemed to be a cultural practice—African Americans believed in walloping their kids. As Hussayn continued to film, the vice principal led us on a tour of the school. Then we left.

■

Three days later, Jabari called a third meeting of our as yet unnamed group. This time he invited two representatives of the University of Washington Black Students Union. They wanted our assistance with a sit-in they had called for June 4 to protest the dismissal of a popular black studies lecturer. There was no mention of what Earl later informed me was Jabari's unilateral decision to cancel the blockade of Meany School. After learning I had notified Dawn Mason and Hussayn of our plans to shut down Meany, he concluded that I also tipped off the police. He then notified Debra, Earl, and the Shiite brothers that the action was called off.

The sit-in was our only agenda item. Once again, there was no discussion of the demands we would make, who would negotiate with the university, how long we would occupy the president's office, how we would get food and water if the protest extended more than a few hours, and who would post bail if we were arrested. The students merely gave us the location—the University of Washington administration building—and the time the sit-in would begin.

■

The morning following our third meeting I had an appointment with my first "undercover" patient since my move to Washington State—at least the first I recognized. I already suspected I was under government scrutiny. A week earlier I received a form letter from King County Medical Society cautioning me about the American Medical Association's truth in advertising policy. As none of my colleagues had received letters, I assumed someone reported me for running an ad in the *Facts*. I was skeptical that any of my African American patients, who all expressed profuse gratitude for the free sessions and antidepressant samples, complained. It was more likely the FBI or police assigned someone to monitor the *Facts* and other minority publications and this person notified the medical society.

During my final year of practice in California, it was not uncommon for the state attorney general to send undercover agents to doctors' offices. The goal was to entrap them into prescribing Valium, stimulants, or narcotics in a manner contrary to state or federal regulations. A friend in Chico, a sixty-four-year-old general practitioner, lost her medical license after prescribing two codeine tablets for a former prostitute with a bad toothache. The woman agreed to pose as a patient as a condition of her plea bargain.

According to my landlord, a prominent trial lawyer, Clara's arrest was part of a public relations ploy to help California Attorney General George Deukmejian position himself for a gubernatorial campaign. My landlord believed the sting operation purposely targeted women doctors, who tend to have lower incomes due to family responsibilities, and are thus more likely to cop a plea.

Shortly before I closed my Chico practice, I myself had visits from two men about a week apart who tried to score Ritalin prescriptions by claiming to suffer from Attention Deficit Disorder. I never saw either of them again after insisting they attend, and pay for, at least three sessions before I wrote any prescriptions. As in Clara's case, it was obvious entrapment and illegal. Both of us performed an important community service by accepting low-income and elderly patients regardless of their ability to pay. Targeting us for arrest—like the FBI sting in which agents pose as patients to try to catch psychiatrists in Medicare fraud—was more typical of the police state tactics I associated with totalitarian states like the Soviet Union or Communist China. It left me questioning if there was anything to redeem in a society that rewards altruistic physicians by handcuffing them and dragging them to jail. Yet there was absolutely nothing I nor my fellow doctors could do, except write letters to the *Chico*

Enterprise Record and be even more careful.

Sheila McIntyre was my first female "undercover" patient. She introduced herself as a private investigator. Unlike the scruffy street types who worked for Deukmajian, Sheila was bright, well-educated, and immaculately groomed in a modest sundress and one-inch heels. I began, as I did with all new patients.

"How can I help?"

"With my depression, I guess," she shrugged. Most patients struggle over how much to reveal at the first visit, but Sheila seemed to have rehearsed what she planned to say. "I have this situation, you see. I believe my ex-lover is stalking me. He's a private detective in New York, and I have just moved here to get away from him. He was my mentor for over a year before we became lovers. He trained me in polygraphy. It turns out he has serious alcohol problems."

Sheila had been studying the floor but looked up to gauge my reaction. "I also suspect he has CIA connections. And he's using these contacts to monitor me in my new home. One of them taped a "missing" poster across from my apartment, with a description and a photo." Her face, neck, and shoulders turned a rosy pink. "It also describes a mole in a very personal place."

Sheila gave me an expectant smile as she waited for my response. I was at a total loss, finding nothing in her history that was consistent with any known mental disorder. The vast majority of patients who complain about the CIA monitoring them are psychotic. However this woman manifested none of the interpersonal aloofness or disorganized thinking that characterizes psychosis. She also seemed surprisingly nonchalant about being stalked.

I tried to elicit more information about her background and education. However, she seemed determined to treat the appointment like a social visit. In fact, she appeared far more interested in my personal life than the issues that led her to seek treatment. She was the first and only patient during my twenty-five years of private practice who spent our sessions wandering around my consulting room, examining my artwork and books. I noticed she paid particular attention to titles related to Marxism, union organizing, and feminism. She pulled several of them out of my bookcase for closer inspection.

In contrast to the two men who tried to score Ritalin prescriptions, Sheila's intentions were never totally clear. Like other "pseudo-patients" who would seek my services in coming years, she seemed to have limited objectives beyond befriending me and gathering information about my personal life and political activities. She ended our first session by telling me about a recent trip to South Africa. I sensed it was a clumsy invitation to talk about my own political beliefs and activities. "I believe apartheid is wrong. And I saw an opportunity to use my expertise in polygraphy to assist black South Africans in their struggle."

Only right-wing law enforcement types, with their obsession with "security" and secrecy, had any use for lie detector tests. If Sheila had been to South Africa as she claimed, the CIA had sent her there to work for the secret police. The comment was reminiscent of the bizarre ideological contradictions government informants came out with when they infiltrated our CISPES meetings. We prided ourselves on our ability to spot the geeky strangers who wore odd assortments of political buttons, took copious notes, and videotaped our protest marches. It turned out we weren't nearly as clever as we thought. It would be more than five years before we realized the FBI had deeply infiltrated both CISPES and ISO and deliberately orchestrated the in-fighting and rumor campaigns that broke up both groups in early 1985.

Sheila came to her second and last visit dressed in jeans and a t-shirt. It now became clear she had a secondary agenda of delivering a subtle but unmistakable message of intimidation.

"It's my cover," she explained. "For my current case." This was her only mention of the assignments she took as an investigator, except for informing me about the gun she carried in her purse. As well as a throwaway comment she made when she got up to study a framed portrait of my daughter. "It's a matter of finding psychological weaknesses you can exploit."

The comment came out of nowhere, totally unrelated to any of the other topics we discussed. I took it as an implied threat against my family. I felt a cold shiver up my spine as I ended the session and told Sheila I didn't think I could help her.

CHAPTER 3

I cancelled all the patients I had scheduled for June 4 and arranged for a friend to pick my daughter Naomi up from kindergarten and keep her overnight. Although I had no intention of participating in illegal activity myself, the presence of supportive bystanders was essential to any successful civil disobedience—mainly to monitor and document excessive use of police force. Jabari, the Shiite brothers, and I arrived early and were inside the administration building at 9:30 a.m. when the protest started. Earl and Debra, who arrived after the police sealed the building, remained outside. Altogether, some fifty black students, reporters, and TV cameramen milled around the lobby while a delegation of students met with UW president William Gerberding. The Campus Police were eager to avoid a potentially violent confrontation. Instead of ordering us out of the building, they simply stationed officers at all the entrances to prevent additional protestors from entering.

At approximately 9:45 a.m., a student approached Amen Ptah and Jabari to complain about a campus cop who had thrown him against a wall. The three of us followed the student to the ground floor, where he pointed out a middle-aged officer with bushy sideburns just outside the entrance. Jabari opened the door to speak to the cop with the retro seventies hairstyle. Without warning, he and two other cops rushed in and attempted to drag him outside.

All four men were still well inside the building, which made it easy for the student and me to block their progress by stationing ourselves in the doorway. I hung on to the doorpost for dear life while the three officers tried to drag Jabari through the two-inch space between me and the student. After several minutes of pushing and shoving, they switched direction to haul Jabari towards the elevator at the center of the lobby. They had only dragged him a few feet when he somehow freed both arms and hit one of the cops on the head with his attaché case. In response, the entire lobby took up a loud chant demanding for the police let him go.

Two of the cops grabbed him again. I didn't see the third officer draw his gun. Fortunately, the Channel Five cameraman caught it on tape and it was shown on the evening news. As Jabari wrested the gun from him, one of the other cops shouted, "Get down. Get back. There's a gun."

The chanting stopped as the students crouched in terror on the floor. Taking full advantage of the lull in the protest, the cops whisked Jabari into the elevator and downstairs to a waiting squad car.

■

With Jabari gone, the sit-in was over. We all filed out of the building to join the one hundred or so protestors outside. Earl went up to the students' makeshift stage to make an announcement over the sound system. "I am happy to report our action has been successful. However we have a fallen brother who will need our help to be released from jail. Come and see me."

I approached Earl as the group dispersed and offered to help with bail. He called me at home around 4:30 p.m. The bond would cost $270. I withdrew the money from a cash machine, picked up Jabari's friend from the Museum, and drove him to Inland Bonding, a black-owned bail bond company across from the courthouse. The whole process took about two hours, as Earl insisted on delivering the bail documents in person. As we waited in the second-floor reception area at the Seattle-King County jail, we continued our earlier discussion about the history of the Museum occupation.

"Royer eventually appointed an African American Museum taskforce as a result of our 1981 occupation," he explained. "The Taskforce met for two years and looked at a number of different sites. Everyone, including the mayor, agreed on the old Coleman School, which closed in 1979. Unbeknownst to us, the city had already promised the property to the Department of Transportation for an I-90 access road."

He paused. "Once wasn't enough, though. The fool also double-crossed us in CAPDA." I recalled reading about CAPDA in a *Facts* article about the I-90 controversy. CAPDA stood for Central Area Public Development Authority. "CAPDA agreed early on that the only way to rebuild the Rainier Valley was for a weighted proportion of I-90 contracts to go to black-owned firms. The occupation was Jabari's idea. The night before we had a particularly passionate meeting during which we confronted Bill Wright, who was the assistant mayor, about CAPDA violating its charter. They were steering all the contracts to Royer's white developer friends." I had heard rumors about this meeting—in which the altercation between Jabari, Earl, and Wright supposedly led to a fistfight. Earl didn't mention this.

"The next morning, Wright called Jabari and warned him we needed to stay out of CAPDA or we could forget the Museum. I had just bought a new fourplex, and Jabari came by to tell me about the phone call. It took about five hours to get four other friends together. Then we tramped through the snow and broke the door down. The rest is history."

Despite giving up his fourplex, car, and real estate business to maintain the eighteen-month occupation, Earl was quite modest about his achievement. "The others left after the first month, mostly out of boredom. After the initial attention from the police and a lot of reporters, there was absolutely nothing to do. After three months the city shut off my electricity and water, thinking that would drive me out, as well." Earl laughed. "Of course, it only made me a martyr. I had black women from every corner of the city bringing me blankets, casseroles, and kerosene lamps."

■

It took nearly twenty-four hours for Jabari to be released. He called me collect from King County Jail the morning of June 5. He was obviously elated about the circumstances of his arrest. "We now have an unprecedented opportunity to profile police racism and excessive use of force. I am claiming prisoner of war status and will appeal to the United Nations and Amnesty International."

He said he needed my help. "I can't make a long distance call from here, so I need you to contact Congressman Charles Rangel in New York right away. Ask his office to notify the Mozambique and Algerian embassies about my arrest." He told me about seeing one of the cops throw me against the wall during the scuffle in the elevator. "I also need you to file your own complaint with the Campus Police as soon as possible. It will help to strengthen my own case."

His time ran out before I could ask why he wanted the Mozambique and Algerian embassies contacted. After hanging up, I obtained the number for Rangel's New York office from Directory Information. A young aid with a Brooklyn accent answered. I gave him Jabari's English and Swahili name and described the unprovoked police attack. The aid, who seemed to have no problem with the request, said he was happy to contact the two embassies on Jabari's behalf.

I waited for my lunch break to visit the Campus Police, who had an office behind University Hospital. After a fifteen-minute wait in the reception area, a female detective escorted me to an interview room. We sat across from each other at a small, unfinished wooden table with two thick metal eyelets in the center, which I assumed the police used to secure a prisoner's handcuffs. She began by showing me the front page of the *Seattle Post Intelligencer*. Under a banner headline, I saw myself hugging the doorpost, my face and that of the campus cop next to me the only white faces in a sea of black ones.

"Before we start I must inform you that you are under investigation for obstructing a police officer." She handed me a Miranda waiver to sign, and a pen.

Without a word I got up and left. My ultraconservative father had drilled me from an early age about my Constitutional rights. I must never invite a policeman into the house unless he had a warrant or submit to police questioning without a lawyer. If Americans didn't insist on their rights, they would lose them.

■

That night I got five hang-up calls around 6:00 p.m. In each case the phone rang twice. However, by the time I picked it up the caller had disconnected. Over the weekend I received calls from two women and a man asking for three different people. I had been getting hang-up calls and wrong numbers for six months. Up until then I'd blamed the problem on moving to a new house. Even after a lesbian activist I treated for depression described similar prank calls.

I had always dismissed Colleen's complaints as paranoia, despite seeing three other women who reported a similar pattern of hang-up and prank calls. I was unaware at the time of Colleen's affair with the ex-wife of an FBI field agent. The other women were technically whistleblowers rather than activists—the first was involved in a product-liability suit against asbestos manufacturer Johns Mansville; the second was the ex-wife of a Department of Defense scientist who engaged in illegal biological warfare research; and the third a retired investigator who had an affair with a member of a secret CIA assassination squad. Two of the women also complained of having mail stolen and break-ins in which intruders stole computers and legal documents. Except for Colleen, who for some reason blamed North Seattle Community College for the harassment, they all blamed the CIA, which plays a prominent role in most persecutory delusions.

However, given the other women's whistleblower status, I found their complaints of prank calls and illegal break-ins perfectly plausible. Yet when all four of them attributed frankly bizarre behaviors to the intruders, such as moving personal items, stealing dirty laundry, ejaculating on armchairs and leaving fecal stains on bath towels, this seemed to invalidate the reality basis of their other claims.

On Monday morning a dry cleaner I never heard of called demanding that I pick up my items. At 5:30 that afternoon I received two calls from a woman who addressed me by name, giggled, and hung up. An hour later I received seven calls from Coast Guard maritime engineers on the same mass paging system—someone had paged all of them simultaneously to my home number. On Tuesday morning I was awoken at 6:30 a.m. by a woman trying to reach Bondo Advertising. After receiving four more calls for the ad agency, I phoned the number listed in the yellow pages. The office manager left the line briefly and came back to apologize. Someone had mistakenly forwarded their second line to my home number.

I had no doubt by now the prank calls were deliberate harassment, presumably in retaliation for my role in the UW sit-in. It made no sense to complain to the police about phone harassment that most likely originated with either the Campus or Seattle police—to "punish" me for interfering in their unlawful assault on Jabari. Especially since none of the callers made overt threats. By complaining that strangers were annoying me by repeatedly dialing my phone number, all I would accomplish was to get myself labeled as mentally ill. A much better solution was to simply increase my political activity in a publicly visible way. The authorities would leave me alone, I reasoned, once they realized I couldn't be intimidated.

On Wednesday morning I phoned Jabari at home to tell him I was forming a Jabari Susalu Defense Fund to raise money for his legal costs. After the massive publicity surrounding his arrest, several white friends warned me about the black activist's emotional instability and unreliability. A year earlier Jabari volunteered to be arrested at the consulate, only for the cops who cuffed him to find a handgun in his jacket pocket.

After the haphazard planning for our two "actions," as well as his abrupt reversal at Meany School, I shared my friends' reservations. The fact remained the Campus Police had attacked an innocent man and were fabricating evidence to conceal their misconduct. The official police report, published in both the *Post Intelligencer* and the *Seattle Times*, stated Jabari opened the back door of the UW administration building to let in more protestors—and hit a campus cop with his briefcase when the officer tried to close it. The police version also claimed it was Jabari who pulled the officer's gun from its holster and that the activist had so-called bomb paraphernalia in his briefcase. At trial this turned out to be a roll of masking tape and two flashlight batteries.

My first official act as chair of Jabari Susalu Defense Fund was to persuade the editor of the *Seattle Gay News* to publish a 250-word op-ed describing the unprovoked police attack as it actually occurred. Like the *Facts*, the *Gay News* was a free weekly with a circulation that included most of the white progressive community, both gay and straight. I based the article, which came out the following weekend, around the video clip Channel Five played the night of Jabari's arrest. It showed him freeing his arms when one of the officers let go to draw his gun—and also that that the activist hit him with the briefcase in self-defense.

As my practice was only half-full, I also used large blocks of unscheduled time to become Earl's unofficial chauffeur and administrative assistant. On Wednesday afternoon I picked him up at the Museum and drove him downtown for a meeting with the assistant director of the Department of Transportation. The DOT still held first option to buy the school property. I found Earl waiting for me on the corner of Twenty-third and Massachusetts in a freshly creased, dark gray pin-striped suit, a dark blue power tie, and freshly shined wing tips. He invited me into the assistant director's office, introducing me as a doctor and one of his supporters. Fortunately, I wasn't called on to say anything. The meeting was the first of many involving complex negotiations that went totally over my head.

When the twenty-minute appointment ended, I drove him to Inland Bonding. At the arraignment Judge McCutcheon re-jailed Jabari and raised the bail to $25,000, after he rejected bail conditions prohibiting him from participating in any political protest activity. Earl had asked me to bring the title deed to my house, and I was prepared to sign it over as collateral. After delivering the bail notice to the jail, we drove to my office. Then based on a draft Earl had written in long-hand, I typed and addressed twenty copies of a letter to the DOT, the mayor, the school superintendent, all nine City Council and all seven school board members, and Jesse Weinberry, the black legislator who represented the Thirty-seventh District.

As I worked my way through the five-page chronology we enclosed with each letter, it became clear the occupation owed its success, not to Earl's willingness to sit in the dark for eighteen months, but from the sustained organizing that began the day he and his friends broke the door down. It was Earl who, using UW black studies professor Dr. Sam Kelly as a facilitator, organized the packed neighborhood meetings that forced Royer to call in a federal mediator. Who forced the mayor to recognize the occupation as a political, rather than criminal, act and to agree to restore the building's electricity and water. It was also Earl who formed the first Museum Support Committee, with help from the women who brought him blankets and food. Beginning in March 1986 they used diesel-powered generators to put on events at the Museum, including a forum on AIDS and racism and films on Haiti and Central America.

Royer had no intention of honoring the commitments he made during mediation. In late 1986 he secretly ordered a police SWAT team to storm the building. After seeing this in the chronology, I asked Earl about it.

"It was Michael Preston who called me," he recalled. "In the late eighties Preston was the only black member of the Seattle school board. I had my phone transferred from my fourplex to the office I set up in one of the classrooms. According to Michael, the police were bragging about having a bullet with my name on it. It was a very spiritual time."

I thought Earl was being ironic. Over the next few months I would learn my new African American friend had a very personal relationship with "Old Massa," as he referred to God. He was saying, in essence, that he prayed for the police to spare his life. Yet even Earl couldn't say so openly to a white activist he barely knew. There is a powerful stigma on the left against any kind of spirituality. It supposedly diverts energy inwards that should go towards organizing.

Earl laughed, clearly relishing the recollection. "I remember the *Seattle Times* reporter who came to interview me. I opened my desk drawer to rummage around for a news clipping. I forgot the gun was there till I saw his reaction. Most white people are actually a light shade of pink. This guy turned as white as this sheet of paper." Earl held up the first page of his notes.

"After phoning me," he continued, "Preston also recruited Sam

Smith to help." In 1987 Sam Smith was the only black city council member. "Between the three of us, we must have generated a hundred calls each to the mayor and chief of police. It was three in the morning when I got Michael's second call. Royer had called off the raid.

"Let's say it was one of our mayor's more rash moments. It's far easier to kill your enemies by putting on a suit and calling a committee meeting. The Museum is ours now. The impasse is keeping the redevelopment under community control." He shrugged and let out a wistful sigh. "We have 50 percent unemployment among black men under twenty-five. And we know the mayor and his cronies too well. If we let the city do it, they will give all the contracts to the same white developers who got the I-90 contracts and revamped Martin Luther King Park."

CHAPTER 4

During Jabari's second jail stay, he and Earl made the joint decision for our group to be reborn as the new Museum Support Committee. In keeping with our new name, we held our fourth meeting at the Museum on Saturday, June 13. Although I had immense respect for Earl's goal of using the African American Museum to generate employment and provide an alternative to drug dealing and gang activity, I was extremely pessimistic about the long-term viability of any group that abruptly changed focus every week. I responded to Jabari's ad thinking he intended to close down the consulate. Instead we agreed to barricade ourselves in Meany Middle School. We proceeded to abandon this action without a word of discussion to participate in a sit-in at the University of Washington. Despite the front-page publicity it generated, the UW protest was a dismal failure. The demand for the university to rehire Dr. Jones evaporated when the quarter ended on June 11, and 90 percent of the Black Student Union left campus for the summer.

The only new person that afternoon was a forty-year-old African American woman named Ruth. I had phoned to invite her after getting her name from a black acquaintance I'd met at an ISO meeting. She came to the meeting wearing two nylon windbreakers, one gray and the other dark blue, a hot pink calf-length skirt, full-length bright red slacks, and a felt hat decorated with multiple bead necklaces and two large crow feathers. As she watched Ruth hand out Xeroxed copies of her poetry, Debra learned over to whisper to me that she was a professional beggar. This confused me. I knew from our phone conversation that Ruth had a master's degree in counseling.

The meeting was a total disaster. Jabari monopolized the entire ninety minutes expounding on his theories that European settler colonialism was and is maintained with terrorism, government mob violence, and deliberate genocide. After my experience in CISPES and ISO, the scenario felt uncomfortably familiar. Once again, male activists were denying me any input into the political work they expected me to take on.

Debra stopped me in the parking lot afterwards. She was just as frustrated as I was with the chaotic meetings and our failure to follow through with the projects we agreed on. I was also alarmed about a warning Jabari gave me about Earl being a hustler and not to trust him with money I raised for the defense fund. The two men were best friends and inseparably linked in the eyes of the community—not only in the Black United Front and Museum occupation, but as former business partners. The idea of forming a separate Women's Support Committee was Debra's. However, I was quick to agree.

Despite our decision to form our own group, I continued trying to raise money for Jabari's legal expenses. When I attended the protest at the South African Consulate the next morning, it became painfully obvious that Jabari's support was limited to Earl and me. After giving a brief speech before the volunteers mounted the steps to be arrested, I collected exactly $35—from two white women. The two African American men I talked to expressed open contempt for Jabari's refusal to agree to the bail conditions. In their view, an activist who took this position had to be willing to do the time—unless his supporters agreed beforehand to cover his legal costs. The next day I scrapped my fundraising efforts and covered the retainer myself for Jabari's first attorney, Rod McGiven, with a personal check for $250.

■

Meanwhile, the phone and personal harassment intensified. In addition to the barrage of prank calls, there was loud static on all of my incoming and outgoing calls, which were frequently cut off. Anonymous callers tied up my office answering machine with long stretches of elevator music. Patients would receive a recorded message telling them that my office number had been disconnected. I saw strangers watching the house from the grassy verge across Third Northwest, while unshaven strangers waited in their cars in my office parking lot and pulled out after me. I often received a single hang-up call after a phone conversation with another activist, and the moment I walked in at night, a forceful reminder I was being monitored.

I awoke nearly every morning at 2:00 a.m. to the sound of car gangs gunning their engines and squealing their brakes as they drove up and down Third, playing rap music or Martin Luther King speeches at full blast on their car stereos. Two mornings in a row I was awoken by solitary drunks standing on the corner nearest my home and swearing at the top of their lungs. I sometimes heard rustling noises in the yard once the car noises and yelling stopped. Terrified one of these hostile strangers would break into the house, I would remain awake the rest of the night.

I was mystified to find myself the focus of so much attention. Such extensive activity was clearly beyond the scope of the Seattle police. It was well documented that the federal government and local police collaborated in spying on anti-Vietnam War activists. Jabari wasn't the first to suggest this practice continued into the seventies and eighties. Angered by the possibility the CIA, FBI, or some other federal agency was involved in the harassment, I was more determined than ever not to be intimidated. My daily routine assumed a manic, driven quality as I tried to be as public as possible about my political activities. In addition to doing Earl's typing and driving, I began volunteering two half days a week at a free clinic in the mainly African American Yesler Terrace housing project.

In the beginning my only real fear, as the subject of an active police investigation, was that cops would appear at my door to arrest me and place Naomi in foster care. However, I addressed this by making sure we were never alone together. My daughter and I spent our evenings at the home of a CISPES friend who was also a single mother. I stayed at Gloria's till Naomi fell asleep and returned at eight-fifteen every morning to take her to school.

It was an ideal plan in theory, except for my inability to fall asleep in an empty house. Many nights I laid in bed fully awake until morning, becoming more and more hypersensitive to traffic noises or rustling in the yard, only too aware I might only be asleep for an hour or so before being awakened by squealing brakes or yet another prank call. After five days without sleep, I found myself dwelling more and more on the suicides and accidental deaths the CIA sponsored death squads "arranged" for union and religious activists in Central America. Bursting into tears as I drove Earl to an appointment at the *Facts* office, I told him about the prank calls and men I observed following me.

"What I find the hardest," I confided, "is not knowing how far they might go." I shared what I knew, through my CISPES work, about CIA-sponsored death squads. "There is always a standard progression, from psychological harassment, break-ins, and property damage to beatings and rape, and eventually kidnapping and murder."

To my surprise he took all this in stride. I picked him up an hour later and he drove my car because I was too upset. We spent the rest of the afternoon cruising around the Rainier Valley and south Seattle, as he talked about going to prison at sixteen for nearly killing a white boy, and his political initiation by the Black Panther Party.

"I was inside at the same time as James Jackson, who was actively recruiting us into the Black Panthers," he said. I already knew Jackson was Angela Davis's lover, having read the love letters she wrote him while she herself was in prison on trumped-up murder charges. "After I got out, the undercover operatives were all over our meetings. We generally knew who they were and why they were there. It was a very elaborate FBI operation called Cointelpro."

He assured me the people following me only wanted to scare me—a nice way of telling me I was overreacting. "The basic problem is making this sudden leap into militant political activity without having a clear sense of what you're trying to accomplish." He went on to tell me about the psychologist he saw in prison who helped him understand the unconscious reasons that caused him to end up there. "Growing up we all watched with immense admiration as the inmates from the local prison went on work release and strolled past us to the factory where they worked. This posed an immediate challenge, though not a conscious one, to all of us."

He turned to look at me when we stopped at a light. "I still think of you on the front page with your arms around a policeman. That's what you were doing, wasn't it? Proving yourself?" It was very embarrassing to have this pointed out, but I knew it was right. "It's okay to want a revolution. However, real political change takes infinite patience."

It became clear as we continued to drive that Earl viewed his life as a continuum of significant relationships. He told me about the prison guard who believed in him and gently nudged him out of his profound, perpetual rage against the white race. And his first white lover, who recognized his skill in drawing and painting and encouraged him to become an artist. And his African American mentor in Portland, who got him to put his talent to good use by helping him establish the first African American museum in the Pacific Northwest.

"He taught me everything I know about organizing, even after the night he put his hand on my knee and tried to seduce me." Earl laughed. "He only tried it once. In an extremely close collaboration that continued a long time afterwards."

We became lovers that night. We drove to my house, where I reheated a chicken stew while Earl sliced and fried two sweet potatoes he found in my pantry. Then we sat in my living room until 2:00 a.m., while Earl smoked and told me stories about his family growing up. I learned about the long discussions his parents had with Earl and his eleven siblings at the dinner table—about current events, political issues, and why people behaved the way they did. He also told me about the white man who shot and killed his older brother shortly after Earl got out of prison—how his mother used the intense bond between them to stop him from going after the killer.

The next morning I felt compelled to tell him about Jabari's warning not to trust him with money. Earl had just finished pressing his trousers and was bringing in the last of the three ten-gallon jugs he had loaded into my car to fill with tap water. The old Coleman School still had no water. Thirty gallons could last a week for drinking and personal hygiene, provided Earl only flushed his one working toilet once a day.

I started to cry as I repeated the awful things his best friend had said. I didn't believe Earl was a hustler. Yet it was hard to be sure where he got money for food and other necessities when the museum occupation took up most of his time. I knew he co-owned a book distribution company that sold black history books. I also knew he was extremely generous before he lost his real estate business—that dozens of people owed him money. Once when he needed fifty dollars for a phone bill, I drove him to a friend's house to collect one of these debts.

Earl's face and voice tightened with anger. "He's at it again, is he?" Apparently this wasn't the first time Jabari had accused Earl of being a hustler. Even though the clear picture I got was that Earl, the stable one, was repeatedly bailing Jabari out of jail for political stunts, as well as rescuing his friend's construction company when his radical politics caused him to lose a major contract with the city.

"Among white activists he has a reputation for being pretty unstable, Earl," I told him. "He can get pretty paranoid at times." I reminded Earl about Jabari canceling the Meany Middle School occupation after deciding I was an informant.

"No more so than any of the rest of us." Earl's reaction, which reminded me of an indulgent parent with an incorrigible child, puzzled me. If a friend accused me of dishonesty behind my back, I would immediately end our friendship. This was a new kind of tolerance I never encountered in the white community. "In the black community it's called a crab pot. You put a bunch of crabs in a big bucket and they all push each other down because it's the only way they can get to the top."

■

The demands of Earl's political life meant he stayed overnight once a week or even less. I was still on my own most nights to worry whether the car gangs who blasted the neighborhood with their car stereos or the disgruntled drunks who yelled obscenities from the corner would try to break in, shoot at the house, or even set fire to it. When the public schools let out in June, I contacted friends in Chico about taking Naomi for the summer. Andrea was my labor coach, and she and her brother Phil had been de-facto godparents before Naomi and I moved to Seattle.

I left the choice up to my daughter. She had come home for a bath before going to Gloria's for the night. I was sitting on the toilet seat waiting to help her rinse her hair.

"You know I'm worried about being arrested for the demonstration?" I asked. My daughter had seen the front-page photo in the *Post Intelligencer*. She gave me a quick nod and pursed her lips, unsure she wanted to have this conversation. "You must know that I want you to stay with me more than anything. But if the police come and take me to jail they might not let you stay at Gloria's." I waited but got no reaction. "Andrea says it's okay if you go to California and stay with them till I figure out what the police are going to do. But it's up to you."

"I want to go to California," Naomi blurted, which was unequivocal. Her clear blue eyes were wide open with terror, and the quiver in her chin told me she was about to cry. My daughter had inherited all her father's best features—a perfectly proportioned heart-shaped face and thick blond hair with a natural curl I styled into a short pageboy.

I didn't blame her. She saw her mother, an unusually resilient and strong-willed adult, nearly paralyzed with apprehension. And she no longer felt safe in our home.

I booked a ticket for Phil to fly to Seattle on June 18, and made Amtrak reservations for June 20 for him to return to Chico with Naomi. I tried to be upbeat about the big adventure, as I helped her choose the clothes, books, and toys she would take, and taught her to wash her hair and cut her nails herself. She took obvious pride in this big step towards independence. This helped counterbalance her misgivings at being separated from her mother for the first time.

I was too big a coward to wait for the train to leave. We said our goodbyes as she and Phil waited in the check-in line. Twice I saw her lower lip quiver as she fought to pull it all back. I was determined to live up to her example. Exerting monumental self-discipline, I turned and walked at a normal pace to the terminal exit. I just made it outside before I broke down sobbing.

■

The next morning Debra and I held the first and only meeting of the Women's Support Committee in my living room. Of the six women I invited, only two showed up—a fifty-year-old African American woman I'd met at the South African Consulate, and a forty-year-old white lesbian I worked with at the Seattle Counseling Service for Sexual Minorities. Debra invited no one. It took about a minute to agree on a goal: to develop a project to help at-risk African American children and teenagers. We then spent about ten minutes brainstorming possibilities. I suggested a latchkey program for minimum-wage African American women who couldn't afford child care and left their kids alone after school.

Debra took offense at the comment as being racist and blasted me with a loud tirade about my insensitivity and inexcusable behavior. "I am sick to death of white women who think they can play Lady Bountiful and decide what's best for African American women. Who think it's okay to condescend to us for our own good. And at the same time are totally blind to their own racism." Then she stormed out of the house.

When I told Earl about her outburst, he said she was most likely a federal agent. We were sitting on my large bungalow-style porch which faced Fifty-fifth. I no longer let him smoke in the house because it inflamed my sinuses. "They do this, you know. Posing as extreme feminists."

I found this very unlikely but kept it to myself. "What if I *am* racist, Earl? Racism is unconscious. Most white people are totally unaware of their racist attitudes."

He shook his head. "Racial intolerance goes both ways if you stretch history back far enough." He went on to talk about a legend the first slaves brought to America about driving white people out of Africa. "The black kings viewed them as a curse on society because they were physically unclean and known for lying and stealing. A group of nobles on camels rounded them all up and forced them to march thousands of miles across the burning sands wearing nothing but a loin cloth."

He then revealed he had phoned Debra prior to our Saturday meeting to confront her about splitting up the Museum Support Committee. "She assumed I told you about my suspicions and created a scene to avoid being exposed."

At the time I dismissed his comments as pure male chauvinism—the formation of a separate women's committee was already a major source of conflict between us. I was unaware then of documents circulating in the African American community linking several prominent black "feminists" with a covert operation allegedly spearheaded by Gloria Steinem. Steinem, a prominent white feminist, had admitted publicly—in the *New York Times* and the *Washington Post*—that she worked for a CIA front group called the Student Research Service in the late fifties and early sixties spying on student festivals. A radical feminist organization called the Redstockings Collective first outed Steinem and the CIA-linked foundations and publishers that financed *Ms Magazine* in 1975.

In 1979 the *Village Voice* reprinted their expose, after Steinem and her powerful friends forced Random House to censor details of her intelligence connections from the collective's 1979 book *Feminist Revolution*. Steinem provoked similar controversy in the African American community after she promoted Michele Wallace's 1979 book, *Black Macho and the Myth of Superwoman*, on the cover of *Ms Magazine*. In addition to demeaning all the black power leaders of the 1960s, Wallace ridicules anti-slavery heroes Harriet Tubman and Sojourner Truth for working alongside black men.

CHAPTER 5

The prank calls and phone disruption persisted, and I continued to be followed when I went out in my car. This puzzled me, as I had ceased any formal involvement with the Museum Support Committee. The group that first formed on May 13 outside the South African Consulate held one meeting after Debra and I withdrew and disbanded. By this time the Jabari Sisulu Defense Committee was also defunct. His attorney, an officer in the National Lawyers Guild, kept my check for a week and a half and returned it. McGiven, who had seen the Channel Five news clip, fully supported our claims that Jabari was defending himself against an unprovoked and unlawful attack by UW Campus Police. Yet after three weeks, the attorney had yet to get a coherent account from Jabari of the events leading up to his arrest. Every time they met, he went on long, fanciful tangents about claiming prisoner of war status as a descendent of slaves and his right to be tried on an Indian reservation.

I still believed I could put an end to the harassment, if necessary by identifying and exposing the people responsible. I knew even then what a daunting task this would be. In 1987 my knowledge of domestic intelligence activities was limited to rumors about CIA involvement in the murder of the Kennedy brothers and Martin Luther King. It was technically illegal for the CIA to engage in any covert operations on U.S. soil. However, in June 1987, along with the rest of the American public, I got a crash course in clandestine CIA activities with the major media attention the Iran Contra scandal received. "Irangate," as it was called, involved the illegal sale of weapons to Iran, which in 1985 was an enemy state, to finance an illegal CIA war against the Sandinista government in Nicaragua. The details of the weapons sales were first leaked to the press in early 1986. A year later, in May 1987, a joint Senate-House select committee launched a congressional investigation into what was clearly a CIA-orchestrated operation to finance the Nicaraguan Contras after Congress cut their funding.

Once I suspected the attention I was receiving involved either the FBI or CIA, in addition to the Seattle police, I began watching the Congressional hearings carried live by C-SPAN and re-broadcast at five every evening for West Coast viewers. I listened to testimony from a range of witnesses that included Reagan's current and former national security advisors, high-level officials in the Pentagon and State Department, CIA officials and contract agents, arms dealers, and pilots who flew the small aircraft delivering rifles and machine guns to the CIA-backed counter revolutionaries in Honduras. It left no doubt that 1973 legislation to curtail CIA involvement in domestic spying and other criminal activity had accomplished nothing. It simply forced the federal spy agency to become more sophisticated by employing non-career "contractors" for most of their illegal operations.

Obviously the CIA's involvement in covert wars and global arms deals had nothing whatsoever to do with my own situation. However, other evidence that surfaced during the hearings revealed that CIA-backed Contras were supplying Columbian cocaine to the

Los Angeles gangs that cooked it down into crack. This electrifying revelation tended to validate claims that Edna Laidlow had made in 1984 about street-level CIA involvement in drug dealing and other criminal activity.

It came as no surprise that the Select Committee on Iran Contra went into a closed executive session to take testimony that the same small planes that flew weapons to Central America transported cocaine, with CIA support and protection, back to the U.S. This meant none of this information appeared on network TV or in any major newspapers. However, the names of pilots and contract agents who supplied the small aircraft and operated the landing strips were leaked to a now-defunct left wing weekly called the *Guardian*, which broke the story in May 1987.

The *Guardian* blamed "Irangate" and the cocaine smuggling on an out of control "Shadow Government"—an unspecified group of power brokers outside the Constitutional branches of government who had ultimate control over U.S. military and foreign policy decisions. In June 1987 the only individual publicly associated with this so-called "Shadow Government" was Colonel Oliver North, who was a contract CIA agent, as well as a Marine and member of the National Security Council. North was also the alleged architect of the scheme to fund the illegal war against Nicaragua through illegal sales of automatic weapons and anti-tank missiles to an enemy state. Although North's involvement in cocaine trafficking never made it into the mainstream media, there was good TV and print coverage regarding his involvement in lesser crimes, including investment fraud, embezzlement, and illegal phone taps and clandestine break-ins that targeted American citizens.

■

The first Saturday in July, after watching the Iran Contra hearings until 2:00 a.m., I called Edna Laidlow at her son's home in Maine. It was the first time we had talked since her move to the East Coast in early 1985. Before becoming permanently disabled in a car accident, Edna worked as a welfare fraud investigator for the state of Washington. Unlike other victims of psychological harassment, she didn't present with paranoia. Her primary complaint was severe depression related to a recent bankruptcy. In her case the harassment started following an affair with a contract CIA operative she claimed was the signaler—the "umbrella man"—in Dealey Plaza on the day of John F. Kennedy's assassination. This meant nothing to me at the time. According to Edna, more than fifty witnesses observed a tall, thin man open a large umbrella, in full sunlight, at the exact moment that Kennedy's limousine came out from behind a freeway sign.

Following her break-up with Edwin, Edna experienced phone harassment, mail theft, multiple break-ins, electronic manipulation of her bank accounts and at least three attempts on her life. Frightened by the aggressive campaign to silence her, I agreed to treat her on condition she not disclose any specific knowledge she possessed about the JFK assassination or other clandestine intelligence activities. I had no desire to be privy to information that might place me or my daughter at risk, and viewed this information as irrelevant to her treatment.

Three years later I was a target in my own right and wanted to know everything she could tell me about domestic intelligence activities. She immediately confirmed Jabari's claims about the CIA and FBI secretly collaborating with the Seattle police in spying on activists and whistleblowers. "They have a group they call the Footprinters and meet monthly at the Corson Avenue Elks Club. Along with undercover investigators from Northwest Security Services and the Welfare Fraud Unit. The meetings are closed to the public." Her voice assumed a weighty, disapproving tone. "And to women, of course."

She continued. "However, the CIA also have their own domestic security operations. Because this is illegal under federal law, they run them through a totally secret division called the Office of Security Services."

She told me a long story I found difficult to follow about an investigation she undertook for former state representative Cal Anderson when he worked for Mayor Royer's office. "When I lived in Jefferson Terrace, it was common for derelicts to follow me and even approach me with vague threats and nonsensical mumblings. They were all fairly young—in their thirties—and obviously unemployed. I was very surprised to discover three of them lived in my building." Jefferson Terrace was a Seattle Housing Authority (SHA) building reserved for senior tenants age sixty and older. "My detective friend at the police department told me two of them were in the Federal Witness Protection program and one was a paid police informant. Numerous people in the building saw all three of them selling drugs. But owing to their special status, they couldn't be prosecuted."

Edna indicated one of the men, who happened to be an assistant manager, was implicated in a bizarre burglary ring involving several SHA buildings. It was this burglary ring that Cal Anderson asked her to investigate. What she discovered was that certain managers made pass keys available to friends when tenants died. With the end result that non-family members would strip their apartments of any valuables before the police arrived.

Edna could shed no light on who might be harassing me or why. "Perhaps one of your patients told you something." Edna was aware I saw former veterans and ex-cops and their wives, girlfriends, and ex-wives and ex-girlfriends who sometimes confided in me about police or government involvement in illegal activities. Like Earl, she believed the men following me were engaged in "conspicuous surveillance." It was intended to intimidate me, as opposed to true surveillance, which was performed without the subject's knowledge.

"In any case," she told me, "the best way to protect yourself is to construct a paper barricade." What this meant was making sure at least one other person had a copy of any "sensitive" information in my possession—in other words information the federal government might not want me to have. "Also, remember to vary your routine, even if you don't think you're being followed. It makes it much harder for someone to set you up for any nasty surprises."

Our conversation was interrupted by a sudden burst of loud, synchronous static from my FM radio, which was playing in the background. I listened to the radio to relieve the drudgery of chopping vegetables and washing dishes—even though the kitchen had the worst reception of any room in the house.

Edna became very grave. "You must never call me from home again. Or your office. Always use a pay phone. Do you hear that noise? There is only one cause for that kind of static—a transmitting microphone. It's most likely in your phone jack."

After we hung up, as Edna instructed, I removed the plastic plate where the phone line connected to the wall. I had no idea what I was supposed to look for. The microphone, if there was one, would remain hidden in the jumble of wires and brightly colored splices.

■

The other intelligence "expert" I consulted that weekend was a forty four-year-old African American named Edward Price. I first met Edward two years earlier when he approached ISO for support in a labor dispute with General Disposal. I had contacted him in mid-June, along with Hussayn and a woman I befriended at a prison reform meeting, to invite them to join the Museum Support Committee. Edward explained he didn't participate in "radical politics" and gave me Ruth's number. After he mentioned seeing my picture in the *Post Intelligencer*, I told him the government was harassing me for my involvement in the UW sit-in. To my surprise he said that he, too, had experienced harassment and thought he could help me.

I called him again after talking to Edna, and he invited me to his Madison Valley home the following afternoon. Edward was darker than Jabari but lighter than Earl and wore his hair in a quarter inch razor cut. Like Earl, he was a meticulous dresser with an eye for high-end casual wear. He invited me into his kitchen where he was preparing to boil a large pile of home-grown mustard greens. After offering me a seat at his kitchen table, he launched into a long, convoluted monologue about his lawsuit against General Disposal. He spoke in a high-pitched expressionless falsetto that had the rehearsed quality typical of someone who has worked hard to speak correctly. The result was full of grammatical idiosyncrasies but bore no trace of his south Louisiana origin.

He began by reiterating everything he told us in 1985—about Mayor Royer de-unionizing garbage collection by abolishing the city garbage disposal service and contracting non-union companies—and about General Disposal firing Edward after they ordered him not to give his Mexican helper a lunch break and he did so anyway. I assumed the harassment he mentioned related to his wrongful dismissal suit, though he didn't say so directly. In fact, after ten minutes of irrelevant detail and references to a half dozen people I never heard of, I was still unclear why the company didn't want his assistant to have a lunch break or exactly what they did to harass him.

His vagueness made me very impatient. "How did they harass you, Edward?" Without responding, he took me into his living room to show me a bullet hole in the outside wall.

Following him back to the kitchen, I sat at the table again while he tended his kettle of greens. I told him about the prank calls I was getting and my earlier conversation with Edna. "In my case we both think the government is responsible. Do you know anything about government harassment?"

He put a lid on the kettle, turned the heat down, and came over to sit across from me. He kept his eyes on his hands, which he folded on the table in front of him. "I used to work with those people. I wanted to see how they operated with all the agents and sub-agents."

When I asked exactly which agency he worked for, he responded that he had traveled all over the world with Jesse Jackson Jr. and other famous black leaders. He looked up and briefly met my gaze. "One thing most people don't realize about these men is they like to hold their meetings in the nude."

As bizarre as this sounded, I was accustomed to patients making off the wall comments to avoid issues they preferred not to discuss. "Are you saying the government paid you to do all this?" I asked.

Edward shook his head slowly and continued in the same monotonous singsong. "I don't keep no secrets. I always warn people when I meet them. A secret is a kind of lie." He rambled on about a female friend at the police department who warned him to have nothing to do with me after seeing my name on what he referred to as a list of subversives. "I also know this security guard at American Building Maintenance who says he does surveillance on your home." Since leaving General Disposal, Edward worked nights at ABM as foreman. "He says you always seem to be writing something." This made sense. My dining room table, where I wrote letters and paid bills, was next to a bank of four windows that faced Third Northwest.

Edward began another long, involved story about the mother of his third child, who tricked him by getting pregnant and then turning him over to welfare. Impatient, I interrupted. "Edward, can you help me stop the harassment?"

He gave me a thoughtful look. "You're giving your power away. This is why I'm spending the time with you. Other people can't make you afraid unless you let them. Both anger and fear are very destructive feelings. They eat away at people from the inside."

I could see where this was leading. I was about to get a "don't worry, be happy" lecture. Irritated about wasting my afternoon on someone who had nothing to offer beyond a pep talk about positive thinking, I got up to leave. Edward also stood up and made a pass. Much to my surprise I responded. My new friend was incapable of normal conversation, much less emotional intimacy. Yet he clearly had links to the local intelligence community. Links I believed he was willing to use to help me.

∎

I didn't tell Earl I was seeing someone else. Nor did I conceal the fact. He didn't tell me he was going to Sacramento for a month to work on a state bill to introduce multicultural curriculum infusion in the California public schools. He simply vanished. I tried his number at least three times a day for ten days and gave up. We had reached a critical juncture in our affair where we spent most of our time arguing, usually over his refusal to discuss where the relationship was going.

He insisted he couldn't be "domestic" because of all the political demands on him. I knew this wasn't completely true, but was tired of arguing. I knew of at least two live-in relationships Earl had had with black women. Though I hated to admit it, I also knew why he insisted on keeping our relationship a secret. African American women, who had always been Earl's main supporters, viewed mixed-race liaisons as a betrayal. An open affair with a white woman would utterly destroy his credibility in his own community.

Edward and I spent three nights together before I realized my new lover was powerless to do anything to stop the people who were stalking me and barraging me with prank calls. All he had to offer was "advice" on dealing with it better. Yet the nature of the advice showed a very advanced understanding of human psychology, a good seven years before the wider psychiatric community embraced Beck's Cognitive Behavior Therapy (CBT) as an effective treatment. What Edward advocated was very similar to the cognitive restructuring that occurs in CBT, as patients learn to challenge negative thoughts and feelings. Somehow, this so-called janitor with no education beyond high school had undergone very sophisticated training in mind control.

We would have sex and lie in bed for an hour or more while he told me long, elaborate stories that either began in childhood—such as the time he hit the family mule to stop it eating the corn, and accidentally killed it, or five thousand years back when he first met me in a prior lifetime. He made frequent mention of knowing each other in a prior lifetime. He claimed a "messenger" came to him in a dream and told him that 5,000 years ago I was some kind of leader who misled everyone.

"We were all killed," he claimed, "but it will be different this time. Through my love we will both become light enough to float away to a less negative planet."

It was never clear if he really believed the New Age psychobabble he came out with or just said it because he thought I did. The cops and prosecutors I encountered in my court work also assumed that as a leftist, I would also be an animal rights activist and a New Age freak.

Aside from all his talk about reincarnation, channeling, and light bodies, Edward was a classic advertisement for free-market capitalism. He talked a lot about his "system" making him rich, his Korean broker, and the ranch he owned in Yakima. How he would make me rich, too, by "smoothing over the rough edges." He always came back to the same themes in the little parables he told about his childhood, his brother the pimp, his past girlfriends, and his four children—themes which, over time, fleshed out a "system" of being absolutely certain of his own intentions and focusing on them relentlessly, no matter how hard other people tried to deflect him.

"That's what you need," he told me. "A system so it don't matter what other people do. My system is to be positive, loving, and truthful, no matter how hard people try to scare me or make me angry. You make a big mistake in trying to figure out who is doing this to you. Be absolutely clear on what *you're* doing. Don't worry about other people."

CHAPTER 6

On July 10, Edward and I had been lovers not quite a week when I had my monthly appointment with my own psychiatrist. A year earlier I asked Nelson, who was chief of psychiatry at St Cabrini Hospital, to put me on Nardil after a severe, treatment-resistant sinus infection caused me to become depressed. Fortunately, the depression resolved within two weeks of starting the monoamine oxidase inhibitor. The idea of doing psychotherapy with Nelson, who had a very traditional lifestyle and values, didn't appeal to either of us. Thus my "treatment" consisted of fifteen-minute visits once a month to monitor my response to the medication.

It was our first visit since the sit-in. My first big mistake was to tell him about the harassment. The second was to share Edna's belief that both the Seattle police and the CIA might be involved. By now I had confirmed the existence of the Footprinters through a security guard I knew at Northwest Protective Services. According to several of my patients who lived in subsidized housing, it was common knowledge that someone with duplicate passkeys was breaking into tenants' apartments when they died. In fact, an assistant manager tried to seduce one of my patients with nylon stockings and dresses from a deceased neighbor who had lived upstairs.

The moment I mentioned the CIA, my psychiatrist decided I was psychotic and refused to listen to anything else I said. "You must submit to immediate hospitalization," he insisted. "If not, I have no choice but to notify the Board of Medical Quality Assurance." Who we both knew would suspend my medical license.

Furious, I told him it was ridiculous to equate a fear of stalking and threatening phone calls with either paranoia or psychosis. "You know perfectly well I meet none of the *DSMIII-R* criteria for either condition," I told him. The *Diagnostic and Statistical Manual* was the official diagnostic manual published by the American Psychiatric Association.

The speed with which my psychiatrist retreated from his ultimatum made me doubtful he knew the criteria without looking them up. Instead he agreed to both of my demands: that he confirm with Edward that the harassment was genuine and that he arrange for a second opinion from one of the academic psychiatrists at the University of Washington.

■

When I returned to my office I also took the precaution of contacting an attorney. Larry Steinglas, who specialized in workers compensation and malpractice, squeezed me in just before five o'clock. Unlike the Soviet Union, where the government diagnosed radicals and dissidents as mentally ill in order to lock them away forever in mental hospitals, the U.S. mental health system was too fragmented to be used to suppress dissent. Nelson's erroneous diagnosis stemmed from pure political naiveté. He had no reason to come in contact with political or union activists, unemployed whistleblowers or the low-income street people that the police, and, I believed, U.S. intelligence, recruited as informants. Nevertheless, I had no confidence in any of my colleagues to objectively assess my mental state. I practiced in a totally different world from other Seattle psychiatrists, who automatically turned away patients who couldn't afford their one hundred dollar fee.

Larry spent about fifteen minutes making detailed notes about my encounter with the UW Campus Police and the phone and personal harassment that ensued. He then called Nelson's answering service and had him paged. My psychiatrist had already scheduled me to see Dr. Al Fields, a psychopharmacologist at the University Hospital, on July 15. The attorney consulted his scheduler and also made an appointment for the two of us to see Nelson together on the seventeenth.

■

The following morning I also called Cheryl Franklin, the *Facts* health editor, and Stan Humbolt, a homicide detective who was investigating Sheila McIntyre's criminal complaint against her former boyfriend. Edna's advice about creating a paper barricade was appealing. She believed that I inadvertently—via one of my patients—became privy to "sensitive" information the government was trying to suppress. I could think of only two, highly remote, possibilities. The first related to my efforts to publicize a potential AIDS treatment I believed was being suppressed. The second to the suspicious death of one of my patients, an activist with the Boilermaker's union. Even with solid evidence, someone of my negligible stature had little hope of exposing heinous government secrets—even if I knew any. Yet, in the face of Nelson's threat to have my license revoked, it felt better to take concrete steps, even relatively futile ones, than to do nothing.

I got an answering machine when I dialed Franklin's number. She called back five minutes later. For weeks I had been leaving messages for both the *Times* and *Post Intelligencer* health editors about recent German research into the use of the ulcer drug Tagomet as a treatment for AIDS. Neither returned my calls. In 1987 Tagomet, which at present is available at any pharmacy or grocery store without prescription, was the most frequently prescribed medication in the U.S. After seeing a letter describing its immune modulating effects in the *American Journal of Psychiatry*, I did a Medline search and discovered more than seventy studies showing the drug had a therapeutic effect in a number of viral illnesses, leukemia, and, in one study in East Germany, AIDS-related complex. Given AIDS was 100-percent fatal in 1987, I found it very puzzling there was no effort to publicize this research in the U.S.

Franklin, who worked from home, said she could see me at one o'clock but refused to give me her address. "I talked with some friends. They say the material you want to give me is extremely dangerous." She told me to meet her outside the *Facts* office at Twenty-third and Martin Luther King Way.

After hanging up I dialed Humbolt's number and was surprised he was in his office on a Saturday. I had found the homicide detective in my waiting room a few days after my first session with Sheila. He wanted to know if she revealed anything that might help in his investigation. The request surprised me. As a police officer he should know that anything a patient told me was privileged. He agreed to meet me at the Ballard Denny's, which was a five-minute drive from my home. I got there first and watched him pull up in his 1980 Ford pick-up with a power mower in the back. Humbolt was a short, burly man of about forty-five, and had streaks of gray in his light brown crew-cut. He wore a short-sleeved plaid sports shirt and new Levis.

He showed me to a booth and ordered two coffees. I began by describing the hang-up and prank calls I was getting. "I really have no idea why people would be harassing me. Sheila gets the same kind of calls. I'm sure she told you this." I paused to look at him but got no response. "Is that why I'm getting them?" I suggested. Humbolt said it was very unlikely, so I continued. "I think it might relate to a former patient who is now deceased. I was trying to help a labor organizer who died under very strange circumstances."

I went on to describe Mark Cranston's alleged overdose on the antidepressant Elavil. There was no suicide note, and he allegedly took the overdose while drinking coffee with friends at the Denny's in Magnolia. According to the police report, with no warning he simply passed out under the table. The restaurant manager called the police, who for some reason sent out a detox van to pick him up. Although the union activist was clearly unconscious, instead of calling an ambulance the detox driver threw him in the back of the van and drove him around the city for five hours. By the time they arrived at the detox facility he was dead.

I looked at Cranston but his face was totally blank. "Is it true the CIA sometimes harasses union and community activists?" I asked.

"The CIA has nothing whatsoever to do with the calls you are getting," he said in a voice that was hard and emphatic, as he locked eyes with me. I found his adamancy perplexing. I knew Sheila had informed him of her ex-lover's CIA connections. If Edna knew about Seattle police involvement in the Footprinters and the Office of Security Services, surely a senior homicide detective did. Why deliberately lie when he could say nothing?

Avoiding any further mention of the CIA, I relayed what Edna and other patients had told me about Seattle Housing Authority managers and assistant managers on the Federal Witness Protection program who dealt drugs and ripped off elderly tenants when they died. Humbolt cut me off. "I'm only interested in unsolved murders." He gave me his card. "Call 911 and file a police report if the harassment continues. Be sure to ask for a case number and then call and leave the number on my answering machine."

■

Two hours later a tall, mahogany-toned woman in a full-length multicolored African gown and matching headdress was waiting for me as I pulled up outside the *Facts* office. The two of us walked three blocks to the nearest deli. I used their Xerox machine to make a copy of the seventy titles that came up on my *Medline* search, as well as twelve journal articles I had ordered from Interlibrary Loan. These included two in-vitro studies showing Tagomet both protected and enhanced functioning of the T4 cells that were essential to a strong immune system—and were specifically targeted by the HIV virus that caused AIDS. In addition, I gave her seven clinical studies showing the drug was effective in colds, hepatitis, shingles, acute leukemia, and an open-label study from the University of Essen in East Germany showing it was effective in early HIV infection.

■

Edward called soon after I returned home to tell me his friend Ruth wanted to see me. Ruth had declined to join the Women's Support Committee Debra and I started, preferring to continue to work with Earl, Jabari, and the Shiite brothers.

"Ruth is very concerned about you. She says she want to clean you out." My lover elaborated with a long, complicated explanation that included references to the "unseen" world and the struggle between good and evil. I knew Edward's friend, who bragged about her maternal grandmother being a "voodoo queen," did some kind of non-traditional healing. I gathered he had told her I was being harassed.

Edward rambled on about Ruth going "too far out" for his tastes. "She says she can only come back if something stops her. Such as going to jail or a hospital."

I already had Ruth's number, and she answered after two rings. She knew I worked during the week and proposed getting together the following weekend. "Do you prefer Saturday or Sunday?" she asked. I told her it made no difference. The sharp reproof in her voice made it clear this was the wrong answer. "It makes a *big* difference."

At first I was bewildered by the point she was making. Suddenly I knew instinctively what she wanted me to do. Within a few seconds I felt myself slipping into an intuitive space where Saturday clearly *felt* better than Sunday. "Definitely Saturday," I said. "At 11:00 a.m."

∎

A week later Ruth arrived on my front porch wearing the felt hat she had decorated with bead necklaces and crow feathers, and no shoes. Otherwise, she was conventionally dressed in a long-sleeved polyester sweater and jeans. Close up, I saw we were exactly the same height and that her complexion was light like Jabari's and heavily freckled. She handed me a business card identifying her as a "MA Psychology, Human Relations Consultant." I took this as a cue to ask how much she charged.

After a brief tour of my combined living-dining room, she announced she would accept a check for seventy-five dollars. "In addition, I want to take some of your house plants home. I also want you to contact the medical director at the King County Jail. I want you to register a complaint on my behalf. They gave me an injection of Thorazine after arresting me for protesting North American apartheid at Northgate Shopping Center. The guards refused to bring me a blanket, and I started singing, 'Go Down Moses, Let My People Go.'" She sang the words instead of saying them. "So they came and gave me a shot."

I agreed to all three requests, and there was an awkward silence. I was still very uneasy with the notion of spiritual healing. Owing to the strong stigma on the left against spirituality, I could never tell my white friends about my session with an African American shaman. I tried to cover my uneasiness with a lame joke about checking my basement for negative energy. "If you check it for me, it might save me from calling the police." I told her about finding what appeared to be a human vertebra while draining the springs that flowed under the unpaved corner of my basement. "If it's human, I really need to notify them."

Ruth took my request seriously. I followed her downstairs to the basement, along each of the four walls of the foundation and out the basement door leading outside. We then circled the house together, as I showed her the peas, scarlet runner beans, and broccoli I had planted among the foxglove and black-eyed gaillardia that grew wild in the old flower beds that bordered the front and back porches. We re-entered the house through the front door and walked through all the rooms.

"The only energy I detect is strong positive bond between you and some of your houseplants." She walked over to the four-tiered glass shelves beside my dining room windows and pulled a handful of toothpicks from her pocket. She stuck four each in a bushy Christmas cactus, a tropical lily my best friend gave me, and a three-foot avocado plant I grew from a pit. "Which is why I want to take them home with me," she explained.

She went out to the porch to bring in a dilapidated boom box and two enormous handbags, which she deposited on my dining room floor. Removing her hat to reveal a tidy, inch-thick afro, she had me sit on the floor across from her. Then she pulled out a candle, which she lit, some small black and white feathers, and a small bottle of odorless oil from one of her bags.

"The Earth Spirit is your strongest connection," she said. I assumed she was referring to my interest in plants. "This is where we will start."

She instructed me to remove my shoes and socks and, to my great embarrassment, began massaging my feet. The self-consciousness was short-lived, replaced by a sudden piercing pain behind both eyes. I almost never experience headaches. Ruth said it was a sign. "You are out of touch with the Sky Spirit, and it's trying to get in."

Going over to the boom box she played a crackly audiotape of John Lennon singing *Come Together*. At the time I had no idea

Lennon himself was a leftist nor that he underwent extensive surveillance and harassment by the FBI, who schemed for years to get him deported. The headache vanished. Suddenly I was overcome with violent sobbing, overwhelmed by a visceral certainty that the government had played some role in the singer's death, as well as the deaths of John and Bobby Kennedy, and Martin Luther King.

"They have killed everyone of any importance to me," I cried.

Ruth said nothing, giving no clue whether she understood what I was saying. It seemed to make no difference. I continued to cry quietly for several minutes after the tape ended. Then I dried my eyes on my t-shirt and the session, which I took to be a modified voodoo ritual, was over. I wrote out a check, and we loaded the avocado, lily, and Christmas cactus into the backseat of her car.

She leaned out her car window as she pulled away. "Just remember to listen to the Universe," she called. This was her first mention of the Universe in the sense of a higher power, though Edward used the term frequently. I assumed she was referring to the intuitive place I went to in deciding where and when to have our session, and where I instinctively returned when we sat down together on my dining room floor. It was the only way I knew how to relate to her. In the rational part of my mind, the things she said and did made no sense.

I knew from my clinical training that women with a history of childhood abuse have an innate capacity for spontaneous trance formation, a form of self-hypnosis. Clearly I have this ability, though I had no idea this was happening at the time. I had also read all Carlos Castenada's books about the altered states he entered with the shaman Don Juan. For the next few months I believed Ruth had endowed me with similar powers to connect with the unseen world. Twelve days later I would use them to thwart two attempts on my life.

■

On Monday morning, as I often did, I took the bus downtown to the Federal Building to testify at a Social Security Disability hearing.

Twice a month the Office of Hearings and Appeals paid me to advise their administrative law judges on claims involving mental illness. Following my session with Ruth, there was an immediate reduction in my anxiety and fear. Still unclear exactly what she meant by listening to the Universe, I found myself attending more and more to body language, patterns of speech, and the energy people gave off, as opposed to what they said and did.

As I boarded a Number 5 across from the zoo, I was immediately struck by the edgy, hyper-vigilant state of the other passengers. All six of them, all men, were much better dressed, in suits and topcoats, than the homeless and disabled riders I was used to seeing at mid-morning. Fascinated by the close scrutiny they gave everyone who boarded or disembarked, for a brief instant, instead of one person following me, I saw six, all assigned to this particular bus to monitor my activities. I shut my eyes tightly and shook my head. When I re-opened them the trance-like feeling disappeared. All I saw was normal passengers, concerned only with their own lives.

When my last hearing ended at 2:30 p.m., I boarded a Number 28 to my office. This time there were five other passengers, all male, all wearing suits and expensive gabardine raincoats, and all with the same pinched, hyper-vigilant demeanor. Again I had a trance-like sense of being disconnected from the scene in front of me. And once again, I momentarily believed they were there monitoring me. I shook my head and refocused. My vision cleared and they became normal passengers.

■

Curious if it would happen again, the next morning I took a 43 from Sixth and Market to my bank in Wallingford. At 10:00 a.m. the bus was empty except for two homeless men at the very back. Three men in designer suits and raincoats got on at the stop after mine and sat two rows in front of me. Two more men, wearing virtually identical topcoats, except that one was gray and the other dark blue, got on at Forty-sixth. Like the well-dressed riders I encountered on Monday, all five rode in total silence, openly inspecting everyone who got on or off, where they sat, and who they talked to.

This time, after being awake all night with hang-up calls and a woman yelling obscenities on my corner, I was too exhausted to throw off my initial perception that they were there for my benefit. Oddly, I no longer saw my "chaperones" as spies assigned to monitor and intimidate me, but as "good" agents who were there to guarantee my safety. Edward had talked about a "revolution" that was occurring at the CIA, which I took as a reference to Irangate. Edna also talked about a "good CIA"—consisting of principled operatives who were trying to rid the agency of its criminal element and sometimes leaked information to assist in her own investigations.

Despite five years as a practicing leftist, I still clung to beliefs drummed into me in childhood that despite great economic inequality, the American political system was the fairest, most efficient, and most transparent in the world. Over time I came to recognize that all spy agencies and all spies were beyond the law because they answered to powerful elites rather than our elected representatives. However, at the time the ramifications were too terrifying. I had to believe the U.S. government was misguided but well-intentioned—or be left with nowhere to turn.

■

I arrived at First Interstate and got in the teller line. I was puzzled to see three times the usual number of patrons in the lobby. It also bothered me that only half of them were waiting in line or sitting with the three account representatives who had their own desks. The rest were milling around or lounging on benches or in chairs. Unlike the smartly dressed professionals I observed on the bus, these non-patrons were scruffily dressed and of both sexes.

Still in the detached, dreamlike state I entered during my session with Ruth, what I saw was a room full of agents and informants with some ulterior agenda for being there. The perception that they were in the bank, not necessarily to monitor me, but to engage in some illegal activity, was real enough that I approached the branch manager.

"Are the people in the lobby normal bank customers?" I asked.

The manager, who sat in a glass-walled office at the back of the bank, was a balding, fifty-plus male with a warm, thoughtful face and an enormous belly that overlapped his belt. Unperturbed by my question, he craned his neck to scan the lobby and assured me they were all regular patrons. He gave me his card.

"Please don't hesitate to call if you have any further concerns."

■

On the sixteenth, I took my car to my appointment with Al Fields, the University of Washington psychopharmacologist that Nelson had arranged for me to see. Though I had no idea at the time I was dissociating, I knew better than to attend a psychiatry appointment in an altered state. I also recognized that the phenomenon only occurred if I deviated from my normal routine. My perceptions remained intact if I avoided busses and unfamiliar streets and neighborhoods.

I was upfront with Fields about my leftist politics, my involvement in the UW sit-in, and the prank phone calls that ensued. I had never told Nelson that I sometimes observed people following me—this would definitely be construed as paranoia—and I didn't tell Fields. Likewise, I made no mention of the CIA, FBI, Cointelpro, or Seattle police spying on local activists—nor my session with Ruth.

"Who do you think is behind the harassment?"

I told him, truthfully, that I had no idea. "I have talked to a police detective, and so far there is nothing they can do."

He called me at my office that afternoon. "It is my impression you are suffering from mania and need immediate hospitalization," he told me. I challenged him, pointing out that I experienced no racing thoughts, flight of ideas, or other characteristic manic symptoms.

"I based my diagnosis on your tangential speech." This was a technical term for rambling speech that included a lot of unnecessary detail. I saw my error in even mentioning my political activism to the psychopharmacologist. The subject bored him, so he decided it was irrelevant. In his written report, the only abnormal findings he cited were that I came over and crouched next to his desk to show him my *Seattle Gay News* article and that my voice sometimes cracked, as if I was on the verge of tears.

He was clutching at straws. Clearly he based his conclusions on the history Nelson gave him, rather than my presentation in his office. The University of Washington psychiatrist put himself at great professional risk by disputing the findings of a colleague. If Fields let me continue practice, and a patient was harmed because of my so-called illness, he could lose his own license.

CHAPTER 7

Three days later Larry was in Nelson's waiting room when I arrived. I knew my psychiatrist had phoned Edward because my lover told me about the call and the assurances he gave my psychiatrist that the harassment was real. I walked into the session believing this input would convince Nelson of my sanity but decided to make one last point about the difference between paranoia and fearful vigilance. "It's like Sherlock Holmes and Moriarty," I started. I was about to add that Holmes's morbid preoccupation with Moriarty made him an even better detective, but Nelson cut me off.

"This woman is insane," he said bluntly. "There is no point in letting her talk." Waving Fields' report in front of me, he delivered his verdict: "She is unfit to practice. Unless she agrees to immediate admission, I will notify the Board of Medical Quality Assurance."

Larry reminded him I could not be hospitalized in Seattle, where I might encounter current or former patients or social workers, nurses, or psychologists that I worked with professionally. "You must find a hospital outside of Seattle willing to admit her." Nelson said this could up to a week or more. "Would you be willing to postpone notification if she voluntarily agrees to suspend her practice? Let's say for a month."

Nelson turned to me. "Are you willing to suspend your practice?" He was clearly surprised when I agreed.

I added that my preference was to admit myself to the University of British Columbia Medical Center in Vancouver. Based on my encounter with Fields, I had already decided it would be far cheaper to agree to an inpatient assessment, which would be covered by my health insurance, than to commence a legal battle with Nelson. It would be extremely difficult and expensive to prove my sanity in court. The outcome in a legal arena was unlikely to be based on evidence, but on the status and reputation of the witnesses. I knew I would have no problem finding other psychiatrists to verify my sanity—there were hundreds of psychiatrists all over the country who made their living providing expert testimony. I also knew the legal expense would bankrupt me.

I proposed Vancouver, as opposed to Portland, Olympia, or Spokane. Jabari and Edna had scared me with talk of undercover operatives pursuing targets into jails and mental hospitals. From my own experience I knew both institutions were a kind of no man's land where adverse events, such as stabbings, beatings, and suicides were so commonplace they were taken for granted. I also naively believed U.S. intelligence wouldn't violate Canadian sovereignty by following me across the border.

Nelson, surprised and pleased I was agreeing to hospitalization, said he would look into it.

■

I drove straight to my office from the Cabrini Towers building where Nelson practiced. After canceling all my appointments for the next four weeks, I called my answering service and instructed them to give callers the message that I would be temporarily suspending practice for a month. I let the Social Security hearing I had scheduled for Monday morning stand, as it involved no direct patient care.

On Monday, July 20, I parked in my office lot and took a 28 to the Federal Building. There were nine other passengers that morning: three men and two women well past retirement age, a man with cerebral palsy in a wheelchair, and a mother with two small children. The youthful minders who were so attentive the week before seemed to have lost interest.

The applicant that morning was a glum, white-haired man in his early sixties with a thick German accent. He was applying for disability on the basis of intractable depression. His attorney led him through the usual questions about his symptoms—insomnia, fatigue, and loss of motivation and concentration. Then the judge asked if I had further questions.

"Where were you born, Mr. Richter?" The written application identified his birthplace as New York City. Thus, the German accent puzzled me.

"New York City."

"Were your parents German? I'm curious how you come to speak with a German accent?"

Richter shook his head. "They were also born in New York. I think you are likely mistaken about my accent." The quaint turn of phrase made the German gutturals even more pronounced. Turning his face away, the court clerk coughed as he struggled to keep from laughing. "I have very precise speech. Americans are unused to hearing English spoken correctly."

The claimant was clearly lying about his German background. However, I had no doubt the clinical depression, which is hard to fake, was genuine. I confirmed that his mood disorder prevented him from performing any type of competitive employment, and the judge granted his claim and adjourned the hearing. Instead of following my normal practice of turning in the evidence file to be shredded, I nonchalantly returned it to the battered attaché case I used to carry medical records. The elderly claimant might have any number of reasons for concealing his German identity. However, I had read an article in the *Guardian* about the CIA smuggling Nazi war criminals into our country following World War II. If this man was in the U.S. illegally or had current or past links with the CIA, any records documenting his current identity and whereabouts might prove very useful.

■

It was around four o'clock in the afternoon when I caught the bus back to my building, only to discover my car had disappeared. I went inside to my office to call the police. At the last moment I decided to call Edward, who worked nights, instead. The lot adjacent to my building was nine blocks long, and I sometimes forgot exactly where I parked my car. Twenty minutes later he arrived in his late-model Mustang to drive me through the half mile of parking lots that lined the west side of Lake Union. We had just completed an initial pass through the four lots to the north of my building when I spotted one of my patients at the front entrance.

Henry Harris was one of three patients I confided in about the hang-up calls and car gangs, and obviously connected my practice closure with the harassment. A high-strung, motor-mouthed disabled African American veteran, he looked very agitated. I got out to talk to him. Shifting his weight nervously from leg to leg, he became even more distressed when he saw who I was with.

"Please don't get back in that car, Dr. B." He said it three times. It struck me now how closely Henry, who always knew a little more about the harassment than I told him, fit the profile of the men Edna and I observed following us. He was bright and streetwise, and, thanks to a generous veteran's pension, had no regular job.

Ignoring Henry I got back in Edward's car. After dragging him out of bed, it made no sense not to continue looking for my vehicle.

Following twenty minutes of slow circling, I located my 1986 Mazda three blocks south of the 1818 building where I recalled leaving it. The lock on the driver's side was broken where it had been forced. It seemed to be another prank, as nothing was missing from the interior. At my insistence, Edward checked the undercarriage and under the hood, and assured me nothing was out of place

∎

I bought a sandwich at the snack bar and spent about two hours in my office responding to messages and opening my mail. Around 7:30 I drove to Edward's to spend the night with him. I regretted doing so the moment I arrived. The scene with Henry had unnerved me too much to have sex with him or even get into the same bed. The people persecuting me had succeeded in getting me labeled insane and driven out of practice. Yet the malicious pranks persisted, along with the incessant calls and booming 2:00 a.m. rap concerts. My activist friends seemed to want nothing to do with me once Naomi left for Chico. In all Seattle, the only support I could muster was that of an emotionally barren ultraconservative who was incapable of normal conversation and was most likely an intelligence operative himself.

Edward said I could spend the night in his spare bedroom and went to his own room to watch TV. I remained on the sofa in his living room, crying, until it got dark. Finding the light switch in the hall, but not the second bedroom, I felt my way towards the bed in the dark. Reaching out with both hands I could feel the sheets and blankets, normally in total disarray, had been straightened and tucked under the mattress. I also discovered two pairs of newly ironed slacks at the foot of the bed and I draped the slacks neatly over a chair next to the wall. Then I got into bed fully dressed. I flinched as I felt something cold and hard next to me. The bed was no longer empty. By this time my eyes had adjusted to the dark. Lying next to me was a fully dressed male mannequin.

Deciding this was some kind of test—another of Edward's techniques to help me conquer my fears—I got up and lifted the dummy to the floor. The moment I got back in bed the light went on in Edward's room. I went out to the living room, where he was just returning from the basement with an old-fashioned insecticide pump.

I asked what he was doing. "There's a mosquito bothering me." I followed as he headed back to his room.

"Please, Edward, don't use it in the house." I assumed the bug sprayer contained an organophosphate cholinesterase inhibitor, a chemical that can be as deadly to humans as to insects. In fact, the Nazis developed the first cholinesterase inhibitors for use in their gas chambers.

In response, Edward raised the pump, aimed directly at my face, and released a line of spray. Acting on some primitive gut reflex, I grabbed my purse and sandals and ran as fast as I could for my car.

Three minutes after I arrived home the phone rang. It was Edward, addressing me in his unreadable sing-song, as if nothing had happened. "All I meant was to get rid of that mosquito. I sure didn't mean to drive my baby away."

He was making a joke. The disconnect between his nonchalance and the viciousness of his actions left a leaden sense of dread in my stomach. "No, Edward, you deliberately sprayed me in the face."

Edward assured me I was mistaken. "I was only spraying a mosquito."

Up until then, I'd had no difficulty relating to the former, and possibly current, federal agent on two levels—on the superficial level of the benevolent friend helping me master my fears, and on the deeper level of a government informant assigned to interfere in some way with my political activities. I now believed he knew exactly who was harassing me—that the same people most likely recruited him to seduce me. I had been so desperate to stop the incessant calls and unwanted attention from disheveled-looking strangers and car gangs, I told myself Edward was my only hope in trying to identify the people responsible. That I would be okay so long as I never revealed any embarrassing secrets they could use against me.

The frightening episode with the insect spray convinced me otherwise. Henry was clearly justified in fearing for my safety. Edward was extremely dangerous. I hung up, determined to have nothing further to do with him.

■

The next morning I awoke at my usual time of 6:30 a.m. It was the first weekday since opening my Seattle practice that I didn't go to my office. In a normal state of mind, the huge uncertainty about my future would have thrown me into panic. However, by this time it had become quite easy to slip in and out of the dreamlike mental state I entered for the first time during my session with Ruth. What I felt that morning was delicious anticipation at the unique opportunity my one-month suspension offered to listen to the Universe, as Ruth called it, without being interrupted by a prearranged schedule. At some point I would get a phone call ordering me to drive to Vancouver and admit myself to the University of British Columbia. However, it seemed unlikely that any of my male colleagues would want to keep an assertive female psychiatrist on a psych ward very long—too much happens in such places that does not bear scrutiny. I figured it would take about a week for them to convince themselves I was rehabilitated and release me.

I turned my TV on to watch the live coverage of the Iran Contra hearings and got back in bed. At 6:45 a.m. I switched the channel to the Cable News Network. I had already watched nearly twenty hours of hearings and despaired over the fact that no senator or congressman had the balls to confront North and his friends about their most heinous crime—smuggling crack cocaine into U.S. inner cities. I normally avoided CNN, irritated by a format that bombarded the viewer with a fast-paced sequence of random mini-features, with the simultaneous distraction of running headlines at one or more locations on the screen. However, in my dreamlike mental state, I found it easy to ignore the news content and focus on the progression of visual images, a process I found strangely pleasurable. When the national weather came on at 7:05 a.m., I zeroed in on the meteorologist's hands, how he extended one, two, or three fingers for different cities.

Before the advent of cell phones, street gangs used similar hand signs to communicate. Mystified who CNN's weatherman might be signaling, it occurred to me that Ted Turner, CNN's founder and owner, might have intelligence connections, like Phillip Graham, the founder and longtime publisher of the *Washington Post*. I could think of only one person who would know exactly what Turner did before he launched CNN and the business contacts that made up his entourage: my mother. A retired schoolteacher who supported herself through her investments, she spent at least five hours a day following the financial markets. I went to the living room to call her.

My mother said she never watched CNN.

"Where did Turner get his money, though?"

"All I know about Turner is that he is heavily *leveraged*. He raised the money to launch CNN through loans rather than issuing stocks."

My mother did not know or care who loaned Turner the money, and changed the subject. "Puerto Rico has just called the coupon on one of my best bonds. And the moving average for Bank One is giving me a clear 'sell' signal." My mother kept a daily chart on the high, low, and volume of the ten companies in which she owned the most shares. This enabled her to make surprisingly precise predictions of each stock's performance. "I can't sell Bank One. It's my only bank stock."

It was hard to tell if she was really distressed about these things or if my mother, who I hadn't seen in four years, couldn't think of anything else to talk about. I let her go on for about five minutes and politely ended the call.

■

I returned to my bedroom. After about twenty minutes, CNN ran a financial update and reported that Bank One had fallen twenty-two points. I told myself it was coincidence and had nothing to do with my recent phone conversation. The government could tap my phone but there was no way they could use the information they gleaned to influence either the stock market or national TV programming. Hundreds of other people, like my mother, got a sell signal and dumped the stock.

However, still fixated on Ruth's instructions to listen to the Universe, once the seed was planted I couldn't let it go. By the time the stock market closed at two o'clock I had made four more calls to my mother in Milwaukee. In each case I believed I was being cued—through a smirk, a raised eyebrow, a hint of irony in an announcer's tone—to ask about a specific stock.

Around 9:00 a.m. I called to ask if my mother owned Smith Kline French. "You know perfectly well I never buy drug stocks." She seemed more irritated by the question than the interruption. "Pharmaceutical stocks are too volatile."

Within fifteen minutes a new announcer with an approving, self-satisfied smile reported that Smith Kline French had dropped more than twenty points. Believing I was cued to do so, I called Milwaukee around ten o'clock to ask about a tobacco stock. A half hour later it dropped twenty-seven points.

It appeared that the people who listened in on my phone were playing a bizarre but intriguing game with me. They had found some way to transmit the stocks I named to brokers and institutional sellers with the capacity to dump hundreds of shares on very short notice. Assuming that listening to the Universe meant acting on what it told me, I continued to play along. By two o'clock all five stocks my mother and I discussed had dropped at least 15 percent.

■

On Wednesday morning I turned on CNN the moment I woke up. Receiving personal messages from TV or radio was a definite sign of psychosis. Yet I still believed I was following Ruth's advice, and the process was too pleasurable to stop. At 8:30 a.m. I called a psychologist friend about a Health Department advisory that came in the morning mail and concerned mercury contamination in tuna fish. Two minutes later, CNN aired a five-minute segment of fisherman in boats reeling in one enormous fish after another. Over the next hour I phoned three more people to warn them about the advisory. Each time I did so, CNN replayed the fishing feature. I was hooked.

At 10:45 a.m. I called Erica, the lesbian counselor I knew from Seattle Counseling Service. I had confided in her about the harassment after our first Women's Support Committee meeting. "Erica," I said, "my psychiatrist doesn't believe me. He thinks I'm psychotic and is forcing me to suspend practice for a month."

Erica said she would be right over. As soon as she arrived I took her to my bedroom. "You need to tell me if you notice anything usual about this TV station."

It was an experiment. The people who were tapping my phone knew she was there. I wanted to know if this knowledge would influence the programming I received. We watched together for about sixty seconds before CNN ran a feature—the only time they did so during the forty-eight hours I spent glued to the channel—about a Catholic bishop who was marrying homosexuals. My gay friend was so astonished she burst into tears.

■

Erica left and I watched CNN the entire day. Because I was focused on patterns and energy instead of content, I have no recall of specific instructions I received or how they were conveyed. My long-distance bill showed that I made calls to personal and old family friends, not only in Seattle, but in New York, Utah, California, and even southern Illinois. The scenario I constructed in my head entailed a massive clean-up campaign, of which Irangate was the primary public manifestation. Somehow I decided a group of "career" FBI and CIA officers were preparing indictments against all the other crooks who, along with Oliver North, had seized control of the U.S. intelligence apparatus. The latter, in turn, were making one last effort to "neutralize" any activists and whistleblowers who were potential witnesses. This meant dozens of activists and whistleblowers were at risk for the same personalized attention Edna and I received.

I only told my liberal and activist friends about the harassment. The others were clearly puzzled by the calls. The main reaction I got from my mother and grandfather was irritation. At 10:30 p.m., CNN played a feature on a recent presidential trip to Texas. I watched TV so rarely that I hadn't seen Reagan since his first State of the Union address. His family and advisors would conceal his Alzheimer's disease well into his successor's presidency. As I watched him stare blankly into the camera, I decided what I was looking at was a medication-induced stupor. I had read in a women's magazine that he took Dyazide, a combined antihypertensive and diuretic that had been recently linked with premature dementia. I recalled with sudden horror that my mother also took it. She wasn't very happy that it was 2:00 a.m. Milwaukee time when I woke her up to tell her to stop the Dyazide.

An hour later, CNN played an ad for a Beatles album that flashed the printed message, "Call Now!" Somehow I missed the 800 number and took "Call Now!" as a prompt to call a close friend, originally from Liverpool, who was in the Socialist Workers Party in the U.K. I had been trying to reach her for two days, curious if the "crackdown" I had conjured up extended overseas. This time she answered.

"What an amazing coincidence." Her voice was breathless. "We have been on holiday for three weeks and just now pulled in the drive."

CHAPTER 8

When I finally fell asleep I dreamed about my great-grandmother, who left Hamburg in 1912 with my twelve-year-old grandfather and his ten-year-old brother. In the dream, Grandmother Sobota, who was orphaned at twelve, was still a teenager and someone was sexually abusing her. Then she turned into Roxanne, a Jewish woman from the Bronx I treated for post-traumatic stress disorder. Roxanne also grew up in an orphanage and was the third patient I treated in ten years who was sexually molested by staff members while in residential care. In addition to the abuse, she also described bizarre experiments in which strange adults gave the children electroshocks or yelled at them while flashing bright lights in their faces.

I awoke with the same intuitive certainty I felt about John Lennon's death that Grandmother Sobota lied about leaving Germany to keep my grandfather and Uncle Otto out of the Imperial Army. Whether through second sight or some other paranormal process, I was convinced my great grandmother knew and worked with the German Communist Rosa Luxembourg and fled Germany because of her radical politics. Years later, shortly before his death, my grandfather validated this burst of insight—

only it was his stepfather, my great grandmother's second husband, who was wanted by the German police for his political activities.

In the next instant it came to me, in that unreal state between sleep and awakening, that the CIA was operating or had operated an experimental program in which they deliberately subjected orphaned children to physical and sexual abuse. At the time the only reality basis I had to go on were strange stories I heard from patients and two colleagues about pedophilia rings involving young girls who mysteriously disappeared out of the foster care system and the involvement of upper-echelon police and military intelligence officers in these rings. I had no conscious knowledge of MK-ULTRA—the top-secret CIA program begun in the 1960s in which CIA-sponsored psychiatrists performed brainwashing and mind-control experiments on unwitting patients, aided by LSD and similar drugs, electroshock and hypnosis. Nor did I know about the even more secretive Monarch project. I would not learn about MK-ULTRA or Monarch until victims of these programs came forward in the early nineties to talk about their bizarre experiences.

Monarch was based on a bizarre and extremely cynical hypothesis that deliberately exposing children to abuse and trauma would turn them into adults with multiple personalities. Theoretically these subjects would reach adulthood with no conscience and would spy, whore, kill, and commit suicide on command. By extension they would also be impervious to torture. The warped thinking behind this theory was that the host personality would have no knowledge of a top-secret message that was given to one of the alters. Therefore, they couldn't reveal it to an enemy even if they wanted to.

■

Believing the Universe was instructing me to do so, I got out of bed, dressed, and drove to the home of a friend whose daughter underwent a sudden personality change two years earlier. Over a matter of weeks, Krystal became depressed, withdrawn, and aggressive with other children. Once I was fully awake, the connection I made had nothing to do with U.S. intelligence but with a day-care center our children attended before they started school. Adrian, who had transferred Krystal to a Montessori program, was never told about the male worker who molested one of the other children.

Even as she ordered me out of her house, I knew nothing compelled me to share my unwelcome revelations with my friend. I made a conscious choice to lay aside rational thought and responsibility to follow random cues and associations. It was a process I found exquisitely pleasurable, a perfect antidote to the unrelenting fear and anxiety I experienced prior to my session with Ruth.

Returning home from Adrian's at 7:45 a.m., I parked in my driveway and took a 28 to my office. Even in my altered state, I recognized the "messages" I received from CNN were of no use in fighting the most urgent threat I faced—the imminent loss of my medical license. Somewhere in other parts of the country other psychiatrists and counselors must have treated whistleblowers, former intelligence operatives, or union activists who experienced the same kind of harassment I did. The best way to prove I was sane and my claims were real was to locate them.

I addressed my letter to Dr Bernie Grosser, a former supervisor at the University of Utah who had recently been appointed Training Director at the National Institute of Mental Health. The body of the letter was only two paragraphs, followed by a page and a half listing the one hundred people to whom I sent copies. The names included every psychiatrist and left of center counselor and mental health worker I knew in Utah, where I completed my psychiatric training, California, and Washington State, as well as all the progressive periodicals I could think of, including the *Guardian*, the *Progressive*, the *Nation* and *The Facts*.

After revealing I was a political activist who recently participated in a protest demonstration organized by the University of

Washington Black Students Union, I briefly described the anonymous prank calls and other harassment that followed. I added that I was treating other activists and whistleblowers with similar experiences. In my last paragraph I asked for Bernie or any of the other hundred recipients to contact me immediately if they knew of similar cases.

I waited until 8:30 a.m. for the building manager to arrive and used her Xerox machine to make a hundred copies of my letter. Then I typed one hundred address labels, folded and inserted my letters into envelopes, and attached the address labels and postage. It was nearly ten o'clock by the time I boarded another 28 to the downtown post office. Recalling advice Edna gave me about mail tampering, I divided the one hundred letters between five mail slots to avoid drawing attention to what I was doing.

■

I continued to listen to the Universe as I left the post office. The first thought that came to me was that there were serious flaws in the "paper barricade" I tried to build around my AIDS research. There was really nothing Cheryl Franklin, a former VA nurse and full-time mother, could do with the complex scientific data I gave her. All I had accomplished in giving it to her was to put Franklin herself at risk. Recalling the urgent call I made to Representative Rangel's office following Jabari's arrest, I headed south on Fifth Avenue to the main library. Jabari clarified his rationale for having Rangel contact the Algerian and Mozambique embassies following his release from jail. He explained that in the sixties and seventies, activists and whistleblowers with knowledge of police or U.S. government misconduct sometimes disseminated the information by leaking it to the Soviet press. According to Jabari, this information pipeline ceased to be viable in the eighties, as a result of covert CIA aid to Eastern block countries.

"As of 1985, any information you hand over to the Soviet press immediately comes right back to the CIA. Which means the only option for getting it out of the U.S. is via non-aligned Moslem and sub-Saharan countries. It was a small Lebanese magazine, you know, that first broke the story on Irangate."

The Seattle library had phone books for all the major cities in the world. I found listings for Mozambique and Algerian embassies in Washington D.C., as well as an address and a phone number for the Algerian embassy in London. I believed a call to Washington was more likely to be intercepted, even from a phone booth. Instead, I copied down the London number, went to the pay phone across Fourth Avenue, and used my Sprint card to direct dial it.

Despite the eight-hour time difference, the phone was answered by a youthful male voice with a slight unidentifiable accent. "Mahmood speaking."

"I have information I need to send you about a potential AIDS treatment." As soon as I'd said it, the line went dead and I redialed. Again, the moment I mentioned AIDS, the call was cut off. In 1987 no one on the left knew the National Security Agency existed, much less electronically monitored all international calls for key words and phrases that posed a threat to "national security." Clearly, "AIDS" was one of them. Four years later, I would have the same problem when I used the words "Kennedy assassination" with a London book agent.

I dialed a third time. Noting the alarm in Mahmood's voice, I avoided any further mention of AIDS. Instead, I spelled out my name and gave him Charles Rangel's address and phone number in New York. "I will send the documentation via certified mail. Be sure to notify Congressman Rangel if you don't receive it within two weeks."

Paranoid that the people monitoring me might steal them, I carried a copy of the journal articles I gave Franklin at all times. I used the library's Xerox machine to make five copies of each. Aside from any political significance, a low-cost AIDS treatment would have major public health ramifications in sub-Saharan Africa, where thanks to poverty, malnutrition, and heterosexual transmission, HIV infection had already reached epidemic proportions. I walked the five blocks back to the post office and certified and mailed four identical parcels to Mahmood in London, to the Algerian and Mozambique embassies in Washington D.C., and to Representative Charles Rangel in New York.

■

I spent the remainder of the afternoon searching the library's microfilm files. For Nelson to believe I was being harassed I had to show him proof that the U.S. government engaged in clandestine intelligence activities, something the majority of the American public was oblivious to. It took four and a half hours to find what I was looking for, four paragraphs buried on page eleven of a March 1985 edition of the *Seattle Post Intelligencer*. It cost me fifty cents to print out an article describing a settlement between the U.S. government and the Committee for Justice for Domingo and Viernes. Although the Seattle police arrested and convicted two Asian gang members for the 1981 killings, the Committee for Justice maintained the murders were a hit ordered by U.S. intelligence. The federal government settled after discovery unearthed declassified documents identifying the killers as agents of former Philippine dictator Ferdinand Marcos. The documents also revealed an FBI surveillance team and an FBI informant who infiltrated Local 37 had assisted the Marcos agents in planning and carrying out the assassinations.

■

By the time I left downtown, it was dusk. The 5 that I boarded at Third and Pine carried its usual mix of nighttime passengers: students, African American women with their children, and single men lugging packs and sleeping bags to the shelter at St. John's Lutheran Church. I took a seat just in front of two twenty-something white males who were whispering nervously about spotting Crips gang members on Second Avenue. The Seattle police denied either the Bloods or Crips, who were expanding their crack cocaine networks northward from Los Angeles, operated as far north as Seattle. Likewise, neither Seattle paper mentioned the drive-by shooting Henry witnessed in mid-June in front of Parnell's on South Jackson.

As we crossed Forty-fifth, I heard a quiet male voice from somewhere near the back. "Be very careful getting off the bus." Expecting to see a frail senior at the back door, I turned. The back of the bus was empty except for three homeless men with sleeping bags.

We made no further stops until I got off, alone, at the zoo. I pushed the walk button and the light changed. I already had one foot in the gutter when it came to me that the warning was directed at me. I hesitated, and a dark late-model Buick with no back plates came barreling through the red light. Missing me by less than a foot, the driver accelerated as he continued down Greenwood.

■

Grateful for the mysterious warning that saved my life, I made no attempt to analyze where it came from—whether from one of the friendly "minders" that seemed to follow me everywhere, or from unseen forces in the distant Universe. All that mattered was that my invisible enemies were prepared to kill me. It was a relief to resolve the uncertainty. This meant it was only a matter of time before they tried to break into the house. I took mental inventory of my options as I hurried down the steep hill from the corner of Fifty-fifth and Phinney. There was no point in barricading my windows and doors, as wallboard does not stop bullets, and there was nothing to stop someone from setting fire to the house or even blowing it up. I had to prepare for all eventualities. This meant finding a hiding place that would give me immediate advantage over an intruder, as well as a quick escape route.

My basement had six-inch thick concrete walls and the fewest and smallest windows. For an hour after arriving home I dragged an old double mattress into each corner of the foundation, hoping for some sign from the Universe. In the end, the southeast corner felt the most secure, and I wedged the mattress between the washing machine and some ceiling-high shelves Naomi used for her toys and art supplies. If I had to get out quickly, I could climb on top of the washer and squeeze through the two-foot square window above it.

I carried a pillow, sheets, and a thin blanket downstairs to make up a bed. Returning upstairs to my bedroom, I watched CNN for more than an hour without seeing anything remotely pertinent to my own life. At 11:15 p.m. the news network showed a preview for a new Japanese cartoon called *Twilight of the Cockroaches*. The plot involves a colony of virtuous cockroaches who thwart a wicked human family that tries to fumigate them. The preview played four times in fifteen minutes. In my rational mind I knew of no technology capable of beaming my own personal TV programming into my bedroom. Nevertheless I still believed I was following Ruth's admonition to "listen to the Universe." In my altered state this, too, was a message. Someone somewhere was trying to warn me. Someone who knew I would connect cockroaches with reincarnation and death. Thus I saw an obvious link between the bizarre preview and a loud, very public conversation I had three days earlier with a group of students on a crowded bus. We were discussing reincarnation, and I made a flippant remark about coming back as a cockroach.

The warning felt so real that I ran next door to my elderly neighbors. Carl was in bed and Florence was in her living room watching TV. I told her about the car that tried to run me down, and my fear that someone might break into the house. The couple took no interest whatsoever in politics, and I saw no point in telling her about the harassment. Florence, who listened to my revelations without comment, was tuned to CNN. For the next forty-five minutes we watched TV together without seeing the cockroach preview again or any of the other bizarre programming I saw at home.

At midnight she wanted to go to bed. When she saw I was too frightened to leave she called the police. Ten minutes later two cops arrived. They were skeptical when I told them about the attempted hit and run. They asked why anyone would want to kill me.

Knowing any mention of the harassment was likely to be construed as paranoia, I told them a disgruntled patient had threatened me. "He says he knows where I live," I lied. "He didn't say what he would do."

The two officers escorted me home and went through the house with me. The older one, a heavy-set man of about forty-five, whose face was permanently flushed, was clearly in charge. "After we leave, make sure to secure all the windows and doors, and under no circumstances go running outside."

I found this to be odd advice. Why issue such a strict warning if they didn't believe me? And why would anyone leave the safety of their home with something lurking in the yard wanting to kill them?

CHAPTER 9

It was 12:45 a.m. by the time the cops left. I returned to my bedroom to watch CNN. At two o'clock the network re-aired the preview for *Twilight of the Cockroaches* four times in ten minutes. When it came on a fifth time, I turned the TV off, grabbed the unzipped sleeping bag I used as a cover, and headed for the basement. I got as far as the kitchen, the only room with second-story windows. An intruder would have no way of knowing I was there without entering the house. Wrapping myself in the sleeping bag, I lay down on the floor and waited.

After twenty minutes I heard the crunch of footsteps on my gravel driveway. I heard them again after three minutes, and a third time three minutes later. Someone was circling the house. There was a noise, a window being forced from below me at the front of the house. Without warning a strong, sickly sweet smell came wafting through the return air duct. It was one I recognized instantly. Farmers use a variety of organophosphate inhibitors in agricultural spraying, but they all have the same distinctive cloying odor. I concluded the intruder saw the makeshift bed and let off a canister of vaporized chemical through the window directly above the washing machine. Delivered at close range, it would have killed me.

I raced into my combined living-dining room and opened all seven of the double hung windows that faced Third. Aware of the target I offered, I then dropped to the floor and crawled to a space under the center left window directly across from the open window in the bathroom. Thanks to a strong cross breeze, it was the one spot in the house with a continuous supply of fresh air. I waited thirty minutes. Failing to detect the odor anywhere in the room, I crawled to my desk, which was next to the front door, pulled the phone to the floor and dialed 911.

I told the woman who answered that someone had let off tear gas in my basement. I knew perfectly well the chemical wasn't tear gas, but this sounded more plausible. Delusions about pesticide poisoning are nearly as common as those involving the CIA. "I need to know if it's safe to remain in the house now that the smell is gone. An officer who came out last night told me not to go outside under any circumstances."

The dispatcher promised to send a patrol car out right away. It never arrived.

At 3:30 a.m., detecting no odor anywhere on the first floor, I returned to my bedroom and turned on CNN. Just before four o'clock I saw a series of images prompting me to dispose of the fake Persian carpet hanging on my clothesline in the basement. The warning made sense. If the rug absorbed the organophosphate, it would re-contaminate the house. Holding my breath, I ran down the basement stairs and dragged it off the line and out the side door into the yard.

I re-entered the house through the front door and continued to watch CNN. At 4:15 a.m. they replayed the cockroach preview three times in seven minutes. Another warning. The intruder was coming back to finish me off. By making the 911 call, I had broadcast over a tapped phone that I was still alive.

I turned the TV off, returned to the kitchen and lay down on the floor. Ten minutes later I heard rustling noises coming from the southeast corner of the basement, then the sound of a bag being zipped, then nothing.

■

By now, from the throbbing in my head and sharp cramps in my lower abdomen, I knew some of the chemical had entered my bloodstream. I weighed the risk of leaving the house to seek medical attention against the possibility that the intruder was still outside in the yard, and decided it was unlikely that I'd absorbed enough to kill me. A victim of cholinesterase poisoning either drowns in respiratory mucous or dies of dehydration due to watery diarrhea. I waited another fifteen minutes and returned to my bedroom, where I continued to watch CNN until daylight.

I saw no more previews for *Twilight of the Cockroaches*—ever again. Instead I was bombarded with promotions, seven in fifteen minutes, for videos about World War II and Nazi Germany. This, too, was a message. I had somehow overlooked the most sensitive and dangerous documents I possessed. The intruder came back, not to kill me, but for the evidence file on the old German.

I ran downstairs to rifle through the stack of old coloring books on the toy shelf where I had hidden it. I had read the cue correctly. The Social Security file was gone.

I returned to my bedroom and continued to watch CNN. After twenty minutes a distinct line of printing appeared at the bottom of my screen: "Where are records related to immigration?"

I got up and went to the living room. Because my line was bugged it made no difference who I phoned. I dialed my answering service. I told the Girl Friday operator I was expecting a call from my mother and I wanted them to give her a message. "Please tell her that there was no immigration material in the file, only medical records."

■

At 5:45 a.m. I got out of bed, bathed, and dressed. I brought my breakfast of granola and milk back to my bedroom and continued to watch CNN. At 6:25 a.m. I received a warning, though a combination of images and the words the announcer emphasized in his voiceover, that the peaches in my refrigerator were poisoned. Twenty minutes later the same announcer advised me to wear dresses instead of pants—that way women agents would find me less threatening and men would want to protect me. At 7:10 a.m. printing appeared at the bottom of my screen directing me to meet someone—in the toilet—of a flight from New York to San Francisco. That line was followed by a flight number, which flashed by too quickly to register. This was followed by six images of buildings exploding into smithereens through controlled demolitions.

Interpreting this cue as a threat, I dialed 911. "I called at three o'clock this morning about an intruder who broke into my basement. They said they would send out a patrol car, but no one came. I want to file a police report." The dispatcher left the line for thirty seconds. There was no record of my earlier call. When I insisted on filing a report, she had no choice but to send another squad car.

Twenty minutes later I told a new pair of cops about the Buick that tried to run me down, the earlier police visit, the odd warning to secure all my windows and doors and not run outside, the sound of the basement window being forced, followed by the house filling up with a smell I recognized as an organophosphate cholinesterase inhibitor. I finished by describing my physical symptoms, which by then included blurred vision, very slight dizziness, and persistent diarrhea.

Then both officers followed me to the basement, where I pointed out rags I had soaking in paint cans in my utility sink. The distinctive sweet smell was overpowering as soon as you got within three feet of the sink. It was obvious the rags had absorbed the chemical. "If possible, I would like you to have them analyzed," I told them.

As before, the cops were skeptical and dismissive. One of them, a beefy heavy-set man of about fifty, scolded me when I showed him the window that was forced. "I thought you were told to secure all your windows." Grabbing a hammer and a roofing nail from a toolbox on the floor, he nailed it shut.

■

They left and I went to my bedroom and packed a small suitcase, both puzzled and alarmed by the cops' contradictory behavior. If they believed I imagined the break-in, why make an issue of the unsecured window? Neither the warning nor the subsequent reprimand made any sense unless the Seattle police had inside knowledge of the break-in. Whether or not they were in league with local law enforcement, the people who were trying to kill me were unlikely to give up after two attempts. With nowhere else to turn, I was desperate to believe an uncorrupted member of U.S. intelligence was communicating with me, God knows how, via my cable system. And was waiting at JFK Airport in New York to take me under his protection.

I walked down Fifty-fifth to Market to catch a taxi, confident someone would cue me with the number of the San Francisco flight before I reached New York. A yellow cab pulled over just as I reached the lights at Sixth. I was about to get in when a passing car gave three sudden honks. In my hyper alert state, I took this as a warning not to get in the cab. I waved the driver on and instead boarded a 43 headed downtown.

As we passed Stone Way there was a disheveled homeless man with his back to Forty-fifth. He had a large white sign taped to his backpack, and printed in large block letters it read: IT'S A DEADLY CENTRAL NERVOUS SYSTEM POISON. Another message. I had told the dispatcher "tear gas." I was being corrected.

It didn't occur to me until I disembarked across from the main post office that I had no idea where to catch the airport bus. In my trance-like state, which was not unlike dreaming, I had no access to the logical processes I needed to figure out the corner where it stopped. A large ad on the back of another bus told me I would find what I was looking for at Seattle Central. I decided to follow this new cue instead. It was much easier to cross Second and catch a Capitol Hill bus to the community college than to fly all the way to New York. Especially as I had no idea which flight to catch once I got there.

Still lugging my suitcase, I spent thirty minutes wandering a maze of corridors at Seattle Central Community College. I was waiting for the next prompt, which never came. I was about to give up and board a 43 home when a young Asian man approached to ask the time. This was how my ex-husband Roy first introduced himself, a cue to get off at Roy Street. At Roy I was prompted—I don't recall how—to follow a woman with long, straight blonde hair. The woman turned right on Harvard, walked six blocks, and disappeared into the courtyard of an apartment complex. I dropped my suitcase behind the courtyard gate, too dizzy and nauseated to carry it any longer, and returned to the street. My next cue was to follow a short stocky male in his twenties with a blond crew-cut back to Roy. I was still behind him when he got in line at the Harvard Exit movie theater.

Obviously unaccompanied, he asked the cashier, in a voice loud enough to be heard ten feet away, for two child tickets. I had just given the clerk a ten-dollar bill for an adult ticket when he walked back and stood over me. His voice was emphatic. "I said two child tickets."

I corrected myself and paid for two child tickets. There was no staff at the door to take our tickets. This later struck me as very strange. I followed the man inside and lost sight of him in the crowded lobby. So I followed a group of chattering women into the main cinema instead. At one o'clock in the afternoon the auditorium was one-quarter full, and I took a left aisle seat in the middle of the center section. In the ten minutes I waited for the previews to start, half of the audience, all in a high state of agitation, got up and changed seats.

The lights dimmed. Still in a dream-like state where I attended to images and ignored content, I watched a series of shots of dolls, vinyl balloons, stuffed animals, and other toys. Suddenly an announcer boomed, "You will be tortured beyond your deepest fears." Then the title of a preview—*Eat the Peach*—came up in big letters with an enormous piece of fruit. Given the earlier cue about the poisonous peaches in my refrigerator, I took this as a cue to kill myself.

My immediate impulse was to do as I was directed. I stood up to leave and was overcome by a deep sense of melancholy. Committing suicide would end the indescribable pleasure of wandering the streets of Seattle following random cues. The sadness was quickly replaced by an equally powerful impulse to rebel. All of a sudden I woke up, as if from a deep sleep. My immediate reaction was horror, at the extent to which I had surrendered voluntary control of my behavior. I knew I was extremely lucky to come out of the experience alive.

Leaving the Harvard Exit I retraced my steps to collect my suitcase, which fortunately was still in the courtyard on Harvard where I left it. I then hiked down Denny to Westlake, where I caught a 28 home.

■

Following Humbolt's parting advice, the moment I walked in the front door I went to the phone and dialed 911. I informed the dispatcher I needed case numbers for the earlier police visits. This time she put me on hold for nearly a minute. She came on the line again and said she was sorry. There was no record of any prior calls or police visits to my home. Owing to my insistence on filing a police report and obtaining a case number, she sent out a fifth officer, a slender, thoughtful man in his mid forties with wavy salt and pepper hair. We sat together in my living room for twenty minutes, as he took careful notes about the five weeks of phone harassment, the Buick that tried to run me down, the two break-ins, the patient file that was stolen, the horrible sweet chemical the intruder let off in my basement, and my lingering physical symptoms. Like the first cops, he expressed surprise at my inability to identify who was harassing me or why.

"I have no idea. That's what I find so exasperating," I explained. We both fell silent as I racked my brain for some explanation he would find plausible. "I'm doing research into a potential AIDS treatment I believe is being suppressed. Perhaps that's why."

His voice became grave. "AIDS is a very dangerous issue. One you had best keep away from."

He gave me his business card with a case number scrawled across the top. He was about to leave when I told him I had wet rags in the basement that had absorbed the organophosphate. Again I asked if the police could have them analyzed. Following me to the basement, he reached gingerly into the utility sink, grabbed one of the paint cans and carried it away with him.

■

I had eaten nothing since breakfast and went to the kitchen to heat up a can of chili. The moment I began to eat the diarrhea started again. Despite drinking a half bottle of Kaopectate, I was in the toilet twice an hour until 4:00 a.m., when I finally dozed off. I was awake again at six o'clock and at 7:30 a.m. I got in my car to drive to the nearest CHEC Medical Center, which was on Denny Avenue at the bottom of First Hill. As I crossed Mercer, which was a freeway access, I was trapped by rush hour gridlock and missed my turn. By now the nausea and dizziness were too overpowering to drive. I turned onto a side street off Boren, parked my car, and walked three blocks up the hill to the emergency room of Cabrini Hospital. I told the clerk at the reception desk that my psychiatrist wanted to admit me and asked for him to be called.

Part II –
The Murder of Oscar Manassa

They can do anything
you can't stop them
from doing. How can you stop
them? Alone, you can fight,
you can refuse, you can
take what revenge you can
but they roll over you
from *The Low Road* by Marge Piercy

CHAPTER 10

I said nothing to the triage nurse about my exposure to cholinesterase inhibitor. I didn't expect to be believed and knew I would receive a complete physical exam as part of the admitting procedure. Meanwhile, if I was on the verge of shock or cardiac arrest, there was no better place to collapse than an emergency room. After taking my details, the nurse escorted me to one of six stretchers in the treatment area, handed me a backless gown, and asked me to disrobe.

It would be three hours before I saw a doctor. The explosive diarrhea persisted, and the only toilet was at the far end of the emergency department near the nurse's station. Reaching behind me to hold my gown closed, I made a total of six trips, all in clear view of ER staff and other patients and their families. The resulting dehydration made me extremely thirsty. A second nurse gave me a paper cup and I went back and forth eight times to the water fountain, which was next to the toilet. After two hours and two quarts of water I experienced a noticeable improvement in my physical symptoms. The blurred vision cleared, the blinding headache subsided into a dull throb, and the frequency of my bowel movements dropped from once every ten minutes to once an hour.

At 10:30 a.m., Nelson came down from Cabrini Towers and took me into the nursing supervisor's office. Since he already believed I was delusional, it seemed pointless to tell him about the intruder or the sweet-smelling chemical he released. Instead, I made up a story about a neighbor spraying insecticide too close to my bedroom window. I told him there was no way I could drive two and half hours to Vancouver. Nelson cut me off as I began to enumerate my symptoms. "I no longer practice inpatient psychiatry," he cautioned. "You will be admitted under a new psychiatrist named Anton Csardas. He is Hungarian but eminently competent."

I returned to my stretcher. Another hour passed before a psychiatric nurse came down from the sixth floor, helped me into a second gown which I wore back to front, and bundled my clothes into a large plastic garbage bag. She then escorted me up the staff elevator to Ward Six.

■

After taking my purse, to be deposited in the hospital safe, she showed me to one of the five bedrooms on the locked side of the unit. Although I was admitting myself voluntarily, assigning new psychotic patients to the locked intensive care unit was standard practice. This minimized any risk they would agitate other patients or try to leave. Except for the full bathroom, my room looked exactly like a prison cell. It had no curtains, window shades, or furnishings other than a small bedside cabinet and a twin-sized bed covered with a single white blanket.

For the first few hours I was having too much fun to notice how scary the ICU was. The nurses, believing I was manic, catered to my every whim. I complained there was no Bible in my bedside table, and someone immediately produced one. I insisted they also give me a *Physicians Desk Reference (PDR)* to look up any harmful drugs they might try to give me, and an aid brought me the copy from the nurse's station. When I demanded to make a phone call, the same aid escorted me to a small window-sized opening in the nurse's station and gave me a princess phone on a fifty-foot connector.

The first person I called was Ruth. Only she would understand how listening to the Universe and following random associations had landed me in a mental ward. I called Gloria next. She had a key to my house and was the logical person to bring my suitcase, which was still packed and sitting in my living room, and find my car and drive it home. My final call was to Girl Friday to retrieve my messages. During my three and a half week hospital stay, there were only three days I failed to contact my answering service and return all my calls. Undeterred by my message about suspending practice, patients and colleagues continued to leave four or five messages a day. Fortunately, I had the foresight to retrieve my appointment book before the nurses confiscated my purse. By the time I was discharged on August 19, I had booked fifteen patients for the month of September.

I returned to my room and opened my Bible. I had spotted a license plate driving up Boren that read "Psalm 32," and was curious if this was another cue. I found the psalm, which was an allegory employing mules to symbolize stubbornness and anger. It seemed to say angry people deserved whatever dire consequences befell them. This was a message of sorts. I should have taken Edward's warning to heart that anger got people locked up. Perhaps I wouldn't be in this mess if I hadn't lost my temper when Nelson accused me of being psychotic.

Deeply disappointed the psalm didn't tell me what to do, I opened the PDR. I flipped through the pages, hoping to recapture the rush of insights about studies different drug companies were concealing. In addition to suppressing research about Dyazide causing dementia and Tagomet's immune-modulating effects, I believed they were also suppressing BCG, an anti-tuberculosis vaccine widely used in Europe and Canada. To my dismay my mind was blank. In the relative sensory deprivation of my stark hospital room, the rush of insights and associations had totally ceased.

At four o'clock a female internist took me to the examining room. I described the dizziness, nausea, and diarrhea that led to my ER visit without mentioning the organophosphate exposure. I knew that Dr. Jones was likely to record everything I said in my chart. It was extremely important not to say or do anything she might construe as paranoid. My original symptoms were gone. I assumed any serious residual effects would show up in my blood tests.

At five o'clock, my new psychiatrist came to see me. Unlike Nelson, who was pushing sixty, balding, and nearly a hundred pounds overweight, Csardas, who was in his early forties, was short and thin and had olive skin and jet black hair. He bowed slightly as he introduced himself. Fortunately, he did not attempt to interview me, as his English was very difficult to understand. He simply delivered his diagnosis: "We will be treating you here for manic-depressive illness. It appears you have been manic-depressive your entire life and were simply unaware of it."

I was dumbfounded he would draw this conclusion without even talking to me. "Wouldn't that interfere in some way with my medical and psychiatric training?" I asked. "To say nothing of ten years of uninterrupted private practice."

Csardas said this was irrelevant. Argumentativeness in patients is equated with psychotic agitation, so I let him continue. "We will be starting you on the antipsychotic, Moban," he explained. That any psychiatrist would be so presumptuous as to start treatment without even talking to a patient left me too astonished to reply. Both Nelson and Fields had recommended hospitalization for observation only.

Twenty minutes later a nurse came to my room with two paper cups. The smaller one, the size of a shot glass, held a small salmon-colored tablet. The other contained water. Although Csardas's diagnosis was ludicrous, I risked losing my medical license if I failed to cooperate. I decided to take one dose. In the absence of true psychotic agitation, I knew I would experience pronounced sedation and dizziness. When this happened, I was confident my new shrink would realize he had made a mistake and discontinue the medication.

Forty-five minutes later I experienced what I recognized as an akathesia, a common side effect of neuroleptics. It started as a painful crawling sensation in my thorax and abdomen, as if something inside me was eating its way out. It was infinitely worse than any natural anxiety state, and nothing I did—lying on my bed, pacing, sit-ups, or push-ups—relieved it. I went to the window at the nurse's station and asked for a stat dose of Cogentin, the most common antidote. A twenty-something nurse with frizzy blond hair left the window to check my chart and came back.

"I'm afraid Dr. Csardas hasn't ordered any. We will have to page him."

Convinced this was the hellish torture I was threatened with at the Harvard Exit, I made the rounds of all the windows in my room and the ICU common area. I was fully prepared to leap out if I found one I could open. However they were all bolted shut with a key lock. In desperation, I shoved my head under the cold-water tap in my sink. After running for thirty seconds, the water produced an icy, stinging sensation on my scalp. This temporarily relieved my inner agony, but after five minutes the effect wore off. Over the next quarter hour I stuck my head under the running faucet three more times.

After twenty minutes a new nurse came to my room. However, instead of offering me Cogentin for the akathesia, she handed me another salmon-colored Moban. I was stunned any health professional would re-administer medication that caused such horrible side effects. Especially to a high-functioning physician who was neither agitated nor overtly psychotic. This time I concealed the tablet in my cheek, waited for the nurse to leave and flushed it down the toilet.

Ten minutes later a third nurse appeared, confronted me with flushing my medication and offered me a third dose of Moban in liquid form. I had forgotten all ICU patients were monitored via a concealed video camera. On the tray next to the cup with the clear pink fluid was a walnut-sized paper cup with a white Cogentin tablet. Convinced I had no choice, I reluctantly accepted both medications.

I was the only patient in the ICU and was totally alone for the rest of the night. Deep despair had supplanted my earlier festive mood. I was at the total mercy of people who clearly had very little regard for my well-being. At around 7:30 p.m., I heard muffled voices and realized St. Cabrini, which was run by the Missionary Sisters of the Sacred Heart, was broadcasting evening prayers. By standing directly under a speaker in the hallway I could just make out the words. For the first time since abandoning my faith at age twenty-one, I prayed along. Some immensely evil force was responsible for both the suicide cue at the Harvard Exit and for an hour of the most terrifying anguish I had ever known. The only way I knew to survive such Evil was to allow that a more powerful force for Good might also exist.

■

The next morning I asked to see a priest. In my mind the Catholics were the experts on the Devil and Evil, given their historic interest in demonic possession and exorcism. At around ten o'clock the chaplain, a short, muscular man with a gray buzz-cut, came to see me in the ICU common area. Without going into detail, I told him I was in the hospital because of problems with harassment. "I asked to see you because of a theological question," I told him. "I've had some very strange experiences in the last few days. I need to know if the Devil acts directly to cause Evil. Or can he only act through a human intermediary?"

The priest gave the same answer I would have expected from Edward. "You must not make the mistake of focusing on the Devil's machinations. Christians are called upon to focus on the greater love of God." He asked if I had any other questions he could help with. I shook my head. He blessed me with the sign of the cross and left.

The second day of my hospital stay was even more frightening than the first. At 10:30 a.m., Csardas came to see me for five minutes. "I'm starting you on Tegretol and lithium, in addition to Moban, as they are more specific for manic-depressive illness," he instructed. I was bewildered that he would order such massive doses of medication for a high-functioning professional who had strange thoughts but no psychotic agitation. However, with my career on the line, I believed I had no choice but to cooperate.

An hour later a large male in his early twenties, wearing brand new jeans and cowboy boots, joined me in the ICU. A second, slightly older man, who was barefoot and whose clothes were dirty and torn, joined us around one o'clock. Both of them were actively hallucinating and far too disoriented to hold a conversation. They paced up and down the hall mumbling to themselves and yelling loud obscenities into the air and occasionally at each other. Although this level of psychotic agitation is frequently associated with random violence, there were no nurses or aids on the locked unit, except briefly when they brought us meals and medication. My psychiatrist and the nursing staff saw no problem leaving me alone with two very angry, confused madmen who, with no warning, could beat me up, rape, or even kill me before a nurse could get the door unlocked.

By my third hospital day I was so heavily medicated I ceased to notice who came and went from the ICU. Despite the extreme sedation and dizziness, my biggest problem was a painful popping sensation that occurred at ten-second intervals in my leg and arm muscles. Csardas assured me the Moban wasn't causing the spasms because the Cogentin prevented this. In my stuporous state, it never occurred to me to challenge him, despite having treated dozens of patients whose neuromuscular side effects failed to respond to Cogentin. Edna had warned me about the possibility of food tampering. Having lost any capacity for rational thought, thanks to my heavy medication regimen, the only explanation I could think of for my overactive nervous system was that someone had doctored my food or drink with some kind of stimulant. The possibilities included cocaine, amphetamine, Ritalin, or possibly small doses of strychnine or picric acid, which were still used in veterinary medicine.

Our meals came up from the kitchen on trays specially labeled with our names. Nearly all the patients, not just the overtly paranoid ones, expressed concerns about the food. Some days the word went round not to touch the meat. Other days it was the salad. There were occasional meals in which all the trays went back untouched. Most of us were forbidden to leave the unit and relied on vending machines in the patient lounge to keep from starving.

When another patient put up a sign not to drink the water, I experimented by collecting water from three different taps in clear plastic glasses. Each glass had its own distinct shade of pinkish gray or yellow. I was already drinking cranberry juice with every meal, believing it would help detoxify me from the harmful effects of my medication. I now ordered a daily six-pack of ginger ale to drink in place of water. I also begged one of the nurses to test my urine for illicit drugs. Obviously perplexed that I would request my own drug screen, she informed me they already had and the result was negative.

By the fourth day I was allowed to leave the ICU and mingle with patients on the open unit, returning to the locked unit at night.

Recalling Edna's and Jabari's warnings about covert agents who sometimes followed their targets into jails and mental hospitals, I encountered only one patient who showed an inappropriate interest in my presence on Ward Six. David was about thirty, attractive, immaculately dressed and groomed, and well-spoken. The reasons for his admission were a great mystery. Unlike the rest of us, he took no medication. During my first evening on the open side, he made a point of sitting next to me as I watched a *National Geographic* special about African elephants. Five minutes into the program he leaned over and addressed me in the same authoritarian tone as the stocky blond man I followed into the Harvard Exit theater. "Stuart," he told me, "I want you to notice which station you are watching."

■

On my fifth hospital day Csardas sent me for an electroencephalogram to rule out organic brain disease, a standard practice in late-onset psychosis. The neurologist observed the procedure from an adjoining room and came in as the technician was removing the electrodes. I expressed surprise on learning the EEG was normal and told him about the continual twitching and popping sensations. His diagnosis, which should have been obvious to a psychiatrist with fifteen years of clinical experience, was a pseudo-Parkinsonian reaction to Moban.

"If the Cogentin doesn't control it, you should stop the antipsychotic," he said.

The next morning I demanded Csardas stop the Moban, and we agreed I would take Mellaril instead. The main side effects of low-potency antipsychotics like Mellaril are dizziness and sedation, but they rarely cause Parkinsonian side effects. Following the change I spent sixty-nine out of the next seventy-two hours blissfully asleep, getting up for one hour each morning to eat breakfast and see my psychiatrist.

I took Mellaril for three days before complaining to my

psychiatrist about the sedation. "I don't see how I can practice psychiatry or take care of my daughter if I sleep twenty-three hours a day. I am already taking lithium and Tegretol. Surely that is enough."

"You have no choice in this," was his reply. "You must take antipsychotics because you are still paranoid." This puzzled me. I took great care never to mention either my political activities or the harassment to my psychiatrist or any of the nurses. "The fact that you sleep on the floor is obvious proof of paranoia."

I had a perfectly rational reason for preferring the floor to my bed but knew my psychiatrist would dismiss it out of hand. The nurses required ICU patients to keep a light on in their rooms at night to allow the nursing station to monitor them via closed-circuit TV. There was a building site not fifty feet from my window. From the banging and clanging that went on all night, I knew homeless people squatted there. I also knew my bed, but not the floor, was clearly visible through my lighted, curtainless windows.

Faced with taking a medication that would make it impossible to work, drive, or care for my daughter, I decided to bite the bullet, take sleeping tablets to overcome my modesty and allow nurses, vagrants, and construction workers watch me while I slept. In essence what "cured" me of my so-called mental illness was the bargain I struck with Csardas: he agreed to stop the Mellaril and I agreed to stop acting paranoid.

Even without the antipsychotic I was left with chronic nausea, which I knew was due to lithium, and a sodden feeling like a bad head cold, which, according to another patient, was due to Tegretol. I complained to Csardas, but he refused to reduce either medication. Rather than argue with him, I decided it was better to put up with a few more days of misery than to do anything that might delay my discharge. After ten years of practice I had come to view male psychiatrists as vain creatures with enormous egos. They were unlikely to declare me sane unless they could convince themselves they had cured me.

■

All patients were required to go on leave to prove they were ready for discharge. Without family or close friends in Seattle, I had no one to fulfill this role other than Edward. My prior resolve to end the relationship crumbled during the first week of my hospitalization. He called twice and I let him visit, mainly out of intense boredom, as I was too heavily medicated to read, do crossword or jigsaw puzzles, or otherwise entertain myself.

I had no intention of ever telling Edward about the messages I received from my cable TV or my strange experiences at the Harvard Exit. However I asked him a question about food tampering the first time he called—continuing a discussion we'd had prior to my hospitalization. After Edna warned me against leaving unopened containers in my cupboard or refrigerator, I also asked Edward how to protect myself against possible food tampering. His response was that the human body could cope with vast amounts of poison—all of us were already exposed to dozens of poisons in our food, air, and water. "The best way to protect yourself is to make sure you are as healthy as you can be physically, emotionally, and spiritually."

What I asked now was whether he knew of any way to poison fresh peaches. My white friends would have found this question quite bizarre and insisted on knowing why I asked it. Not Edward. He didn't miss a beat. "A peach with a split pit can be poisonous. The pits contain cyanide."

When he came to visit, he asked to go to my room, interacting as a lover and special friend as if nothing untoward had happened between us. We lay down on my bed, and he attempted to fondle my breasts and belly under my clothes. Startled when I pushed him away, he gave me a long penetrating look. "Speaking of peaches, I don't keep no secrets."

It was pointless to ask what he meant because Edward never explained himself.

■

I had been at St. Cabrini exactly three weeks when Csardas gave me a pass to accompany Edward to Ruth's wedding to a tall, balding white man with shoulder-length blond hair. They got married in her home on Lake City Way. Her yard resembled a plumbing salvage outlet, with numerous discarded toilets, sinks, pipes, and bathroom and kitchen fixtures, along with odd pieces of furniture and car parts. It was the only time I ever saw Ruth dressed up, in a sheer rayon blouse and a tailored skirt. She was busy dancing in and out of the house, while simultaneously playing bongo drums and singing. She didn't seem to notice I was there.

CHAPTER 11

Two days later I was discharged. Edward drove me home and we went straight to my bedroom. Following my hospitalization, I resumed our affair partly out of fear and partly out of grandiosity. At one level I saw it as a kind of insurance against further attempts to kill me, or, more importantly, attempts to kill or harm my daughter. After five fruitless contacts with the police, I had nowhere else to turn. At another level I still believed Edward might inadvertently disclose who he worked for and what they wanted with me. At the same time, I was deeply ashamed of my own indecisiveness, which was totally uncharacteristic. I knew I would have to conceal our relationship from my feminist friends, especially after the assault with the insecticide pump.

As before, the sex was an expectation, the price I paid not to be home alone with constant prank calls and the threat of another home invasion. Edward viewed all women as one-dimensional creatures who bartered their sexual favors for a variety of material and emotional needs. Determined this wouldn't occur with us, he made sure all our time together revolved around the sex act. It didn't occur to me to object. I had no interest whatsoever in sex—a new side effect I had no opportunity to experience in the hospital. Nevertheless, my vagina lubricated and I submitted passively to intercourse. If my lover noticed that I got nothing out of it, he didn't let on.

As I watched him dress, I was alarmed to discover it wasn't just my libido that was gone. The medication seemed to have wiped out my capacity for a whole range of emotions—warmth, curiosity, anticipation, excitement. I listened for the front door to slam and got up and emptied the lithium and Tegretol tablets I was given down the toilet. It was okay to vege out in the hospital, where someone else looked after all my needs. In the real world I had a child to support. In a mental state devoid of any joy or excitement, I would never get out of bed in the morning.

After flushing the toilet, I went straight to the phone to call my answering service. I told them to cancel the message that my practice was closed. My one-month suspension ended the day of Ruth's wedding.

∎

The hang-up calls resumed within hours of Edward's departure, a painful shock after my three and a half week reprieve from prank calls, car gangs, and break-ins. I left the hospital wanting to believe Csardas was right, that I would arrive home to discover the harassment was an invention of my paranoia. The daily pattern of five to six hang-up and prank calls continued unchanged from the weeks prior to my hospitalization. In addition, I noticed an ominous shift in the content of the calls. While I received no overt death threats, I got eight calls in two days about funeral insurance and burial plots.

My first night home I was awakened at 12:30 a.m. by squealing brakes and a car stereo blaring Martin Luther King's "I Have a Dream" speech. I heard the vehicle make the circuit down Market, up Fifty-fifth, and down Third Northwest back to Market. Ten minutes later it stopped in front of my house. After two attempts on my life, I faced the very real possibility the occupants would try to enter the house. I got up to call Edward, who had the night off, my head spinning with terrifying images.

"Please, Edward. It's started again. I'm afraid they will break in. Please come and stay with me."

My lover refused, speaking slowly and with practiced patience as if addressing a child. "I want you to know that I love you. But I can't do this for you. You can only do it for yourself. The only solution now is to prepare yourself to die."

This was neither as heartless nor sinister as it sounded. Edward was referring to a story he had told me about nearly choking on a piece of meat. He was at a dinner party and the harder he tried to cough it up the more tightly lodged it became. Eventually, he resigned himself to the inevitability of his death, his throat relaxed, and the meat popped out. It was a point he came back to many times. If the people who were harassing me were intent on killing me, I only increased my suffering by getting so upset about it.

I saw no alternative but to follow his advice. After hanging up, I sat down at my desk, took a blank piece of stationery from the top drawer, and tried to visualize the unfinished business I would take care of if I had a terminal illness. The first item on my list was to complete and submit the application for the People's Memorial Association that had sat on my desk for nearly a year. This was a local funeral cooperative that offered bargain rates for burials and cremations. The second was to make a copy of my will for Gloria and give her a key to my safe deposit box. Number three was to change the message my answering service gave out to patients. If I knew for certain I was about to die, I would put an immediate stop to the 3:00 a.m. hang-up calls by unplugging my phone. Whereas previously I prided myself on being available to patients at any hour of the day or night, from now on Girl Friday would instruct them to contact the Crisis Clinic after 11:00 p.m., as the public mental health clinics did.

By the time I found the most recent copy of my will, which was buried in the bottom drawer of my desk, filled out the PMA application, wrote them a check for fifteen dollars, found a stamp, and called my answering service, it was 5:30 a.m.. I pulled slacks and a sweater over my nightgown and drove to a nearby convenience store to copy the will. From there I drove straight to Northgate to leave the will, key, and contact details for Andrea, who became Naomi's guardian on my death, in Gloria's mailbox. I returned via Third Northwest and sat in the parking lot of the Greenwood Fred Meyer's until the store opened at seven o'clock. A month earlier I had seen air purifiers on display that made a continuous low-pitched noise that was louder than a babbling stream but softer than a waterfall. I bought one for $24.95, took it home and plugged it in next to my bed. As I anticipated, the white noise drowned out all sound outside my bedroom. There was nothing I could do to thwart people who were genuinely determined to hurt me. Instead, I would render myself oblivious to their presence. I was resigning myself not so much to my death as to my powerlessness.

■

On Wednesday at 9:00 a.m. I drove to SeaTac airport to meet my mother's flight from Milwaukee. From the very beginning she was the only person in my life who believed there were real people calling and following me who sought to do me and my daughter harm. It was only after her death that I discovered the log she kept in a tiny notebook in her underwear drawer. It was a record of strange phone calls, five of them all together, that she herself received while I was in the hospital. One of them was from Jabari. I didn't give her number out to any of my friends and I wondered how he'd gotten it.

The next morning we boarded a southbound Amtrak Starliner for a four-day trip to Chico to see Naomi. An hour out of Seattle I observed a tall, slender man with thick reddish-blond hair and a designer knit polo shirt who got up and followed me every time I left the coach for the snack bar or the scenic lounge. When we stopped at Roseberg he took the armchair next to me in the lounge. I knew he was studying me as I watched families greet each other on the platform. In fact it came as no surprise when he commented on what he saw.

"It's fascinating, isn't it, to observe other people's lives?"

I ignored him. At midnight he pursued me to the snack bar and asked permission to sit at my table. With only one table, it was hard to refuse.

"Are you traveling alone?" he asked. I told him I was with my mother. "And you're on your way to California?"

"Chico. To see my daughter. She's spending the summer with friends."

"I'm on my way home to San Diego. I was just in Seattle for a conference. I'm a psychologist specializing in pain disorders." The blond stranger lost no time establishing his interest wasn't romantic by bringing his wife into the conversation. "I have a private practice in San Diego, and my wife and I have just built a home there."

Because he was obviously pursuing me, I assumed he had some connection with the people responsible for tapping my phone and harassing me. However, I could see no particular danger in talking to him. I naively believed if I was totally open and convinced the FBI, CIA, or whoever sent him I wasn't a communist and posed no threat to national security, they would leave me alone.

From then on he bombarded me with progressively intrusive questions about the kind of work I did, where my mother lived and what she did, how I spent my leisure time, and the friends I was visiting in California. I made no mention of my hospitalization or the events leading up to it. Otherwise, I was totally candid about my political beliefs and activities.

After about ten minutes his questions became more personal and open-ended. It was clear he wanted me to discuss my relationship with my mother. However, I had no intention of doing so. He made a general comment about families and communities coming together after a long period of being alienated from one another. It wasn't exactly a question. However, it was clear from his expectant look and smile that he wanted me to respond. It suddenly occurred to me that he had no interest whatsoever in my politics. He was assessing my mental state, presumably to determine whether I was still psychotic or not. I recalled an oblique comment Edward made at Ruth's wedding, suggesting that I had deliberately faked my illness. I could see why this might alarm my psychiatrists. However, I could see no possible reason for U.S. intelligence to worry whether I was truly insane or just putting on an act.

■

Our train pulled into Chico at 2:00 a.m., and Andrea kept Naomi up to meet us. I felt a bittersweet ache in my ribs when I saw how thrilled she was to see me. Despite all the psychoanalytic literature describing the romance between mother and infant, I hadn't expected a six-year-old to be this demonstrative. She insisted I sleep in the sofa bed she made up for us in Andrea's living room. In the morning she brought me a scissors and demanded I cut her hair. During her entire two months in California, she refused to let anyone else touch it.

Surrounded by trusted friends, I could speak openly for the first time about the bizarre circumstances leading to my hospitalization. Andrea's boyfriend Paulus, who was in his mid-twenties, looked like a hippie with his straight shoulder-length blond hair, unkempt beard, and torn jeans. He was actually a brilliant biochemist and biophysicist who was pursing advanced degrees in both disciplines and who manufactured his own amphetamine salts to help regulate his mood. He also suffered from bona fide manic-depressive illness.

Unlike my three psychiatrists, he had no difficulty pinpointing a plausible biochemical cause for my brief psychosis.

"The stress of the harassment obviously caused a massive increase in your pressor amines," he diagnosed, "while the monoamine oxidase inhibitor you were taking totally obliterated your ability to degrade them."

Andrea and Naomi were outside with my mother while she smoked a cigarette. Paulus and I were alone at the dining room table drinking our third cup of coffee. He continued. "Given sufficient environmental stress and dislocation, all human beings, not merely people like me with bad genes, are capable of psychotic disorganization. If they weren't, psychophobia wouldn't be so universal." He explained the term coined by the controversial Scottish psychiatrist R.D. Laing. "Homophobia is the irrational belief homosexuality is contagious. Psychophobia is the fear of becoming psychotic. Not only do people believe they can catch mental illness, but they have a deeply engrained fear that psychosis is always lurking just around the corner. Why else do human beings cling so tenaciously to routines and rituals except to keep their mental life in order?"

As comforting as I found all this, I was more interested in his take on Edward and his role in my so-called illness—the dummy he left in the spare bed, the bizarre assault with the insecticide sprayer, the repeated previews for a cartoon about cockroaches being attacked with pesticide, the release of a cholinesterase inhibitor in my basement, followed by the mysterious appearance of a homeless man with a large sign about "nerve poison."

"I know it all sounds really bizarre," I admitted. "Do you think I imagined this stuff as a result of my psychosis? If it really was a conspiracy, it was an extraordinarily complicated one. I can't think how any government agency or group could affect so many areas of a person's life. Besides, what possible motivation could they have?"

It was clear from Paulus's tight-lipped response that he was uncomfortable with this topic. "I think this man is an evil magician and you need to stay away from him," is all he would say. Taking his cup to the sink, he grabbed his cigarette papers and foil-lined packet of rolling tobacco and joined the others outside.

■

At 3:00 a.m. on Sunday, my mother and I boarded Amtrak again, without Naomi. I could resign myself to my own death but not my daughter's. Bringing her home was unthinkable until I found some way to protect her from the people targeting me. We arrived in Seattle on Monday afternoon. On Tuesday I had appointments with both Nelson and a psychologist named Hanan Berman. I got Berman's name from an African American social worker at the Asian Counseling Service. He left a message with my answering service while I was in the hospital, after someone showed him my letter to Bernie. Berman was a former Veterans Administration psychologist who specialized in treating Vietnam veterans for post-traumatic stress disorder. By now I was beginning to suspect my so-called psychosis was actually a dissociative episode, a common feature of PTSD. The only effective treatment for PTSD is psychotherapy—in essence talking and working through the trauma that triggers it. Yet despite seeing three psychiatrists and spending three and a half weeks on a mental ward, I had yet to discuss the break-in or the attempts on my life with anyone but Paulus.

My mother accompanied me to both appointments. We saw Berman first, an obviously Jewish man of about forty with wavy brown hair sprinkled with flecks of gray, and a short gray beard. He knew why I was there and introduced himself by talking about ex-GIs he treated who fought in Cambodia when it was illegal for them to be there.

"Government agents still visit them twice a year to remind them what will happen if they tell anyone," he revealed.

I began the session by telling him how ashamed and humiliated I felt that I had been briefly psychotic and believed I was getting messages from my cable TV. His response surprised me. He thought there might be a technological explanation for the strange programming and printing I saw on my TV screen. "It involves inserting a 'patch' where the cable feed leaves the street," he explained.

We saw Nelson in the afternoon. In my mother's presence my psychiatrist was more circumspect about interrupting me. He let me tell him about the old German I encountered at the Office of Hearings and Appeals, and the intruder who broke in and stole his file. It seemed better not to mention that this person had also let off a cholinesterase inhibitor in my basement. My psychiatrist would find that much harder to believe.

"You were harassed, then." Obviously perplexed, my psychiatrist related his side of the conversation with Edward. "He told me he was a janitor downtown and denied he ever had problems with harassment himself. He said he could never tell if you were in fantasyland or not."

I was neither surprised nor disappointed to learn Edward had lied about vouching for my sanity. In fact the plan to railroad me into the hospital struck me as quite ingenious. I still believed whoever planned the break-in meant to kill me with the organophosphate. However, if for some reason I survived, they had a foolproof fallback. They assumed I would inform the police—and Nelson—about the incident with the insecticide pump, the odd cockroach cartoons, and the homeless man with the sign about nerve gas. Claiming someone had let off nerve gas in my basement was bizarre enough. Linking it to such a freakish and improbable chain of events would be taken as proof I was delusional.

I was quite surprised that Nelson didn't object when I informed him about stopping the lithium and Tegretol. In fact, on learning that a psychotherapist was monitoring me weekly, he agreed to write a new prescription for Nardil. It was obvious to both of us I had lapsed into depression. I was convinced that my medical career was most likely over—that no one would give me a job or send me referrals once word got out about my psychiatric hospitalization. Nelson also took down Berman's name and contact details. At our second visit my psychologist presented me a written agreement the two of them had drawn up for me to sign. It stipulated I would only see patients for medication management and perform no psychotherapy prior to January 1, 1988.

■

On Wednesday, August 26, my mother returned to Milwaukee and I resumed practice. My first appointment was a new patient, a well-spoken, immaculately dressed and groomed African American in his early thirties. He said he called my office after seeing my ad in the *Facts*. The *Facts* editor, viewing free treatment as a community service, continued to run my ad for eighteen months without charge. Yet, like many of the fictitious, "undercover" patients I saw over the next fifteen years, the man in front of me couldn't tell me why he had come. Instead, this young black male with perfect teeth and diction launched into a series of very direct questions of his own—where I trained, how many years I had been in practice, and whether I had a subspecialty within psychiatry. As with the psychologist on the train, his tentative tone and appraising silences told me he wasn't interested in the answers—he was reading me for nonverbal cues of my mental state.

I saw two patients on Thursday, two on Friday, and a total of seven the following week. During the five and a half weeks my office was closed I had lost half my caseload, as well as two contracts with the Social Security Administration. This meant I would have to find part-time work to cover basic living expenses for myself and my daughter. None of the local clinics would hire a new psychiatrist without at least three references. I had only one. Of all my professional colleagues, only Erica knew the real reason for my hospitalization. By now most of the mental health community knew, somehow, about my stint at St. Cabrini. Many of them told me openly that a psychiatrist who had been psychotic would never be fully competent to see patients again.

Ironically, I fell back on Edward's advice in overcoming the stigma I faced. Although he offered it in the form of long, convoluted stories about his family or past girlfriends, in reality it was quite simple: if I was unflinching in the view of myself I projected to the world, I could force other people to see me that way. In doing so I had to be absolutely clear what I was trying to accomplish. I saw this now. First and foremost I had to restore my professional credibility, resurrect my practice, and look after my daughter's material and emotional needs. Once I met these goals, I could exact my revenge from the people who attempted to destroy my sanity and my career.

Over the next month my former terror transformed itself into a relentless single-mindedness that left no room for slackness, doubt, or uncertainty. Although there were many days I had no appointments at all, I disciplined myself to arrive in my office promptly at nine o'clock. Except for trips to the toilet and snack bar, I remained at my desk till six o'clock to make sure I answered the phone personally for prospective patients. That first month I was lucky to get three calls a week and spent most of my time sending out resumes and bills on delinquent accounts, updating my ledgers, preparing reports for other doctors and agencies, and auditing my patient files to make sure they all had typed assessments and medical histories and documented referrals for physical exams and lab tests. When there was no more paperwork to do, I removed all the books from my shelves and dusted them, as well as all my plants and pictures. Then I brought my mop and vacuum cleaner from home and moved my desk, shelves, and file cabinets into the waiting room while I shampooed my carpet and my two upholstered armchairs.

I engaged in the same exhaustive housecleaning and yardwork when I arrived home in the evenings. I waited for rush hour, when a hundred cars an hour head towards north Seattle along Third, to bring out my heavy wrought-iron push mower. My purpose was to make a big show of my upper body strength, by pushing the mower up the steep hills in my front and side yards. I wanted to send a clear message to anyone contemplating a second home invasion. I wanted them to know that I would have the psychological, if not physical, advantage—and that they were unlikely to escape the encounter unscathed.

■

Two days after I resumed practice, Mark Watson, a known copious note-taker who frequented ISO and various coalition meetings, called and said he had to see me. On the surface it was an odd request. Mark was nothing more than a face I occasionally saw at meetings. In fact, it had been two years since we'd had any contact at all. Nevertheless, I agreed to his request. Mark had a well-established reputation as an informant, and I was open to any potential opportunity to glean information about my invisible enemies.

I asked him come to the house at 5:30 p.m. while it was still light. I waited for him on the porch, determined to remain in full view of two sets of elderly neighbors. I offered him a seat and went inside to make him a cup of herbal tea. When I returned, he started talking before giving me a chance to sit down.

"Stuart, I want you to know that I understand exactly what you are going through. I've been through it myself."

I had no idea what he was talking about. I never discussed my personal life with known informants, and Mark and I shared none of the same friends. His face was unreadable. Mark had piercing blue eyes, a short military-style haircut, and the classic stone face I associated with men who wore military style haircuts in 1987, before short hair became fashionable again. He gave me a few seconds to say something. Then he continued with a long, bizarre story about a forty eight-hour "spiritual quest" he undertook in 1982, by following random "signs" through the streets of Buffalo.

There was an awkward silence when he finished. I was still at a total loss what we were talking about. It occurred to me he wanted me to disclose my own experience of following random cues that directed me to wander through Capitol Hill with a suitcase. Obviously, I had no intention of doing so. I had told no one, not even Paulus or Berman, about the subliminal cues that led me to the Harvard Exit. Any knowledge Mark had about my strange "adventures" came from the people who arranged them for me.

"This is a prison planet, you know," he continued. I had no idea where this came from, either. I think Mark, like Edward, assumed I was a New Ager and eager to discuss my beliefs. It irritated me that the people spying on me equated being a Marxist, which was a perfectly logical system of thinking about the world, with New Age spirituality, which was totally irrational and superstitious. "There are profoundly evil forces in the universe that sentence people here for crimes in their past lives. They try to get you to kill yourself because that way you are forced to repeat your sentence."

Mark waited about half a minute for me to say something. I had no idea what to say. So he got up, drained his tea mug, and left.

■

I noted a distinct change in Edward following Mark's visit. We were never alone together after that, except in bed, and he no longer made any effort to conceal his contempt for leftists and progressives. After making love one night he told a long, complicated story about the mothers of his four children and how he turned three of them into successful business women.

"My love will do the same for you," he said. "That way, you can give up radical politics. People only turn to that kind of thing out of envy. Because they don't know how to be successful."

"I'm sure all three of my psychiatrists would most likely agree with you," I said. "They also blame my political views on mental instability."

I felt Edward stiffen when I said this and heard a distinct edge in his breathing. This happened whenever I broached topics relating to my hospitalization or the events preceding it.

"There is no question you are a supremely intelligent woman," he went on. His tone of awe and mistrust told me he really meant "supremely deceptive." It also gave me the sense that he was speaking for others beside himself. Presumably, he and whoever he worked for concluded, based on my rapid recovery, that I merely pretended to be psychotic—as part of some devious scheme to entrap them. This was pure projection, of course. Edward and his friends were so caught up in their own deceit and intrigue that they automatically attributed their own motives to me.

CHAPTER 12

The daily prank calls and phone disruption continued. Calls I initiated were cut off or interrupted by loud static. Strangers tied up my office answering machine with long stretches of elevator music, while patients complained of getting a disconnect recording whenever they tried to call my office. When I complained to the U.S. West customer service representative, she assured me there was no way this could happen with a working number.

If car gangs continued to visit the neighborhood, I was oblivious to them. The house was still watched or I was meant to think it was. At least three times a week I received a hang-up call within seconds of walking in the door. On September 5, someone broke into the house while I was at work. The only item they took was an ad I clipped from the *Christian Science Monitor* for a wrap-around skirt. Three days later the clipping mysteriously reappeared on the mantelpiece where I left it. However a *New York Times* clipping about the Christic Institute's lawsuit against the CIA that disappeared off my desktop that day was never returned. The Institute, representing two reporters injured in the La Penca bombing in Nicaragua, used the suit to expose the extensive involvement of the Contras, the CIA, and military intelligence in cocaine trafficking.

A week later I experienced a third attempt to either kill or permanently disable me when I came within a foot of colliding with a young blonde in a red corvette convertible. It appeared to be one of the "arranged" accidents Edna had warned me about. I was heading north on Third when I saw a disheveled looking vagrant, presumably the "spotter," in front of the steep wooded bluff between Market and Fifty-fifth. Puzzled at seeing a stranger in an overgrown area with no foot traffic, I slowed to fifteen miles per hour to investigate. A few seconds later, the blonde zoomed into my lane from a hidden driveway across the street. At a normal speed I would have totaled my car.

■

It would take four weeks to lay the groundwork to bring Naomi home. By now I was confident of my ability to dissuade potential intruders from messing with me in the middle of the night. Ensuring my daughter's safety when she was out of my direct supervision was more difficult. The week school opened I walked the three blocks to West Woodland Elementary School to enroll her and inform the school secretary she would be starting one month late. I also put her on the list for a first grade playgroup and signed myself up for the Parent Teacher Student Association. It was dangerous to limit my acquaintances to fellow leftists. For the sake of my own and Naomi's personal safety, it was important to convince as many mainstream yuppies as possible that I was a happy, well-adjusted professional—people who would ask awkward questions if I suddenly committed suicide or succumbed to some freak catastrophe.

On Friday, September 25, I drove to Olympia to testify at a Senate Health and Long Term Care Committee hearing on Senator Lorraine Wojahn's bill to regulate antipsychotic drugs. Her bill would have prohibited psychiatrists from prescribing antipsychotics without obtaining written consent, comparable to the form patients sign for surgery. My decision to testify was a frontal attack on the stigma surrounding my hospitalization, as well as an opportunity to demonstrate to one hundred legislators, lobbyists, and reporters that I was happy and well-adjusted. I was given exactly two minutes to describe how I was coerced to accept treatment with drugs I didn't need and which caused excruciatingly painful side effects. The success of my testimony was clear from the dead silence that fell over the packed hearing room. If a high-functioning psychiatrist could be coerced to accept treatment that caused harmful side effects, it could happen to anyone.

The final issue I had to resolve related to the criminal charges stemming from the UW sit-in. Unbeknownst to me, Csardas had contacted the presiding judge after a friend who was collecting my mail delivered the court summons to his office. When the judge learned I was on a psychiatric ward, he ordered the charges stricken. Csardas told me all this three days before my discharge, during our first and only discussion about the harassment. I was surprised to discover my psychiatrist already knew about the sit-in and my tussle with the police. His tone was dismissive. "You were obviously psychotic to be up there in the first place."

I wanted written proof that the charges had been dropped, and I drove straight from Olympia to the public safety building for an official copy of my rap sheet. The transcript, which cost fifty cents, contained a single entry dated July 15, 1987 for "Obstruction of a Peace Officer." This was partially obliterated with the purple stamp, "Stricken," followed by the judge's signature and the date August 4, 1987.

■

I pulled out of my driveway at 5:45 a.m. the next morning and arrived in Chico at 10:30 p.m. Saturday night. Naomi and I began the return trip on Sunday just before noon, spent the night in Roseberg, Oregon, and arrived home at 3.30 pm on Monday. The next day I had a second near-collision on my way home from work. This time the "spotter" was a woman with a black leather jacket and spiky orange hair. By the time I noticed her on the northwest corner of Third and Fifty-fifth, I was in the middle of the intersection. A half second later a blue pick-up ran the stop sign. With no room to brake, I steered a hard left and hit the truck's rear fender. Instead of stopping, the other driver gunned his accelerator and sped away.

From then on I left my car in the driveway and took my bicycle to work. A bike was virtually tamper-proof because I could take it inside with me. Cycling to my office also made it much harder for people to follow me. I only observed two cyclists shadowing me over the next two years. In both cases I forced them to pass by slowing up. I was totally unprepared for the possibility someone would try to ram me with their bike. In early November, I was pedaling west along the ship canal when a twenty-something cyclist with waist-length brown hair and heavy motorcycle boots darted out of an alley and headed straight for me. I braked hard and, by some miracle, dismounted without falling. The other rider pedaled away, pretending not to notice me.

In early December I was set up for a fifth near-miss, which I believe was actually an elaborate prank, as it involved a child. I was cycling east on Leary when a tall, middle-aged man came running out of the florist shop opposite Sixth with a ten-year-old boy. The man shouted to the child to take cover, and they both ducked behind the passenger side of a dark Honda sedan. Suddenly there was an ear-splitting crack from a truck on my left. It was a little after nine o'clock and all the sidewalks on both sides of Leary were deserted. Thus there was no question the gunshot, if it was real, was meant for me.

■

After bringing Naomi home, I responded to these threats with the ferocity of a female bear protecting her cub. Still determined to identify and expose the specific agency or group responsible, on Berman's advice I filed Freedom of Information Act requests with the FBI, CIA, and Seattle police. Both federal agencies denied the existence of any records under my name. The police sent me a form letter acknowledging they kept a file on me. However, because it related to a criminal offense, they could only release it if I requested and signed a privacy document.

It seemed a safe assumption that I was targeted for engaging in political activities my anonymous admirers found objectionable. Yet here, too, I drew a blank. If the harassment related to my collaboration with Earl and Jabari, surely it should have ceased the day Naomi and I returned from Chico. Earl phoned that night for the first time since my hospitalization. He wanted me to organize a fundraising banquet for the Museum. The call surprised me. I assumed Earl had written me off as a result of my so-called mental illness, as most of my white friends had.

I declined his request to organize a banquet for him. "I can raise as much money for the Museum as you want," I told him. "But I have to do it my way, using proven fundraising techniques. Putting on a banquet requires a significant outlay of cash. Which neither of us have. And public events are very unpredictable. You can put a massive amount of work into them and still lose money."

My response clearly annoyed him. "No, it has to be a banquet," he insisted. "The next time you decide to occupy a public building, we'll do it your way."

I replied calmly and firmly that I wasn't about to commit money I didn't have. "I have virtually no income now, Earl."

"I'll call you back later. It sounds like this isn't a good time."

I lost it. I was working hard to control my temper, as well as my anxiety and fears. But not when men patronized me. Earl and I shouted at each other for a few minutes and he slammed the phone down. It would be our last conversation for four years.

The only way I could think of to identify my invisible tormentors was to figure out exactly what I was doing that they found so threatening. It seemed the best way to go about this was to simply resume the activities that seemed to provoke a response in the past. If this produced a new, more intense reaction, there was always a possibility someone would inadvertently leave evidence behind or provide some other clue of their identity. They obviously had concerns about me keeping the old German's file, or they wouldn't have broken in and stolen it. And I already had direct input from Cheryl Franklyn and the last cop who came out about my interest in AIDS being dangerous. Thus it seemed logical to pursue both avenues.

The file was gone, but I still had a billing sheet and social security number for the elderly Social Security applicant who denied his German identity. Six months earlier, *Frontline* broadcast a documentary about the Simon Wisenthal Institute in Los Angeles and their work tracking ex-Nazis who entered the U.S. illegally. In mid-October I Xeroxed and mailed them a copy of the billing sheet, with a cover letter explaining the circumstances of my encounter with Richter. The Institute's eight-month investigation ultimately failed to connect him to specific war crimes. However, it did turn up German documents revealing he had served in Hitler's army, for which he still received an army pension. They forwarded this information to the Social Security Administration, which in turn revoked his disability award, fined him $10,000, and disqualified him from ever reapplying.

Alerting the medical community and public to a safe and potentially life-saving AIDS treatment was more complicated. I began by contacting Smith Kline and French and requesting copies of all existing studies regarding the effects of Tagomet in HIV infection. What I got back was the University of Essen open-label trial, a preliminary report from their current double blind study and a cryptic letter from one Smith Kline researcher to another regarding the pharmacokinetic interaction between Tagomet and AZT.

I followed up with a request for Smith Kline to fund my own open-label trial in five patients with AIDS Related Complex (ARC). Before the advent of antiretroviral treatment, ARC was diagnosed when a patient had demonstrated HIV antibody, along with evidence of chronic illness—usually fatigue, night sweats, weight loss, swollen lymph nodes, and high susceptibility to colds and other minor infections. Patients only qualified for a diagnosis of AIDS once they developed a life-threatening secondary infection. The latter was inevitable as the HIV virus totally destroyed their immune system.

I knew I had no hope of getting a medical journal to publish such a small study. However, Elizabeth Taylor had just started a non-profit organization in San Francisco that collected and publicized information about alternative AIDS treatments for patients unable to tolerate AZT.

Although Smith Kline ignored my second letter, their detail man, who supplied antidepressant samples for my indigent patients, was happy to provide Tagomet samples as well. I performed all the baseline physical exams myself, which meant my only cash outlay was to Swedish Mini Lab for quarterly blood monitoring. Within three weeks of starting 1200 mg of Tagomet a day, all five of my subjects reported that their fatigue, night sweats, oral thrush, and swollen lymph nodes had vanished. One patient, who had suffered for months with herpes simplex lesions all over his body, woke up after two weeks to find they had crusted over and healed. A diagnosed Kaposi sarcoma on the cheek lining of another patient disappeared after three weeks on the drug.

In March 1988 I submitted these findings to Project Inform, which circulated them to support groups across the country that were investigating alternative AIDS treatments. In March 1989 the Gay Men's Health Center in New York presented my study, along with the University of Essen studies and other research into Tagomet's in-vitro effects, at the International AIDS Conference in Montreal. Two months later the AIDS Coalition to Unleash Power (ACT-UP) conducted a civil disobedience, in which they laid down in the street in front of the corporate offices of both Smith Kline French and Glaxo, who produced the H2 blocker Zantac. Glaxo eventually funded a $600,000 double blind trial of the effect of Zantac in HIV.

In the U.S., the lifesaving antiretroviral drugs that became widely available in the mid-nineties eclipsed the Glaxo study. It was left to the developing world and a group of Thai scientists to continue research into H2 blockers and other low-cost treatment alternatives. The vast majority of AIDS patients live in the Third World, where they have no hope of ever receiving antiretroviral medications costing more than $15,000 a year.

■

I was very frustrated that my contacts with the Simon Wisenthal Institute and my AIDS study produced no particular increase or decrease in the intensity of the harassment. I concluded there must be something about me personally or the kind of work I did that the U.S. security apparatus objected to. Although I participated in no organized political activities for two years following my hospitalization, my psychiatric practice itself was quite politicized. There was no question my status as a physician strengthened the credibility of whistleblowers and labor activists I assisted with lawsuits and workers compensation and disability claims.

Unfortunately, my medical credentials proved of no benefit whatsoever when I was subpoenaed to testify in Jabari's defense. It was November 1987 before the activist finally went to trial on the charges stemming from his arrest in June. In August, Judge

McCutcheon laid the additional charge of contempt, after Jabari repeatedly disrupted his preliminary hearings with long ideological harangues. McCutchen also issued orders prohibiting him from representing himself pro see and remanding him in custody pending a psychological evaluation. It took Earl ninety days to raise the eight hundred dollars to pay the psychologist's fee to get the report released. Which meant Jabari had already served his sentence by the time he went to trial.

Without the Channel Five videotape, which mysteriously vanished after the public defender subpoenaed it, my testimony alone was insufficient to convince the jury the police attacked Jabari, rather than vice versa. Following the guilty verdict, McCutcheon sentenced him to time served and released him. Jabari spent the next five years appealing, unsuccessfully, to remove the conviction from his record.

■

The same week Jabari went to trial, I was subpoenaed to a deposition hearing on Len Stone's wrongful dismissal suit against Swedish hospital. Stone, who was a shop steward, had been a maintenance engineer at Swedish for eight years before he lost his partner to AIDS. His supervisors and co-workers only realized he was gay following Steven's death. They retaliated with approximately eight months of vicious harassment and ultimate dismissal.

When Stone filed suit for wrongful dismissal, Swedish Hospital countered that he was a troublemaker with "personality problems," and demanded he undergo a psychiatric assessment. Strict labor laws made it difficult to fire union activists. However, it became very common in the Reagan-Bush era to brand them as mentally unstable and require them to undergo psychiatric treatment as a condition of employment. I found it interesting that many of my colleagues made very similar errors in diagnosing labor activists, as Nelson, Fields, and Csardas made in my case. Although there is a clear financial incentive to diagnose conditions that require lengthy ongoing treatment, I blamed their erroneous diagnoses on their relative ignorance of the social class they were dealing with. Psychiatry is a rich man's specialty. For the most part my colleagues in private practice had limited contact with working-class clients.

As I often did in labor disputes, I requested a copy of Stone's personnel file. Along with seven years of commendations and superior performance reviews, I found two handwritten memos regarding his alleged misconduct that were obviously backdated and inserted following his dismissal.

In addition to describing the forged documents, I used my report to detail five incidents in which supervisors yelled and swore at him, wrote him up for non-existent infractions, stole his tools, and deliberately sabotaged repairs he made. I went on to briefly summarize the objective findings that led me to diagnose Major Depressive Disorder, in remission with antidepressant treatment. I summed up with a short paragraph explaining the DSMIII-R criteria for a diagnosis of "personality disorder" and why Stone didn't meet them.

The deposition was held in the plush, panoramic offices of Perkins Coie on the twenty-second floor of the Union Square building. Unlike a court hearing, there was no judge, though Stone and his attorney were present, as well as a court reporter who administered the oath. Stone's lawyer, a thirty-something, fashionably thin woman, wore a conservative linen skirt suit and the slightest hint of make-up. The Swedish attorney was a short, older man. He had almost no hair, and the fluorescent glare turned his bare scalp a ghoulish orange pink.

I was floored by his first question, which was whether I took mind-altering medication that could interfere with my ability to testify. Obviously, news of my hospitalization had traveled well beyond the medical community. I told him no. This was an honest answer.

Nardil greatly improved my mental acuity. Though I made no mention of this personal information, as it had nothing to do with my testimony.

The hospital attorney proceeded to lead me paragraph by paragraph through my report. For the most part he picked out statements at random and challenged them as biased or exaggerated. After nearly forty-five minutes of cross-examination, he could find no factual errors or discrepancies in a document that left no doubt that Stone's superiors had systematically harassed him. And won him a $150,000 settlement and reinstatement.

■

The second labor activist I helped that fall was an African American postal worker named Oscar Manassa. I already knew Oscar had a grievance against the U.S. Postal Service, due to extensive coverage it received in the *Facts*. Oscar had an exemplary ten-year history with the Postal Service prior to his transfer to the all-white Queen Anne substation in 1984. What followed was a sadistic campaign by his immediate supervisor to get him fired. Oscar's paralegal, Dean Gordley, a striking, heavy-set African American woman who wore designer suits and styled her hair in thick, soft curls, made the preliminary appointment on December 2. She introduced herself by handing me a copy of my letter to Bernie.

"This woman repeatedly wrote Oscar up for minor offenses and then gave him progressively longer suspensions," she told me. I had attended Mount Sinai School of Medicine on the Upper East Side and had no difficulty recognizing the woman's harsh South Bronx vowels. "After his third suspension—after more than two and half years of harassment—he became too depressed to work. I helped him file his first worker's compensation claim. The Department of Labor denied the claim, of course, and I persuaded Anne-Elizabeth Foley to take his case pro-bono." I recognized Foley's name. She was a prominent Bellevue labor attorney.

What the *Facts* never made clear was that Oscar, like me, was being barraged by prank phone calls, as well as being stalked by hostile strangers. "I know they're Postal Inspectors because I've seen them," Dean insisted. "They follow me sometimes after Oscar and I meet together."

Dean wanted Oscar to see me because the depression had become so severe that he was virtually incapacitated. "He misses appointments and loses paperwork," she explained. "Anne and I want to file an appeal. In his current condition, he's unable to meaningfully participate in the appeal process."

■

I arrived at my office the following morning to find a tall, thin African American in his early thirties in my waiting room. I knew it was Oscar. His light blue trousers with a slightly darker blue stripe on the outside seam identified him as a letter carrier. As I had no appointments scheduled, I escorted him into my office.

He couldn't tell me why Dean wanted him to see me and was too nervous to make eye contact. "She tells me the post office has been harassing you," I said. "Do you have any idea why they're harassing you, Oscar?"

After a long hesitation he answered, in a lilting, barely audible south Alabama accent. "I think the reason is me being a shop steward. I be very serious about my union work. When someone axe me to file a grievance, I follows it through till they does something. My supervisor, she take it very personal and keep giving me routes that was too long. When I don't come in on time she write me up. When I complain, she write me up for insubordination. She also write me up for stupid stuff. Like I don't dispose of trash at my work station."

The morning of our appointment, he was on a special disciplinary leave, which amounted to being on call six days a week. If his supervisor wanted him to work, he had forty-five minutes to arrive at the Post Office or face immediate dismissal. At other times he was banned from Post Office property. Two weeks earlier they had him arrested for trespassing when he tried to pick up his paycheck.

The interview progressed slowly through standard questions about depression and suicide ideation. Oscar admitted to feeling hopeless about his future, but denied that he ever thought about killing himself. He saw what his aunt went through when his cousin committed suicide.

"I couldn't never do that to my own mom," he said.

CHAPTER 13

I wrote Oscar a prescription for Elavil to help him sleep. Two days later he discontinued it. He drove a cab on the days the Post Office didn't call him in to work. Even a tiny dose of ten mg. left him left him so groggy he rammed his taxi into the back of a Honda Civic. He refused to try other medication, preferring "talking treatment" to pills.

As in Stone's case, Dean asked me to prepare a report to assist in the appeal. In addition to Oscar' personnel file, she provided transcripts of all his grievance hearings and a copy of an evaluation by a psychiatrist the Post Office sent him to. At both hearings the union rep established that the Post Office fabricated many of his so-called "infractions." An affidavit from an elderly woman on his route revealed her name was forged to a complaint about his rudeness. The union also disputed a write-up accusing him of slashing a supervisor's tires. They cited the absence of witnesses or material evidence linking him to the vandalism.

The first psychiatrist diagnosed him with Character Disorder and Antisocial Personality. Despite the absence of criminal history this diagnosis required nor any explanation how someone with a ten-year exemplary work record could suddenly develop a character disorder. Dr. Pitt also overlooked Oscar's classic symptoms of Post Traumatic Stress Disorder—flashbacks, intrusive recollections and nightmares, hyper-vigilance, and withdrawal from usual activities and relationships. I pointed out all these discrepancies in my own report. I concluded by enumerating the diagnostic criteria for Post Traumatic Stress Disorder, which Oscar clearly met, with workplace harassment as the precipitating trauma.

I made copies for Dean and Oscar's lawyer and submitted the original to the Department of Labor's Office of Workers Compensation, along with a claim form for the evaluation and therapy sessions. The latter was a mere formality. The Department of Labor didn't recognize claims for psychiatric conditions.

■

Performing "talking" therapy with Oscar technically violated my agreement with Nelson and Berman. However, as neither had African American patients or friends, his legal battle with the Post Office was a non-event in their lives. Nevertheless, it underscored the major threat the ongoing scrutiny of my mental health posed to my livelihood. As a result of an argument or misunderstanding, either of my shrinks could declare me unfit to practice without a shred of evidence. Although Berman accepted the harassment was ongoing, he didn't share my political values or appreciate how important they were in defining who I was. After leaning I was being set up for accidents, he suggested it was time to give up radical politics.

"You should look at it as a tour of duty that is ending," he said. "You have done enough for the progressive movement."

■

I stopped the Nardil, out of pure vanity, when Jabari went to trial on November 23. I put on my only skirt suit the morning I went to court and was unable to button the waistband. I weighed myself and found I had gained fifteen pounds. Berman believed I was calmer and more focused without medication and wrote to Nelson informing him of his impressions. I had an appointment with my psychiatrist the following week. He was clearly offended a psychologist would question his clinical judgment.

"You have to take antidepressants because you're depressed," he argued.

"Nelson, it was the Nardil that made me psychotic in the first place," I said.

We both knew I had grounds for a malpractice suit, and my psychiatrist beat a hasty retreat.

"All right," he conceded. "We'll stop it on a trial basis, then. But only with the understanding you will contact me immediately if the depression recurs."

Berman and I terminated psychotherapy at the end of December when my insurance ran out. Nelson made me come and pay cash for one last appointment the second week in January. As I still manifested no symptoms of either psychosis or depression, he had no choice but to release me from treatment and all practice restrictions.

■

Two days later I tried to break up with Edward. The exhilarating sense of freedom I felt on liberating myself from mental health treatment and scrutiny only heightened my frustration with a personal relationship that provided no emotional support, companionship, or sexual gratification. We had just spent Saturday night together and were arguing over his unwillingness to spend any time with me on his day off. All of a sudden my lover, who I had always regarded as an emotionless automaton, burst into tears. Guilt stricken as I watched mucous stream from his nose, I immediately relented. As a member of an oppressed minority, surely he had suffered enough without me breaking his heart. What bothered me even more was a nagging sense that I had led him on by embarking on a relationship with someone I knew was incapable of emotional intimacy.

It would be the last time we had sex. Edward knew I didn't climax, and I wasn't remorseful enough to make love with someone who was indifferent to my emotional or physical needs—and who put on his clothes and went home whenever I broached the subject.

■

Our affair officially ended in mid-April when, with exactly five hundred dollars left in savings, I accepted a part-time contract at Eastside Mental Health. In landing an outside job I had finally overcome the last major threat—which was financial—to my career. With my license and practice secure, I was ready to do serious battle with the people who had targeted me.

My new position consisted of four six-hour days per week, as well as a thirty-minute commute to and from Bellevue. This left Thursdays, evenings, and weekends to see all my private patients. The only upside of a fifty-hour work week was that it left no time to see Edward. After leaving messages on my home machine for six weeks, he came by unannounced one evening in early June. I was on the porch hemming my new wrap-around skirt. He wanted me to go inside and make love with him. I refused.

Edward's jaws tightened with anger as he turned and started down the steps. "Well, I guess I can't rape you." As always, my now ex-lover had no ability to conceptualize women—or men—as having needs of their own. It made no difference whether I enjoyed sex. If he wanted it, I should want it, too.

■

The visits from fictitious patients resumed within weeks after my lover's final visit. The first was an African American named Arthur Whitman, who was in his early forties and had a Charlie Chaplin moustache and skin the color of a deep tan. Most of my pseudo-patients came with an apparent goal of befriending me and eliciting information about my personal life. A few, like Whitman, sought to lure me into illegal or unethical activity.

My new patient told me about seeing my ad in the *Facts*—an obvious cue not to bill him for the visit. Unlike many of my fictitious patients, he had no problem telling me why he was there. However, I faced an immediate dilemma, given that his specific complaint—impotence—didn't qualify for free care under the "grant" I was advertising. In twenty-five years of practice, Whitman was the only patient, male or female, to seek my help for sexual dysfunction. It is more typical, and appropriate, for men to consult their family doctor or a urologist for this problem.

Whitman gave me no time to respond before launching into his history. Owing to the unusual nature of his complaint, I already suspected he had an ulterior agenda. Curious what he might reveal about the people who sent him, I let him continue.

"I honestly think it's the massive stress I'm under," he explained. "I'm what they call a mortgage broker. Do you know that that is?" I nodded. "I've had my own firm for about five years now. I'm unusually good at it, if I say so myself." He gave me a self-satisfied smile. "My immediate problem is I happen to be facing federal charges for falsifying a credit report."

Whitman was obviously in a lot of trouble but was surprisingly upbeat about his situation. He gave me a seductive grin, as if to indicate the type of help he had in mind. "Prior to my arrest it was unheard of for me to have problems in that area."

He quickly moved on to talk about his ex-wife and the interpersonal conflict that led to their divorce, and to identify numerous reasons for preferring the single life. Then he began telling me about an African American friend, a commercial banker, who also faced charges for accepting the phony credit report. "I'm hoping you will agree to perform a pro-bono psychiatric evaluation on my friend." I immediately sensed this was the real purpose of the visit. "Perhaps with your help I can get him to plead guilty. If the court accepts emotional problems as a mitigating circumstance, we can keep him out of prison."

There was no mention at all of Whitman's impotence at our second visit. He began the second session by quizzing me about the grant I advertised in the *Facts*. His edgy defensiveness reminded me of Henry Harris, and like the ex-GI he carried both sides of the conversation. "Of course, you have no obligation to reveal who is funding you. Unless you want to."

Abruptly switching tack, he told me he was launching a new venture in mortgage products. He needed financial backers. "I don't suppose there's any chance you would be interested?"

I told him it was unethical for psychiatrists to do business with patients. I think he already knew this. He cocked his head as if questioning my sincerity. "As a doctor you are bound to have friends who are interested," he pushed. I also considered it unethical to involve my friends in my patients' business ventures but didn't argue the point. The man struck me as totally amoral. He wasn't in my office for legitimate reasons, and I had no interest in wasting any more time on him.

The following morning he drove out to Bellevue to deliver the prospectus in person at Eastside Mental Health. I was determined Whitman and whoever he worked for should know as little as possible about my second job and intercepted him in the parking lot.

■

I did agree to see his friend, Harold Black, who in his spare time was a well-respected minister and director of a small Central Area church school. Black called to make an appointment soon after my last visit with Whitman. He was heavier, darker, and more personable than the mortgage broker. Like Whitman and Jabari, he was born and grew up in Seattle and spoke perfectly grammatical English with no identifiable accent.

He began the interview by apologizing. "To be honest, I only came out of curiosity. I have no intention of pleading guilty. I told Arthur that. I must admit, though, I was curious what you might have to say."

Black related exactly the same history as Whitman. I found it surprising it hadn't occurred to him that his best friend had set him up. It seemed so obvious. I resisted the temptation to flaunt the strict confidentiality laws I operated under to set him straight. Although Whitman was a liar and thief and possibly much worse, I was ethically bound to protect his privacy.

Black knew that even if he was found not guilty, his banking career was over. Unlike Whitman, he was totally candid about the intense grief he felt over this loss. He also expressed profound gratitude over the solid support his wife and extended family gave him. "Without it I don't believe I could survive an ordeal of this magnitude." We also talked at length about his early experiences growing up in Seattle, as well as the difficulties he faced as the first member of his family to go to college. There was nothing we discussed in our thirty-minute conversation to suggest he had a diagnosable mental disorder. I suspected Whitman knew what my findings would be when he asked me to see his friend. Perhaps he assumed that as a leftist I would bend the truth if it meant keeping an African American male out of prison.

Because Black stuck with his decision to demand a jury trial, I was never called on to produce a formal report. He was found guilty and spent a year in a federal penitentiary. Whitman, as the instigator, pled guilty and served no time. Troubled by this turn of events, Black visited my office a second time shortly after his release in 1989. I found him in my waiting room one Thursday as I finished with my last patient.

"I know I don't have an appointment. However, I only want a few moments of your time." I invited him into my office and encouraged him to sit down. "I thought it important to let you know about a discovery I made when I was in prison," he said. "It appears there are federal agents conducting undercover operations in Seattle's African American community. Without mentioning names, I felt obligated to warn you of my suspicions."

Without waiting for a response he got up and left.

■

The encounter only strengthened my resolve to identify and expose the men who attempted to kill me and settled for destroying my career. In Black's case, some higher-up in the intelligence hierarchy had given the order to destroy the career of an upstanding pillar of the black business and church community, an operation that clearly had nothing to do with national security, the only legal justification for domestic intelligence operations. Unlike Earl and Jabari, Black was no radical. The former commercial banker was centrist Democrat who, like many of Seattle's black ministers, openly opposed the Museum occupation and the other militant activities Earl and his friends engaged in.

Nevertheless I was still at a loss where to start. Prior to the Internet, published material regarding illicit intelligence activities was scarce and difficult to locate. The works of disaffected CIA veterans like Phillip Agee and Victor Marchetti only allude to illegal domestic operations without providing any detail regarding the government entities or individuals who ran them. The *Guardian* provided my first significant lead, an ad in July 1988 for a new book called *Cointelpro Papers*. It was written by a Native American professor at Colorado State University named Ward Churchill and published by an alternative publishing house in Boston called South End Press. Because I received a catalogue along with my book order, I realized Churchill had published a book called *Agents of Repression* in 1987. I immediately ordered that one, as well.

In his first book, Ward Churchill reveals that he was targeted for extensive harassment as a result of his involvement with the

American Indian Movement (AIM). His meticulous research, based on Freedom of Information Act documents and letters and memos stolen when activists turned the tables and broke into an FBI field office, makes it clear Cointelpro didn't end when Congress allegedly shut it down in the seventies. *Agents of Repression* reproduces extensive correspondence between J. Edgar Hoover and FBI field officers and agents about specific operations they undertook to sabotage and discredit AIM, the Black Panther Party, the Socialist Workers Party, and a handful of other leftist groups. The additional letters and memos in *Cointelpro Papers* reveal that between 1945 and 1985 the U.S. government systematically infiltrated and crushed every left of center organization—including CISPES—that held publicly notified meetings.

The systematic personal harassment the FBI undertook against Black Panther leaders Huey Newton and Stokely Carmichael was even more eye-opening in view of my personal experiences. Both men broke with the Panther leadership after becoming overtly paranoid, which was clearly Hoover's intent. In the FBI director's own words, the goal of continual phone interference, break-ins, mail tampering, and "hot" or conspicuous surveillance, was to make radical activists "see an FBI man behind every mailbox."

Cointelpro Papers also documents the fifty-plus FBI-sponsored death-squad killings on the South Dakota Pine Ridge Reservation in the early seventies. I still found myself questioning if the attempts on my own life were real or if the government merely wanted me to think they were trying to kill me. For some reason I had to see it in writing before I could fully accept the U.S. government murders its own citizens.

I also saw frightening parallels between my own ordeal and the racially motivated vendetta the FBI director undertook against actress Jean Seburg. Seburg, who was white, became a target after donating $10,000 to the Black Panther Party. Playing on her history of emotional instability, Hoover planted bogus stories in the *Los Angeles Times* that her unborn baby was the illegitimate offspring of a Black Panther. The rumor mongering ultimately resulted in both Seburg's and her husband's suicide.

Yet the pages I kept coming back to were those displaying photos of fifty of the three hundred known FBI agents who infiltrated the Black Panther leadership in the early seventies. The main reason my affair with Edward continued for nine months was my difficulty convincing myself he really worked for U.S. intelligence. Despite mounting circumstantial evidence, I found it mind-boggling that any African American could knowingly ally himself with a security intelligence apparatus that was well known for persecuting dark-skinned people. As I studied the stoic, expressionless faces it dawned on me what should have been obvious from Edward's affected speech and preference for white women. Edward didn't see himself as black. Nor did Whitman. Because neither would ever be fully accepted by the white men they sought to emulate, they disowned the entire human race. It wasn't a question of disloyalty when they betrayed a lover or best friend. They trusted no one, formed no attachments, and, as Edward liked to remind me, kept no secrets.

■

When I phoned Edna Laidlow on Sunday August 7, it was our first contact in over a year. Churchill's work clearly confirmed the inability of either the courts or Congress to contain the criminal element that had taken over U.S. intelligence. Even if I identified the agencies or individuals who gave the orders for the attempts on my life, I had little hope of bringing them to justice. Despite what felt like an immense personal defeat, I had to resign myself to reality. I was very unlikely to be successful where two highly competent individuals with extensive experience with U.S. intelligence had failed.

However there was no reason not to create a public record, as Churchill did through the *Cointelpro Papers* and Edna through her lawsuits, of what they did to me. In 1977 the former investigator set out to make a permanent record of the lengthy harassment she experienced by filing a series of lawsuits pro se. Staff at the UW law library referred her to relevant legal code and case law. By the time we had our first appointment in 1984, she could produce an affidavit on her word processor that was indistinguishable from the briefs I received from any downtown law office.

Edna was very excited to learn someone had published a major expose regarding illegal FBI undercover operations. She promised to go out and buy both Churchill's books right away. "This is the major breakthrough we've been waiting for," she exclaimed.

She was even more enthusiastic about my proposal to chronicle, like Churchill, both my own and Edna's experiences, along with the illegal operations she uncovered during her fifteen-year investigation. A year after the fact I entertained three equally plausible explanations why the government targeted me for harassment. The first was the threat that I, like Seburg, posed in supporting two black radicals; the second was my discovery of a conspiracy to suppress a lifesaving AIDS treatment; the third was my relationship with a Kennedy assassination witness. While I had no reason to favor any one of these possibilities, I was far more likely to reach a mainstream audience by focusing on the assassination.

"Let me know what I can do. I'm happy to help in any way I can," said Edna.

I told her I was mailing a consent form releasing me from confidentiality. I explained that unlike *Agents of Repression* and *Cointelpro Papers*, I would have to write and market my book as fiction. That for ethical reasons I had to give Edna a fictitious identity. Although I only learned the details of her relationship with the so-called "umbrella man" following her move to Maine, it was a breach of confidentiality to reveal she was ever under my care.

Edna promised to sign and return the form as soon as it arrived.

CHAPTER 14

The signed release sat unopened on my desk for three months. The day after we talked, I made a perfunctory start on the six inches of legal documents Edna began sending me in June 1987. Every time Edna filed an affidavit with the court, she built her own "paper barricade" by mailing copies to a half-dozen friends and supporters.

She filed her first complaint against Sharp in 1977, after a business venture they formed went bankrupt, resulting in the loss of her home, savings, and a vacation property on the Kitsap Peninsula. The original complaint describes Edwin Sharp as a "dollar-a-year" man—the CIA paid him an annual fee of one dollar while shielding him from prosecution for any financial scams he ran on the side. Edna's complaint alleges that his "cover" was teaching watchmaking at Seattle Central Community College. He also used these skills to assemble timing devices for bombs used in "hits" he undertook with Irving Stone, a second CIA contractor who was also a Manhattan attorney. I knew from prior conversations that Edna never met Stone. However, Sharp introduced her to other contract agents, including a CIA psychologist who bragged about intercepting activists' mail at the Post Office to assist in constructing their psychological profiles.

The complaint alleges that Sharp deliberately befriended Edna to cause her financial ruin. I found this credible, given the uncanny similarity to business offers I received from Whitman and one other "undercover" patient. As a welfare fraud investigator, she had just exposed a scam, involving the governor, a U.S. senator and the Department of Social and Health Services, to divert federal block grant funds into private development projects. Her first complaint refers to phone records she possessed linking Sharp to a mysterious explosion in a Minneapolis Honeywell factory in 1976, as well as photographic evidence establishing his strong resemblance to a tall, thin man in a suit who, according to numerous eyewitnesses, signaled with his umbrella immediately before Kennedy's limousine entered Dealey Plaza.

"Despite the grainy quality of the photos," her brief continued, "the height and build are the same, as well as the distinctive curvature of the spine. It looks exactly like a turtle coming out of its shell."

A second affidavit filed in early 1979 outlines the all-out campaign of phone and personal harassment that began within weeks after Edna filed her first complaint. In addition to the prank calls and verbal abuse by unshaven derelicts, it describes a series of break-ins in which intruders stole legal documents and her word processor, and in one case jammed the drum of her electric log fire, intending for it to catch fire when she turned it on. The 1979 complaint concludes by describing her meeting with comedian and activist Dick Gregory when he spoke at the University of Washington in 1978. Gregory was on a tour of college campuses with a bootlegged copy of Abraham Zapruder's home movie of the assassination. The film shows clearly that the fatal shot struck Kennedy from the front, which meant it was fired by someone other than Oswald, who was in the School Book Depository behind the motorcade. Edna goes on to reveal that Gregory sheltered her in his Massachusetts home for a month while he flew to Minneapolis to confirm Sharp's involvement in the Honeywell explosion.

■

Putting my own experiences on paper proved much harder. After seeing patients fifty hours a week, it took enormous willpower to spend my weekends sitting in front of a blank notebook. Continual interruptions by my seven-year-old daughter, who was incapable of entertaining herself longer than twenty minutes without bursting into my bedroom, made it even harder to call up words for occurrences that were totally out of the range of experience of most Americans. By Christmas I had typed a total of fifty pages on an old Underwood manual. I did far more revising than writing, and all fifty sheets were cut into thin ribbons and re-taped with multiple revisions.

In many ways I felt like a guinea pig whose knowledge of the world is limited to the faceless hand that keeps it confined. I had come to accept that ultimate political power didn't rest with our elected officials, as I was taught in high school. It had been seized by an unelected Shadow Government, which exerted political control through a vast, mostly invisible intelligence security network. I also knew, mainly from articles I clipped from the *Guardian*, about various secret societies of corporate elites, such as the Trilateral Commission, the Foreign Relations Council, the Bohemian Grove, the Bilderbergers, and Skull and Bones—groups that seemed to make all the important foreign and domestic policy decisions for Congress to rubber stamp. I suspected these groups were powerful enough to run their own intelligence security operations. What I found difficult to visualize were the lines of authority that presumably extended from these elite groups to covert FBI, CIA, and police operations—and from the official spooks to the marginally employed petty criminals who were paid several hundred dollars a month to infiltrate and disrupt meetings, videotape demonstrations, make prank calls, follow and pester whistleblowers and activists, and entrap doctors into prescribing controlled drugs.

On paper the CIA and FBI answered to the president. Yet in 1963 when the CIA murdered John Kennedy, clearly someone else was in charge. Likewise there was no way Reagan, who already had advanced Alzheimer's at the beginning of his second term, gave the orders to target Edna for harassment.

■

Edward continued to call twice a month. Determined to capture the high-pitched monotone and saccharine turn of phrase, I made no effort to discourage him. Sometimes he rambled on for ten or fifteen minutes, repeating the same flowery speeches I had heard a dozen times about how much he loved me, how beautiful and disciplined my daughter was, how he had known us both in past lives, and how we would all be together again 5,000 years in the future. To prove that he, too, engaged in "community organizing," he often bragged about his role in the police-sponsored Neighborhood Watch and the street parties he organized to help his neighbors drive the drug dealers off Thirty-third Avenue.

Ten days before Christmas he came to the house with a potted poinsettia with three large scarlet blooms. Wisely anticipating I wouldn't let him in, he simply handed me the plant and left. Fifteen minutes later Naomi summoned me from the kitchen to show me it had lost three leaves. The other leaves and petals fell as we watched and within an hour its stems were totally bare.

I knew instinctively this gift, of a terminally ill plant, was a threat, not unlike the black calling cards South American death squads delivered to potential victims. The next morning I canceled my first appointment at Eastside Mental Health, left five minutes later than usual, and took a new, longer route to the Interstate. Thus it was 9:28 a.m., instead of 9:15, when I crossed the ship canal overpass and all the cars ahead of me slowed to a crawl. After inching my way through the Mountlake tunnel, I had just reached the 520 bridge when the two drivers ahead of me shut off their engines and got out of their cars. A third driver was walking back from the center of the bridge, while three ambulances, with lights flashing and sirens wailing, crept up the far left lane. Five of us crowded around him as he informed us the drawbridge had opened without warning in the middle of rush-hour traffic.

According to the press statement issued by the Department of Transportation (DOT), tower staff members were holding their daily bridge-opening exercise and someone forgot to disable the button that raised the bridge decks. This made no sense as the gate and flashers were automated to activate with the opening mechanism. The deck on the Bellevue side lifted first. It was six feet in the air when the woman in the eastbound lane slammed into it. She was killed instantly. Nine people in the six cars behind her were critically injured.

There would be no criminal charges or disciplinary action against any of the tower staff. The DOT made a quiet settlement with the woman's family, and the incident vanished from public view. I never had any proof the bizarre accident was connected to Edward's gift of a dying plant. Yet had I left home at the normal time and taken my customary route, my car would have been at the exact center of the bridge when it opened.

■

Oscar got no warning, at least none we recognized. He left treatment in June 1988 after resigning from the Post Office and returned to his family home in Alabama. He arrived back in Washington state in January 1989, spending two months in Tacoma, where he worked in the Salvation Army shelter. He was on the front desk when a call came in from an officious sounding male. "This is the Tacoma police. We're coming to pick up Oscar Manassa." The Tacoma police later denied any record of the call.

On March 13 he came to my office with a psychiatric disability form he wanted me to complete to help him qualify for general assistance. He was staying at the YMCA and had signed on to the casual-labor pool at the Millionaire's club. He had already been to see Dean and his lawyer, who helped him reopen his workers compensation claim, as well as filing for reinstatement at the post office. I was amazed at the new self-confidence in his demeanor as he talked about two prank calls his mother received shortly after he arrived home.

"Both of them was men, two different men," he told me. "They says her son Oscar is crazy and she need to get me locked up. She tell my sisters and brother-in-law. They all believes me then."

Again I saw clear parallels with my own experience. When his mother also received prank calls, Oscar immediately ceased to be paranoid in the eyes of his family and their small close-knit community. As in my own case, re-establishing his credibility proved far more therapeutic than any professional treatment.

Three days later he was dead. Because there was a card for our next appointment in his pocket, the King County Medical Examiner left a message on my office machine for me to call. I was in Bellevue that day but contacted him during my lunch break when I picked up the message.

He asked if Oscar was one of my patients. I confirmed that he was. "The police found his body in an alley at 6:00 a.m. Could you tell me if he was suicidal? There were no witnesses but they concluded he jumped from the fifth floor of the YMCA."

I assured him that Oscar never at any point expressed suicide ideation. "He was experiencing vicious harassment," I said. "People were stalking him."

"We will make sure to make a note of it." The irony in the pathologist's voice said it all. The case was closed. The police had no intention of investigating his death.

■

I lay awake till 3:00 a.m. that night, unable to suppress my growing apprehension that Oscar's supporters would be powerless to bring his killers to justice. I no longer had any illusions about who they were and what they represented. The most powerful country in the world was run by sociopathic thugs who, like Hitler's Brownshirts, were unaccountable to the rule of law. Anyone who posed a threat to the status quo was relentlessly persecuted, harassed, and even murdered by a faceless security force accountable only to a handful of ruthless criminals who were the real government.

At some point I drifted off. I forgot to turn the phone off and at four o'clock I was awakened by a call. A voice I couldn't quite place informed me a woman on the corner had a radio-operated detonator and was about to blow my house up. I rushed to my daughter's bedroom, reached out to roust her, and stopped. Was the call real or had I dreamed it? If we left the house where would we go? With an eight-year-old in tow there was no way I could pack a suitcase and flee as I had in July 1987.

With my heart beating so hard my sternum hurt, I felt my way through the dark to the living room. From the south facing window, I had a clear view of Fifty-fifth and Third in four directions. Both streets were empty of any cars or pedestrians.

■

I was still awake when the alarm rang at 7:30 a.m. Dean called soon after I arrived in my office. She gave me a phone number with a 205 area code and said that Oscar's mother wanted to talk to me.

"Thank you so much for calling. I won't take up too much of your time." Mrs. Manassa's voice was nearly as low-pitched as her son's, the melodic singsong of her broad, drawn-out vowels both measured and unhurried. As Oscar's psychiatrist I was obligated to call and she knew it.

"I want you to know how grateful I am that you helped my son."

She also knew as well as I did that the psychotherapy sessions had very little impact on Oscar's emotional state. She was thanking me for my willingness, as a white professional, to advocate for a young African American in distress.

I said I was sorry I couldn't do more. "I saw Oscar three days before he died and I don't believe he killed himself," I told her. "It's more likely that he was murdered by the people who were harassing him. I think we need to pressure the police to open a homicide investigation. The only way to do so is to publicize the vicious harassment they put him through." I told her I wanted to go to the newspapers. "Because of patient confidentiality laws, I can't do that without your permission."

There was a long pause. "No, they young children in the family." There was a grim resignation in Mrs. Manassa's flat, emotionless voice. Oscar's death was just another lynching. It wouldn't be the first in her lifetime, nor the last. "You can't help us by talking to no reporters."

■

Two days later Dean called an emergency meeting of Oscar's legal team at her home on Martin Luther King Way. Dean and her husband Tyrone, to my surprise, were the only African Americans present. Jolinda Stephens, the *Facts* reporter who covered Oscar's grievance against the Postal Service, was a forty-something white woman with large, translucent framed glasses and two blonde pony tails. His lawyer, who was in her mid-thirties, had just left court and wore stockings, low heels, and a fine-weave tweed suit. Next to Elizabeth was a third, much younger woman with a cluster of acne scars on both cheeks. Dean introduced Cherie as one of Oscar's "postal patrons."

I walked in as Dean was explaining that the Postal Inspectors had claimed jurisdiction over the investigation on the basis that Oscar was a former postal employee. "They walked into the downtown precinct this morning with a federal warrant and seized the evidence file."

This confused me. "I don't understand. Oscar no longer works for the post office. Besides, I thought Postal Inspectors were limited to investigating mail fraud."

Dean informed me that the U.S. Postal Inspection Service performed a security and intelligence function nearly identical to that of the FBI and CIA. "Except that the Postal Service is an autonomous, federally owned corporation. Which means the Postal Inspectors aren't accountable to Congress. Or anyone else, for that matter. What I find alarming is that there's already a clear precedent." According to a union activist Dean knew in New York, there was an epidemic of violent suicides among postal workers. "In three years there have been four in Salt Lake City, three in Palm Beach, two in San Diego, and one in Oklahoma City. In every case, the Postal Inspectors usurp jurisdiction from local police and seize the evidence."

■

Ten minutes later the meeting was over. Oscar's attorney turned to address Dean as she stood up to leave. "I will send Oscar's legal files over by messenger, and you can ship them to Alabama."

Only then did I realize the full significance of Dean's revelations. With the investigation in federal hands, the option of lobbying the Seattle police to open a homicide investigation was off the table. There was nothing more we could do.

I had no choice that night but to rely on the other women's superior knowledge of the law. I now know we could have challenged the Postal Inspectors' claim of jurisdiction in federal court. Our decision not to proceed with a long, expensive legal battle was a simple matter of priorities. I doubt if any of us consciously weighed our chances of success against the personal cost—in my own case it would have meant giving up my private practice; in Jolinda's, the lawsuit her African American husband had filed against Boeing, and in Dean's, her own workers compensation claim against the Postal Service. But, in the end, this is what we did.

■

A week later Oscar's sister phoned me from Alabama. "Here's a medical question for you," she began. "The coroner gave me a look at Oscar's autopsy pictures when I was out to Seattle to get his body. They has both his eyes all bruised and bloody. I be wondering how this can happen—how a person that fall five stories come to land squarely on both eyes."

There was no mistaking the accusation in her tone. Unlike her mother, she held me partly to blame for allowing other white people to murder her brother. "Then this man call me the night I get home," she continued. "He won't say his name. But he tell me Oscar he don't jump from his own room. He tell me my brother's room was on the second floor."

Five days later I received notification from the Department of Labor that Oscar's worker's compensation claim had been approved. A strange woman called my home that night asking about a picture I supposedly took of Oscar in a Chinese restaurant.

I told her she was mistaken. "I was his psychiatrist. It's unethical for me to socialize with patients." She claimed I told her about the photo myself. I demanded that she identify herself and she hung up.

The timing of the prank call was no coincidence. Dean, Jolinda, and I were highly visible advocates in a number of similar cases. The chilling message was clear. For all our combined ingenuity, victory would elude us so long as the government could preemptively murder our clients.

Part III –
Revelation, Enlightenment and Despair

> But two people fighting
> back to back can cut through
> a mob, a snake-dancing file
> can break a cordon, an army
> can meet an army.
> Two people can keep each other
> sane, can give support, conviction,
> love, massage, hope, sex.
> Three people are a delegation,
> a committee, a wedge. With four
> you can play bridge and start
> an organization. With six
> you can rent a whole house,
> eat pie for dinner with no
> seconds, and hold a fund raising party.
> from *The Low Road* by Marge Piercy

CHAPTER 15

Oscar's death affected me far more than anything they did to me in 1987. The photos in Naomi's baby book speak to the siege mentality that pervaded our home after his murder. Prior to March 1989 there are photos of bright sunlit rooms filled with gaudy bouquets of red, orange, and gold nasturtiums and black-eyed gaillardia. Later pictures depict gloomy, colorless rooms where the drapes are never drawn. I made no conscious decision to live like this. However, I couldn't help feeling partly responsible for the postal worker's murder—for encouraging him to confront the people who were persecuting him. This meant I was also obligated to find some way to bring his killers to justice. Guilty and ashamed over my powerlessness to do so, I could allow myself no pleasure or happiness.

The notion our government was free to brutalize and kill their own citizens with no fear of legal repercussions left me with a diffuse pent up rage—without a specific focus where I could direct these feelings. For the first few months after Oscar's death I directed my fury at the mainstream media and cancelled my subscription to cable TV, the *New York Times*, the *Seattle Post Intelligencer* and the *Christian*

Science Monitor. I decided the TV networks and big city newspapers were the main culprits in permitting the transformation of a once democratic society into a criminal despotism. United States intelligence could engage in heinous criminal activity in total confidence their activities would be concealed from public view. I was certainly not the first activist to question the apparent government control over public information. On the surface this made no sense, as the U.S. has never had an official censor like totalitarian countries, such as the Soviet Union, Communist China, and Cuba. However, by the late eighties it was well known on the left that a handful of corporations owned all the U.S. newspaper chains, TV and radio networks, and publishing houses—the same corporations with major financial interests in big oil and the defense industry.

There was also increasing evidence that the CIA itself played a direct role in controlling public information. I had recently learned about Project Mockingbird, via an unauthorized biography of the ultraconservative Patrick Buchanan, given to me by a friend who belonged to Workers' World. It claimed that Mockingbird was a top-secret operation launched by the first CIA director Allen Dulles and *Washington Post* founder and publisher Philip Graham in 1948—to assert "strategic" control over the news stories that reached the American public. Their goal was to both recruit and "plant" CIA-friendly journalists at both wire services, *Time*, *Newsweek*, and *US News and World Report*, and various big city newspapers. In 1954, Buchanan and a CIA official named Tom Braden formed a new front group to replace Mockingbird called the Congress for Cultural Freedom. This new entity continued to pay these CIA-friendly "reporters" a monthly stipend to publish stories written by the CIA's Office of Public Affairs.

After Braden left the CIA in 1958, the two men went on to co-host "Crossfire," CNN's long-running public affairs program.

However, neither CNN nor Braden, the program's designated "liberal," ever informed viewers of his longstanding intelligence connections.

■

I was helpless to confront the entrenched power of the career criminals who wielded the instruments of government. However, I still had total control over the information that entered my home, and in April 1989 I bought my first shortwave radio. Prior to the Internet, this was one of the few unbiased daily news sources available to leftists. A libertarian lawyer who worked in the office next to mine helped me rig up a thirty-foot antenna behind the house. This gave me good reception for three hours every night to the BBC World Service, the Canadian Broadcasting Corporation, and two California peace and justice stations.

Shortwave became my lifeline. On April 13, 1989, I was one of several hundred Americans to learn the results of the congressional investigation Senate Foreign Relations Committee chairman John Kerry launched in 1986 to investigate CIA and Contra links to cocaine trafficking. The Kerry Committee took testimony from dozens of witnesses about the small aircraft the CIA and Contra leaders commandeered to smuggle Columbian cocaine into small rural airports in Arkansas and northern California. Thanks to the Congress for Cultural Freedom, or whatever the CIA called it in 1989, the mainstream networks and papers boycotted the Kerry Committee's explosive findings. As a result the vast majority of Americans remained oblivious to CIA narcotics trafficking until 1998 when Gary Webb published his "Dark Alliance" series in the *San Jose Mercury News*.

■

The emotional upheaval triggered by Oscar's murder also prompted my return to organizing, for the first time since my hospitalization. My two-year quest to identify and expose the culprits behind the harassment Edna, Oscar, and I were subjected to had brought me full circle to my original views—that true reform was only possible through collective political action. It was pointless to seek redress for Oscar's brazen murder by publishing yet another book on the government's criminal enterprises. The only way to end the extrajudicial murder of innocent Americans was to remove the criminals responsible for these activities from power—and the only way to make this happen was for a critical mass of Americans to refuse to go about their daily lives. The peaceful removal of Philippine dictator Ferdinand Marcos via a massive public protest in 1986 gave me reason to believe this could also happen in the U.S.

In January 1989 the founders of Physicians for a National Health Program (PNHP) published a study in the prestigious *New England Journal of Medicine* showing the U.S. could save several billion dollars by replacing 1,200 competing private health plans with a single publicly financed system. I didn't see the article until a month after Oscar's death. However, there was no question that health care was in crisis in the U.S.—with the number of uninsured Americans reaching 44 million in early 1989. Moreover, the ability to access medical care was an issue affecting all Americans, irrespective of their income, social status, or ideological perspective. Which meant it also was one of the few issues with the potential to draw a million people into the streets.

In June 1989, nine other doctors, a social worker, and I met at Country Doctor Community Clinic, with the goal of creating a Washington State chapter of PNHP. We formed a five-person steering committee to write bylaws and articles of incorporation and apply to the Internal Revenue for non-profit status. In November we officially incorporated as Health Care for All, and the Steering Committee appointed me to chair a Speakers Committee. Our role was to develop a slideshow presentation and train other members to make public presentations.

I also joined the Tyrone Briggs Defense Committee the same month. Thanks to Jolinda Stephens, the case of the shy, eighteen-year-old basketball star from Garfield High School had received extensive coverage in the *Facts*. Tyrone's first trial ended in a hung jury; the second was thrown out on appeal for juror misconduct. Although both the *Seattle Times* and the *Seattle PI* persisted in calling Tyrone the "Harborview Rapist"—on the basis the alleged assaults occurred near Harborview Hospital—none of the formal charges involved sexual assault. Tyrone was charged with three counts of purse snatching and one of "kidnapping." The latter charge related to a bizarre scenario in which a black male dragged a white woman into an abandoned shed, "stared" at her for one hour, and released her. Jolinda, who had read the entire transcript of both trials, believed Tyrone's first attorney made a serious error in failing to challenge the police identification. Especially as there was no physical evidence connecting Tyrone with any of the attacks. In their initial statements, all five prosecution witnesses described a well-spoken perpetrator with a short afro, whereas Tyrone had a pronounced stutter and wore his hair long in a Jeri curl.

My decision to facilitate Tyrone's release from jail by pledging my home on his bond grew out of my developing friendship with Oscar's paralegal, Dean Gordley. A few weeks after Oscar's death, Dean, who was starting her own tailoring and alteration business, offered to give Naomi free sewing lessons. Every Saturday we drove to Dean's home on Martin Luther King Way. While I sat on a stool in her cluttered sewing room, the African American woman taught my eight-year-old daughter to pin and cut out patterns, thread the bobbin and needle on her state of the art Bernino sewing machine, and gently feed the fabric while massaging the foot pedal that ran the motor. Some Saturdays there were no lessons. Instead the three of us just sat in the living room talking, drinking coffee and juice, and eating cookies and watching "Style" on cable TV.

Over time I realized Dean's main purpose in offering my daughter sewing lessons was to monitor our welfare. Although I never told anyone other than Paulus or Berman about the attempts on my life, Dean somehow sensed, or at least suspected, something more serious than prank calls had occurred. During our little talks, I sometimes felt a tight suffocating sensation in my chest, as I became fully conscious of the total emotional isolation I had endured. I didn't dare tell any of my leftist friends about the attempts on my life. In the weeks before and after my hospitalization, my friends took on the perverse role of reporting all my "bizarre" behavior to my psychiatrist. I believed they wouldn't hesitate to call him even so long afterward. Moreover, because I was no longer a patient, Nelson would lose no time in notifying the Board of Medical Quality Assurance.

We arrived for Naomi's lesson the Saturday after Thanksgiving to find a large Canon copier in the middle of Dean's living room. Dean used Jolinda's Master Card to pay for the copier and a fax machine, intending to return them once Tyrone's third trial ended. The two women were engaged in a campaign to raise a $100,000 equity bond to release him from jail. Dean had a word processor set up next to her ironing board. While she helped Naomi sew the sleeves on a dress she was making for my mother, she asked me to type and print out a flier she and Jolinda planned to distribute at all the black churches the next morning. It was an appeal for African American property owners to offer their homes on the equity bond.

■

In the end, Tyrone's bond was secured with two homes—mine and a rental belonging to Tyrone's high school math teacher. A certified appraiser who was also an elder at Mount Zion Baptist Church, volunteered to perform the court-ordered appraisal on our properties. The combined valuation on our homes was $170,000, well in excess of the amount required for the equity bond. The final requirement was for the teacher and me to appear in court, which according to Tyrone's new attorney, Richard Hansen, was unprecedented.

Dean picked me up at my office and drove me to the courthouse. John, the math teacher, was already in the courtroom when we arrived. After about five minutes the judge, a dark-haired, sensitive-looking woman in her early forties, summoned both of us to the bench. "The district attorney will question you now. He must determine your fitness to pledge surety." She signed the document in front of her, handed it to the bailiff, and ordered him to escort us to a small conference room at the back of the courtroom.

John and I found the assistant prosecutor, a short reptilian-looking man with slicked-back blond hair and thick glasses, Tyrone's attorney, and the court reporter seated around a large wooden conference table waiting for us. The court reporter, a heavy-set woman in her mid-fifties, administered the oath to both John and me simultaneously. I was questioned first. The snake-faced man made no secret of his contempt for me. In fact, it was immediately obvious the sole purpose of the interrogation was to intimidate us into withdrawing from the bond. Obviously, the willingness of two white professionals to stake their homes on Tyrone's reliability greatly strengthened the case for the defense.

The assistant prosecutor man began by demanding that I enumerate all my assets. He was seated next to me and wrote the amounts on his legal pad as I listed them. "I have $70,000 equity in my house. That has already been established. I also own a 1985 Mazda outright and have a $5,000 IRA and $4,500 in savings."

"Is that all?" It was clear from the tone used this was an insult, not a question. "Tell me, have you ever heard of a fire sale? If the state has to sell your home in a hurry, they might not get market value." The implication was clear: if, for any reason, Tyrone missed a court appearance, the government would seize not only my home but everything I owned.

I looked up at Tyrone's lawyer for help. Surely this was illegal. The assistant prosecutor saw me hesitate. He moved forward in his chair, certain I would reverse myself and withdraw my home from the equity bond.

My usual response to intimidation was stubborn defiance, and this was no exception. I had waited more than two years to strike a blow at the police security apparatus that had nearly destroyed my career. I might not get another chance.

"I'm sorry," I said. "What was the question?"

In a tone of utter disgust and scorn, the assistant prosecutor told me I was dismissed.

I left before John testified, and Dean and I waited for him in the lobby. He was nearly six feet tall and had shoulder-length, curly black hair. As he stepped out of the elevator his face, which was white with rage, mirrored my own stubborn defiance at being treated like a criminal. Two days later Tyrone was fitted with an electronic shackle to monitor his whereabouts and left jail for the first time in three years.

■

Dean prepared a press release about the white doctor and teacher who put everything they owned on the line to guarantee the right of the so-called Harborview rapist to a fair trial. She was all ready to blast-fax it to sixty newspapers and radio stations across the country when Bush the elder announced plans to invade Panama. The official justification for declaring war on the tiny Central American country was to capture Panamanian president General Manuel Noriega and transport him to Miami to stand trial for cocaine smuggling. With the coming war crowding out all national and local news, Dean knew no mainstream outlet would have space for our human-interest story.

For six straight days, the unprovoked U.S. attack on Panama was the only story on the six and ten o'clock news and on the first four pages of every major newspaper. However, nowhere was there any mention that the U.S. Air Force killed more than 3,000 civilians when they firebombed Panama City, nor that the U.S. Army forcibly evacuated 20,000 working-class residents from the capitol, as well as arresting thousands of political activists, journalists, unionists, and university professors suspected of leftist tendencies. This information was only available on shortwave from the BBC and California peace and justice stations. As was Noriega's twenty-year stint on the CIA payroll and his immense popularity with the Panamanian people for his legal, economic, and military reforms—despite his portrayal in the U.S. media as a vicious dictator.

In this respect, the U.S. war on Panama was a unique experience for me—the first time in my life I had access to war commentary from a perspective that differed from the one trumpeted by the corporate media. It was my first exposure to dissident commentators like Noam Chomsky and Michael Parenti. Both men offered cogent arguments, backed by extensive historical data, linking the invasion of Panama to the CIA overthrow of other democratically elected leaders in Guatemala, Iran, the Dominican Republic, Indonesia, and Chile. From their perspective, the U.S. wasn't really a democracy any more, but a vast military empire that "occupied" more than thirty-five foreign countries with more than six hundred military bases.

■

It took the U.S. military six days to find the Panamanian president, whose ingenuity in thwarting his powerful adversary only increased his status as a folk hero. While the BBC provided no background regarding Noriega's history as a populist nationalist, the tone of their reporting echoed the strong affection he enjoyed among the local population.

Naomi, who was nine, was just starting to make sense of the broadcasts I listened to on shortwave. On the third day of the manhunt she got out an old Aunt Jemima doll, now naked and sexless because my daughter had lost her clothes. Naomi kissed the doll and buried it under the cushion of her favorite armchair.

"I'm hiding Noriega," she said. "That's the real reason George Bush can't find him."

Once Bush increased the reward to one million dollars, a disgruntled former mistress betrayed the Panamanian president. It was well known that Bush himself had ties with narcotics traffickers during his time at the CIA. It was also widely believed that he intended to kill Noriega rather than capture him, lest he disclose any unsavory secrets in open court. However, once again the general outwitted the greatest military power on earth by fleeing into the Vatican Embassy and claiming sanctuary.

The U.S. army's two-day siege of the Vatican Embassy was the lead story on all four TV networks. Bush wisely discarded the option of storming or bombing it. Instead, a U.S. Army Special Operations unit lined the perimeter of the property with their jeeps, turned their car stereos on full volume and blasted everyone inside with continuous, ear-splitting heavy metal. Two days later, the wily general surrendered—in front of two million TV viewers.

CHAPTER 16

The U.S. occupation of Panama, which continued for nearly a year, vanished from the nightly news on January 10 with Noriega's capture. Two days later, Dean faxed her sixty press releases. The *Philadelphia Enquirer* was the first to run a small feature about the white doctor and teacher fighting to stop the Seattle police from framing an innocent black high school basketball star. The *Enquirer* was also the first mainstream paper to disclose that the police had concealed evidence from Tyrone's lawyer at the first two trials. The public now learned there was a sixth victim, identified only as "Jane Doe," who was adamant her attacker was someone other than Tyrone. And that the police lifted the fingerprints of a known felon from one of the crime scenes. The Associated Press wire service ran the story the next morning. Two days later it appeared in both the *Times* and the *Post Intelligencer*.

The death threats against John, Dean, and Jolinda began the evening the *Enquirer* published its article. I, strangely enough, got none. In fact, within weeks after pledging my home on Tyrone's bond, the hang-up and prank calls suddenly dropped from a frequency of three or more per day to two or less per week. Moreover, after July 2, 1989, I experienced no further attempts on my life. That was the day a six-ton road grader ran the red light at Eighth and Market. I narrowly escaped being crushed by braking hard, steering a hard right, and skidding into a telephone pole on the other side of the intersection.

Tyrone's trial began on May 17, 1990, and lasted three weeks. The jury deliberated for four days and informed the judge that they were deadlocked 10-2 for acquittal. Three days later, county prosecutor Norm Maleng announced his decision not to seek a fourth trial. That afternoon the front page of the *Times* featured a large photo of Tyrone and the parole officer who removed the electronic shackle from his ankle. It was the first and only time I saw him smile.

■

On June 9, 1990, I resigned from Eastside Mental Health. By now my practice income was more than adequate to cover my office overhead and a modest, but comfortable, lifestyle for Naomi and me. I used the ten hours a week this freed up to resume my novel. I had more or less abandoned the book a year earlier, unable to write coherently about anonymous activities I couldn't connect with specific people or agencies. This changed in early 1990, when I began to receive visits from patients who openly acknowledged their involvement with U.S. intelligence and who, unlike my pseudo-patients, had genuine psychiatric problems for which they desired help.

The first was a thirty-four-year-old career officer from a South Carolina Special Operations Unit. In March 1990, Lieutenant Harding used a seven-day leave to hitchhike across the country to make an appointment with me. Although he arrived at my office in civvies—a high-end lavender polo shirt and designer jeans—Harding had the erect posture and precise gait characteristic of men who spend their adult life in the military. Harding, who had an advanced degree in electronics, began by telling me about his extensive reading about mood disorders and his belief that he suffered from a bipolar II disorder. In this condition cycles of severe depression alternate with very brief periods of elevated mood.

"I am much more troubled by my down periods," he said. "They are starting to get really severe. They are also lasting longer and starting to affect my work performance." Based on his research, he was skeptical that antidepressants would work for him. "I understand that lithium is the treatment of choice for this condition. However, I can't possibly ask an army shrink to prescribe lithium. It would mean instant discharge on medical grounds. What I want to do is take it secretly for three months to prove I can still carry out my duties. Then I will confront my commanding officer. If the army tries to discharge me, I will sue them under the Americans with Disabilities Act."

After taking a complete family, social, and medical history, I told Harding I agreed with his self-diagnosis, as well as his opinion that lithium was more likely to help than antidepressants. I wrote out the prescription he asked for, along with a lab order for a lithium level and routine blood screening.

He wrote out a check to pay me, and I complimented him on the successful Special Ops campaign in Panama. I had an ulterior agenda in doing so. I assumed he knew I was a radical under government scrutiny. I saw no other way he could know of my existence, much less choose a psychiatrist 3,000 miles away when there were hundreds he could see closer to his base. What I wanted to know was whether he also knew about the harassment directed against me and whether he himself had any links with the individuals or agencies responsible. There was an uncanny similarity between the strategy used in the Noriega capture and the decision, in 1987, to blast my house with loud rap music and Martin Luther King speeches.

"I know what the boys were up to in Panama." It was a careless remark, accompanied by a smug smile. It obviously didn't occur to him what I was really after — some nonverbal "tell" suggesting he knew something about my own situation. Recalling how stiff and defensive Edward became when I tried to feel him out, I decided Harding was out of the loop on the specifics of my case.

■

Two months later I saw two more operatives who deliberately sought me out for professional help—an undercover Drug Enforcement Agency Operative who developed disabling panic attacks while stationed in the Middle East, and a retired Air Force general with a background in military intelligence who asked me to see his mentally ill son. In July I saw a fourth for chronic back pain and depression. Lowell never told me exactly who he worked for. However, at fifty-two, he had no formal employment history, allegedly supporting himself for twenty-five years as a professional gambler. The fact that he had to go on welfare after his back injury suggested he was a contract operative. As a legitimate federal employee, he would have been eligible for government health insurance, as well as a federal pension and Social Security Disability benefits.

While he never discussed the details of his undercover work, I sensed a strong undercurrent of resentment at being abandoned in this way—after devoting twenty-five years of his life to a dangerous, high stress occupation of questionable legality. Lowell, a history buff, knew of my interest in the Kennedy assassination and loaned me his hardcover edition of *On the Trail of the Assassins*, by former New Orleans District Attorney Jim Garrison.

■

Until Lowell loaned me his book, I had purposely avoided the so-called conspiracy literature. It was a field dominated by right-wing paranoiacs, who traced all twentieth-century assassinations, and numerous plane crashes, to the KGB, the Trilateral Commission, the Council on Foreign Relations, or the Illuminati, a secretive sub-group of Freemasons that supposedly masterminded the French revolution. However, the back cover of *On the Trail of the Assassins* featured a photo of the author—a judge on the Louisiana Superior Court—in his judicial robes. In reading the caption, I was astonished to learn that in 1967, as District Attorney for the Parish of New Orleans, Jim Garrison had prosecuted one of the CIA co-conspirators for Kennedy's murder.

The main focus of Garrison's bestseller is the chain of evidence he compiled for the grand jury—responsible for indicting Clay Shaw in 1967—establishing there was more than one shooter in Dealey Plaza. However, the allegations that most intrigued me related to evidence, which, for some reason, Edna never mentioned in any of her affidavits, that Oswald himself was a U.S. intelligence operative and still on both the CIA and FBI payroll in 1963 when Kennedy was shot. Like Mark Watson and other Seattle area informants who flitted from one leftist tendency to another in total disregard of their conflicting ideologies, in New Orleans Oswald involved himself simultaneously in the Fair Play for Cuba Committee, the Socialist Workers Party, the Socialist Labor Party, and the Young Socialist Alliance.

On the Trail of the Assassins also addresses the real mystery: how the government managed to conceal the truth about the murder of the thirty-fifth U.S. President for nearly thirty years. The demise of at least eighty witnesses closest to the conspiracy—by murder, accidental death, or unknown or suspicious causes—was obviously a major factor. However, although Garrison never refers to it by name, it was clear that the operation launched by Allen Dulles to infiltrate the major media outlets was alive and well in 1967. Garrison describes how both CIA and FBI agents penetrated his investigation, stole his case files, and leaked them to the *New York Times*, *Time*, and *Newsweek*. All three ran nearly identical editorials accusing Garrison of being irresponsible and "power-mad" and wasting taxpayer money on the Clay Shaw case as a publicity stunt.

After an NBC producer tried, unsuccessfully, to bribe several of Garrison's witnesses to retract their grand jury testimony, NBC reporter Frank McGee broadcast a fabricated news story about three other witnesses failing lie-detector tests. Garrison, of course, challenged the allegations. Although the network failed to produce any evidence to support them, they refused to retract the story.

Clay Shaw was ultimately acquitted. Garrison had no difficulty persuading the jury—agreement was unanimous—that there was more than one sniper in Dealey Plaza. By definition this made the president's murder a conspiracy. However the CIA blocked subpoenas for Shaw's CIA records, which remained classified until the House Committee on Assassinations reopened the investigation into Kennedy's murder in the late seventies. Without this evidence, Garrison was unable to establish that Shaw had CIA connections. Thus making it impossible to establish motive.

■

A fellow activist I met purely by chance that summer provided the last missing piece to the puzzle that refused to come together in my head. Wil Clough, the founder and president of National Association of Federal Injured Workers (NAFIW), accompanied one of his members to an independent medical examination the first week in July. It was Wil, in shedding light on the epidemic of violent suicides among postal workers, who offered the most likely motive for Oscar's murder.

Ted Jacobsen was a VA pipefitter who was applying for workers compensation because of a work-related back injury, chronic pain, and depression. As in Oscar's case, the Office of Workers Compensation repeatedly denied—four times in six years—that any of his problems were work related. No lawyer would take the appeal because the Department of Labor prohibits contingency fee agreements in which the claimant pays the lawyer's fee out of the final award. As a last resort he approached the NAFIW, Wil's 15,000 member-strong organization. Wil, in turn, contacted the Department of Labor, who asked me to perform an Independent Medical Exam.

Wil, an intense, heavy-set man in his mid-thirties, had driven more than three hundred miles from Grants Pass, Oregon, and handed me a NAFIW newsletter as he introduced himself. He accompanied many of his members to Independent Medical Exams, to protect them against what he referred to as "medical prostitutes"—doctors who derive substantial income from Department of Labor referrals because of their willingness to declare injured workers fit to work.

Although five other doctors, including two psychiatrists, had authorized him to return to work, the former pipefitter was obviously depressed. He hadn't slept for days. Except for dark circles around his eyes, his face was pale and his speech was slow and labored. His unblemished twenty-year work record argued against a prior history of mood disorder. While a detailed review of his personal history uncovered no alternative explanation for his depression, other than the back injury, pain, and loss of his livelihood.

■

I completed the interview and was explaining my findings when a column entitled "Postal Bull" on the front page of the NAFIW newsletter caught my eye. It referred to a tracking study of violent suicides by postal workers. As of June 1990, the total had reached twenty-two. I asked whether the tracking study included Oscar's death. To my surprise, Wil was unaware of the Seattle postal worker who was brutally harassed for four years and in March 1989 took a five-story drop from the fifth floor of the YMCA. After I described the autopsy findings and the seizure of the evidence file by the Postal Inspectors—as well as the prank calls, stalking, and an ugly run-in with the Texas Rangers—Wil drew the same conclusion as Oscar's legal team. That the thugs who were stalking Oscar took him up to the fifth floor of the YMCA, beat him up, and threw him out the window.

"Did he have a workers compensation claim?" he asked. I nodded, curious why Wil would make that connection. "Nearly all the violent suicides are linked to workers compensation claims. I also have a dozen statements from postal workers who have been systemically harassed after filing claims. They describe incidents in which Postal Inspectors threatened them, flattened their tires, or beat them up. They threatened one guy at gunpoint. In another case they gang raped a female letter carrier."

"It seems rather extreme, doesn't it," I asked, "to kill dozens of postal workers simply for filing for workers compensation?"

Wil told me about a former FBI agent who had recently joined NAFIW following a disabling hip injury, an individual whose security clearance allowed him access to classified documents. "He says the order to discourage postal workers from filing claims originated at the highest levels of the Reagan-Bush administration," said Wil. "He has seen memos regarding the diversion of funds from the Office of Workers Compensation Programs (OWCP) account to bank accounts linked to the Nicaraguan Contras. This is why it's so important no new claims are filed."

It was a revelation I found highly plausible, following Pete Brewton's February 1990 *Houston Post* expose about CIA links to the savings and loan debacle. During his two-year investigation, Brewton traced billions of dollars of fraudulent loans to CIA shell corporations, contract agents with offshore accounts, and ultimately covert mercenaries in Nicaragua, Afghanistan, Angola, and Chad. After Congress cut off legal funding for the Nicaraguan Contras, in addition to orchestrating illegal weapons deals with Iran and trafficking cocaine, it seemed the CIA had also tapped the lucrative savings and loan industry. According to Brewton, CIA embezzlement played a major role in the collapse of at least twenty-nine savings and loan associations.

I had a leaden, sinking feeling in my stomach when I realized Dean and I sealed Oscar's doom by reopening his claim. The high-level officials who raided the OWCP fund held human life, especially African American life, very cheaply. When Oscar won his workers compensation award, they had no compunction about killing him to avoid political ruin and likely criminal prosecution.

Wil seemed to sense my discouragement and assumed a somewhat forced cheeriness. "On the positive side," he said, "they have promised us a Congressional Investigation."

I knew what this meant—that after more than two years, a possible avenue had opened to expose Oscar's killers and bring them to justice. "Our classified documents," he added, "the tracking study, and sworn affidavits from postal workers experiencing ongoing harassment are now in the hands of two members of the House Committee on Education and Labor. They have both the guts and the clout to make it happen."

Wil and I agreed that I would prepare an affidavit regarding the circumstances of Oscar's harassment and violent death and that NAFIW would include the document in their submission to the House Committee on Education and Labor. I told him about the book I was writing about illegal domestic intelligence activities, and he also promised to send me copies of the classified documents that NAFIW had uncovered regarding the diversion of OWCP funds.

■

Dean kept Oscar's legal records, rather than shipping them to his mother. She delivered the three bankers boxes to my office the following afternoon. A week later the attorney next door notarized my three-page affidavit, which I sent via certified mail to Wil's home in Grants Pass.

I heard nothing for two months so I phoned him. "I'm sorry," he said. "The whole thing is called off." I asked why but Wil was vague and evasive. "The two congressmen and the former FBI agent are being 'pressurized.'" I asked if NAFIW still had copies of the classified documents regarding the diversion of OWCP funds. "I'm sorry, dear. I'm afraid I have nothing to send you."

It was an enormous letdown but totally predictable, given the total disinterest Congress showed in 1988 regarding the Kerry Committee findings documenting CIA involvement in cocaine trafficking. It appeared U.S. intelligence had the same iron grip on our elected officials as on the media. If a pressure group of 15,000 couldn't persuade the House to investigate a systematic terror campaign against federal injured workers, I had to accept there was no legal means of addressing the pervasive corruption within the executive branch of government. Once again, the specter of violent revolution raised itself as the only possible solution. It was one that I found distinctly unpleasant, and I put it out of my mind.

CHAPTER 17

By Christmas 1990, Bush the elder was preparing for yet another war—against Iraq. This time he faced massive public opposition. The night before the President bombed Baghdad, the Church Council of Greater Seattle organized a candlelight procession through Capitol Hill. A column of 15,000 of us extended the length of Broadway, as dozens of groups who had never collaborated before joined forces. In addition to the religious activists and the Marxist-Leninists who attended all political protests, there were Generation X anarchists and punks, peace, social justice, and anti-nuclear activists and old Vietnam antiwar protestors from the seventies. It was the first protest that all my non-political friends attended—all the counselors who worked in my building, Naomi's friends from school and their parents, and even her third grade teacher. Once again, I had visions of a million Americans converging on Washington D.C. to dislodge the criminals who controlled our government. It had happened in the Philippines and now in Eastern Europe. I still believed this could happen in the U.S. if there were enough of us.

The sudden blossoming of a vibrant anti-war movement, which held marches and rallies every Saturday, opened up a wealth of opportunities for health-care reform and other social justice issues. After a year and a half in Health Care for All, I found myself in fundamental disagreement with the other doctors. Joel Kaufman, who had a "Today is a Great Day to Smash Imperialism" poster on his refrigerator, was an exception. The other doctors adamantly opposed grassroots organizing as a strategy. They didn't believe our low-income and unemployed patients were capable of organizing to improve their lives. They felt it was up to enlightened intellectuals like us to bring about political change on their behalf. Which meant the only appropriate role for an organization of professionals was to advise legislators on crafting health-care legislation.

Most of the doctors in Health Care for All joined the Education Committee to research and write "white papers" on health-care systems in other countries and other economic and health-policy issues. Most of the non-doctors joined the Speakers Committee, where I was the only physician. When the war started, Catherine LaDuke, a Group Health visiting nurse on the Speakers Committee, and I used the Apple IIe I bought just after Christmas to produce a flier we handed out at all the rallies and marches. The flier explained how Canadians all had free health care and how Bush could easily provide free health care for all Americans with the billions of dollars he wasted in Iraq.

Catherine was a tall, broad-shouldered woman about five years my junior. She belonged to a small splinter group called the Communist Labor Party and was one of the few people in Health Care for All who shared my vision of using health-care reform to create a mass movement. More than one male activist suggested we were romantically involved, presumably because we both had short hair and no make-up. However, my relationship with Catherine, who was happily married with two boys, was purely political. Until the break-in that summer, which led me to confide in her about the harassment, my affair with Edward, and the attempts on my life. She, in turn, talked about the unsolved murder of her activist brother in Detroit. This provided instant commonality between us, as well as insight into our shared passion for grassroots activity. There has to be some outlet for the grinding guilt and rage people experience when the government murders their friends and family members—and does so with absolute confidence they will face no criminal penalties.

Naomi used our new computer to make her own flier urging people to "Stop Oil War I," a slogan she saw at the candlelight procession. She used Paintbox to draw a large peace symbol and a stick figure on a bicycle. At the bottom she typed two bullet points urging people to use less gasoline and ride bicycles more. I took her to Kinko's to print out fifty of them. The clerk, a young man in his twenties with purple hair and two nose rings, was so impressed he faxed a copy to the White House at his employer's expense.

■

In April 1990, U.S. troops withdrew from Iraq and the anti-Gulf War movement collapsed. Catherine and I and other veteran activists failed in our efforts to link the ballooning defense budget to the deep cuts Reagan and Bush had made in health care, education, and social services. We were unsuccessful in persuading them that the government's military adventurism wouldn't end with Iraq—or, more importantly, that homelessness, child poverty, and violence don't merely impact-low income Americans. These immense social problems are an insidious cancer that gradually destroys the quality of life for the entire society.

After the exhilaration of marching shoulder to shoulder with thousands of other progressives, Catherine and I found it impossible to settle back into Health Care for All's anemic agenda of rubbing elbows with elected officials. The group had spent most of 1990 lobbying for the Washington Health Care Reform Act, one of the nation's first state-based, single-payer proposals. Bellingham representative Dennis Braddock drafted the bill. He did so with the support of the traditionally conservative Washington State Medical Association and Washington State Hospital Association, following an epidemic of bankruptcies of rural hospitals and clinics. By eliminating numerous tariffs and import quotas, Reagan had enabled dozens of Washington manufacturers to shut down and move their factories overseas. This forced the workers they left behind into minimum-wage jobs with no health benefits—and no way to pay the hospitals and clinics that provided medical care for their families. Rural health providers offered them free care until their soaring overhead costs exceeded their revenue and they were forced into bankruptcy.

For all our lobbying efforts, the governor rewarded us with a line item in the final budget creating a blue-ribbon commission to do a "feasibility study" of a state-based universal health-care system. The one thousand calls and letters we generated over the next three months resulted in the appointment of exactly one single-payer supporter—former nurse and union activist Cyndy Zehnder—to the governor's blue-ribbon Health Care Commission.

Exasperated by this enormous waste of energy, Catherine and I, along with the wife of one of my brain-injured patients, started a third unofficial committee of Health Care for All. We called ourselves the Committee for Health Care Rights. For four months in 1991 we held monthly meetings in neighborhood libraries and leafleted welfare offices and shopping centers.

■

I reserved Sundays for the sixth draft of my novel. I composed on the computer and made revisions with a word-processing program instead of scissors and tape. I was still no closer to identifying the agency or group responsible for tapping my phone, sending fake patients to my office, and making six attempts to kill or seriously injure me. Thanks to the *Cointelpro Papers* and a recent expose by the Center for Constitutional Rights, it was now public knowledge that the FBI and the Jewish Anti-Defamation League (ADL), a conservative, pro-Israel lobby that collaborated with them, had infiltrated all the major CISPES chapters during the years I was a member. Yet no one else in Seattle CISPES was personally harassed.

In May 1991 the *Guardian* featured a front-page article about Wackenhut, a private security contractor that operated out of Coral Gables, Florida. According to the *Guardian*, Wackenhut employed former CIA, FBI, DEA, and military intelligence agents to maintain files on "dissident" Americans and undertake "dirty" jobs that were too politically risky for their parent agencies. This raised the disquieting prospect that my invisible enemies didn't actually work for the government but for a private right-wing group, such as the John Birch Society or the Anti-Defamation League, or even a private corporation. If the harassment originated with a private entity, the perpetrators would be free agents unaccountable to any governmental authority. It was unlikely they kept any paper or electronic record of their activities. Which meant that, short a death-bed confession, I had little hope of ever identifying them.

Likewise I could never conclusively pinpoint the agency or group responsible for infiltrating Washington's single-payer movement— whether the federal government, the police, or some private security company hired by the insurance lobby, which was our most powerful adversary. I had opposed the Steering Committee's decision to exclude non-health care providers from Health Care for All. Mainly because it shut out dozens of career activists from Gray Panthers and the Puget Sound Council of Senior Citizens, who had far more leisure time than doctors for the doorbelling, phone-banking, and envelope-stuffing necessary to launch a grassroots campaign. However, an unanticipated benefit of limiting membership to doctors, nurses, and allied health workers was that it made Health Care for All impervious to infiltration—the credentialing process for a health professional is so vigorous that it's virtually impossible for an undercover operative to pose as a doctor, nurse, or social worker. In fact, it was something that never even occurred to either of us until Catherine and I attempted to broaden Seattle's single-payer movement to the general public.

Scott Hancock was the first of more than a dozen uninvited strangers who found inventive ways to disrupt our work. After my experience with Edward and a dozen undercover patients, I seemed to have an instinct for picking them out. Ironically, the covert agents were always much more eager than the true activists to take on take on the labor-intensive person-to-person contact essential to serious organizing.

A self-employed carpenter in his mid-forties, Scott attended his first Health Care for All meeting in early May 1991, a few days after Catherine, Anne, and I first agreed to form the Committee for Health Care Rights. Scott was a conservative dresser with a striking lack of variety in his wardrobe. He typically came to meetings in new Levis with a light blue, light green, or gray plaid sports shirt. His short, wavy hair, fastidiously cropped, salt and pepper beard, and large oblong eyeglasses all exaggerated the square shape of his face. After being asked to introduce himself, Scott apologized, twice, for not being a health-care professional. He then gave a long, rambling account of a massive heart attack he suffered in 1987 and the $25,000 debt he incurred because he was uninsured.

The rest of the group reacted to Scott's brief outpouring with embarrassed silence. It was a classic survivor's story. The Speakers Committee collected similar tales for our public presentations. However, the manner in which he told it left everyone at a loss as to how to respond. Despite a sprinkling of warm fuzzies that seemed to invite intimacy, Scott's whiney, effeminate voice broadcast a continual undertone of complaint. People sensed instantly that he felt enormously distrustful and put upon by others.

Catherine and I found him waiting for us in the corridor as we left the meeting. "I just wanted to tell you guys about the new health-care coalition I'm trying to organize," he said. "One of my frustrations with the Washington Health Care Campaign is the absence of a clear grassroots focus." The Health Care Campaign was the name of the coalition formed to lobby for Braddock's bill. "I think the three of us should get together some time and talk."

Catherine and I gave our usual pat response—that any decision regarding Health Care for All's involvement in coalition work had to go through the Steering Committee. However, as we walked to my car, we both agreed that he was most likely angling for an invitation to join the Committee for Health Care Rights. It raised the disturbing question of how he knew of our plans to form a new grassroots group. We had yet to advertise our first public meeting and had informed no one other than Anne of our plans. It was a pointed reminder that my phone—and possibly Catherine's—was still tapped.

■

Three days later Scott showed up at my house for a Speakers Committee meeting. A female friend in her late thirties accompanied him. Charlotte was heavily made up, had shoulder-length bleached blonde hair, and wore a gingham sundress with silver designer thongs. She introduced herself as an unemployed hairdresser and the ex-wife of a famous Seattle sculptor. Like Scott, she felt compelled to justify her motives for attending a meeting of health-care professionals. In Charlotte's case, she wanted to see health care nationalized because her insurance company refused to cover in-vitro fertilization (IVF) for single women. This was quite an unorthodox rationale, as it ran contrary to the egalitarian belief system most single-payer activists subscribed to. We took as a given that the primary function of a publicly funded system is to guarantee that everyone receives basic services. Unlike the current private health system, which allows the wealthy to monopolize scarce health-care resources for boutique-type treatments such as cosmetic surgery, orthodontia, and IVF.

Charlotte was no different from many of the operatives who sought to involve themselves in our work and was eager to volunteer. For six months the Speakers Committee had been looking for someone to help contact the fifty groups on a contact list I drew up of local progressive organizations. I put out a proposal at every meeting to split the list with anyone willing to take half the names. There were no takers until Charlotte showed up and agreed to take the entire list.

Like Sheila McIntyre and my other female undercover patients, Charlotte also seemed intent on forming a personal relationship with me, presumably by convincing me we were kindred souls. She lingered more than an hour after the others left to tell me a long, complicated story about her ex-husband dumping her because she was infertile, and the heartache and despair she experienced over her inability to bear children.

After my cool response to her overtures, we never saw Charlotte again. Fortunately, I kept a duplicate copy of our contact list, aware that names and phone numbers of activists are highly valued among FBI and police informants. I called her after a month to ask for it back. Her flippant, dismissive response betrayed her true feelings towards me and the single-payer movement: "I'm sorry, but my cat peed on it."

■

Two weeks later someone broke into our house and stole our computer while Naomi and I were on vacation in California. The intruders entered by smashing the window of the back door opening into the kitchen. The police had already been there when we arrived home from our trip. I found a yellow carbon of their report among the glass splinters on the floor. In both bedrooms, all the bureau drawers and closet shelves had been emptied onto the floor. Yet only the computer was gone. In hoisting the console, which housed both the computer and monitor, the thieves disconnected and left the printer behind. They also ignored the color TV, the VCR, my rare penny collection, the clear-glass piggy bank in which my daughter kept her silver dollars, and the $1,800 antique slot machine in the basement. Nothing was stolen but an Apple computer, for which there was no commercial software, and which had no resale value except to a school or library. I had bought an Apple IIe, the model Naomi used at West Woodland, knowing she would have to teach me to use it.

Later that day I discovered someone had broken into my office and disconnected the call forwarding. Fortunately, nothing was taken or moved. When I told Catherine about the break-ins, she agreed with my theory that the thugs who took the computer were unaware that an Apple IIe, unlike the IBM clones, has no hard drive. I had saved my novel to a floppy disk, which I hid in a secure location whenever I left home. On learning my computer had no file-storage capability, the intruders re-entered the house and ransacked our closets and drawers looking for the disk. Unsuccessful, they broke into my office to look for it there.

We also agreed it was my own fault the computer was stolen. I had gotten tipsy at a Fourth of July picnic and confided in a fifty-something stranger about the book I was writing about my affair with a U.S. intelligence agent. The dapper-looking stranger with tortoise-shell glasses introduced himself as the house guest of someone who worked with the woman, an old CISPES friend, who hosted the picnic. He supposedly lived in Los Angeles and wrote TV quiz shows. He refused to tell me which quiz shows. He assured me there was no way I would have heard of any of them.

■

Six days after the break-in I had my third appointment with Adele Stevens, a single, unattached, former exotic dancer with an odd mixture of complaints that resembled no known psychiatric condition. Adele, who had straight shoulder-length blonde hair and dressed in shapeless second-hand dresses from the Salvation Army, wool socks, and Birkenstocks, spent most of our sessions venting her anger with Medicaid for their refusal to pay for her in-vitro fertilization—as well as her great sorrow over her infertility. My deep attachment to my daughter must have been obvious to the men who watched my house and office and listened to my phone conversations. However, unlike Charlotte and Adele and presumably the male chauvinists they reported to, I didn't view children as material possessions that I had to "own" at all costs. I became a single mother because I place a high value on all close relationships, of which parenthood is merely one form.

Adele chose this visit to inform me that she was working on a novel about the crime bosses who ran her strip club. On the surface her comment was purely coincidental, as I never discussed my book or the break-ins with any of my patients. However, given Adele's failure to cop to any psychiatric problems, I already suspected she was a pseudo-patient. Her clumsy attempt to claim some aspect of my personal life merely confirmed it.

It turned out Adele also used an Apple to work on her novel. "I save it on a floppy disk, which I hide to keep my sister from reading it." Bursting into tears, she revealed she had totally forgotten where she hid it. "I've looked everywhere. I spent three years working on that book and now I have to start all over again." She wiped her eyes and gave me a hopeful look. "Unless you could somehow help me remember."

CHAPTER 18

Edna never gave her reasons for leaving her son's place in Maine in late 1991—a decision that would be the death knell for my four-year effort to publish an expose regarding U.S. intelligence abuses. I had no idea the former investigator was in Canada until someone called me in late November from the Mennonite House of Friendship in Montreal. They were assisting her with an application for political asylum. In view of all her talk about CIA harassment, they wanted reassurance she wasn't a paranoid nutcase. I heard nothing more until mid-January, when Edna called from Columbus, Ohio. After the Canadian government denied her petition, she took a bus to Ohio and discovered the second cousin she planned to stay with was in Florida. She checked into Motel 6 but only stayed two nights.

"I came back from breakfast to learn that a federal marshal had been there," she explained. "In plain clothes, with a warrant to search my room." She said she immediately packed all her things and moved downtown to a homeless shelter. "It was a very unfortunate decision. There were some women staying there—some self-described Satanists—who left me threatening notes and pounded on my door in the middle of the night."

It was clear that Edna believed these women deliberately targeted her, owing to her efforts to expose Edwin and his involvement in a CIA assassination squad. However, there was no need for her to be explicit. We both knew the presence of street-level police and intelligence informants in homeless shelters was a common occurrence.

"I waited for my January check and rented a small studio apartment in the red-light district," she continued. "It was all I could afford but it was clean and quiet—until a week later when a mentally ill Mexican moved in next door. It's awful. The man is up all night pounding on my walls and yelling and swearing in Spanish. Last night I heard him at my front door trying to jimmy the lock." Her voice caught as she tried not to cry. "I worry they may be setting me up for a hit."

It was an operational strategy that the former investigator described in one of her affidavits. I had heard something similar from a former patient who did time in the penitentiary at Shelton. The CIA or military intelligence, which also engaged in extrajudicial murder, recruited an assassin to pose as an emotionally disturbed vagrant with an obsessive preoccupation with the target. After weeks of increasing agitation in the victim's presence, accompanied by nonsensical yelling and swearing, the act of stabbing them with a Samurai sword, or hitting them over the head with a brick or tire iron is nearly always attributed to mental illness. The assassin pleads not guilty by reason of insanity, spends a few years in a mental hospital and returns to the streets $50,000 richer.

Edna and I both knew it was pointless to call the police. With no money or family or friends to stay with, she had no option but to return to the homeless shelter and endure hounding and pestering from the government's endless supply of street-level informants. I had never heard her in such a panic. After receiving a similar distress call from Oscar shortly before his murder, I believed I was hearing a replay of his last months on earth. Thus, I took a long shot. I had no way of knowing what reaction I would get.

"I don't suppose you've heard of the New Black Panther Party?" I asked. During the surge of activism that accompanied the first Gulf War, I signed up for as many anarchist and black-liberation mailing lists as possible. The New Black Panther Party sent me their quarterly newsletter. In 1992, their main focus was freeing Mumia Abu Jamal, a black journalist on death row in Philadelphia for a murder someone else confessed to; Geronimo Pratt, whose conviction was finally overturned in 1997; and twenty other Black Panther leaders the police and FBI had framed for political reasons.

Edna said she heard of the Black Panthers but thought the FBI had shut them down.

"They've started up again and they're holding their national conference in Chicago this weekend." I hesitated. "I don't know how you would feel about this. But the government has openly murdered dozens of their members. If you were to go to them and let them know about your own situation, perhaps one of their members might take you in—like Dick Gregory did." I reminded her of her brief stay with the African American comedian turned activist in 1978.

I told her I was happy to pay her airfare and lodging and was a little surprised how quickly she agreed. I took my car to work and drove to Western Union over lunch to wire her eight hundred dollars.

Two days later she called again. "I have bad news. Someone broke in and stole the money. I won't be going to Chicago after all."

The day of the conference I got a third call. She had found the money in a book. The intruders had merely moved the money as a prank. She promised to mail me a money order the following week, but it never arrived. Months later, I learned she used it to move her belongings out of her son's home in Maine.

The last week in January she phoned a fourth time, more distressed than ever. "I get no sleep at all now because my neighbor pounds on my door all night. Yesterday he threw a mug of hot coffee at me and narrowly missed my head."

It was obvious she had lied about the break-in. I assumed she had second thoughts about throwing herself on the mercy of a strange group of black militants but was too embarrassed to tell me. However, in view of the deliberate fabrication about the money I wired being moved, I began to have misgivings about other claims, particularly those that involved ongoing attempts on her life. I had no doubt she continued to be harassed, as I was, by prank calls and belligerent strangers, including her Mexican neighbor. However, it seemed unlikely he intended to kill her. It made no sense that the U.S. government, with unlimited access to the most proficient assassins in the world, would spend fifteen years making unsuccessful attempts on a retired investigator.

I was very torn. I couldn't be absolutely certain that her enemies would stop at threats and intimidation. If I did nothing and the Mexican killed her, I would be lumbered with the burden of her death as well as Oscar's. Her limited finances meant her only chance of reprieve was to find friends or family to take her in—where someone else would answer the phone and deal with any weirdos who knocked on the door or yelled outside her window in the middle of the night.

I made the offer because I saw no other alternative. "If you can pay your own airfare to Seattle, you are welcome to stay here until you can make other arrangements."

■

Naomi and I created a makeshift bedroom for Edna in our daylight basement. The house was built into a steep hill and the southeast corner of the foundation stood at ground level. We moved a queen-sized bed, chairs, chest of drawers, TV, and bedside table into a fifteen-foot square, walled-off area with two full-size windows. Edna and I came to an agreement that she could live there rent-free so long as she arranged to be at the house at 3:45 p.m. on school days. This meant that Naomi, who was eleven and detested her after-school program, could come straight home on the school bus.

It soon became clear that our guest was clinically depressed. Edna was five years older than my mother. In most respects she was indistinguishable from other women I knew of her generation, except for her preference for thick wool socks and Birkenstock sandals. She dressed in nondescript cardigans and polyester slacks, wore her short gray hair in a granny perm, along with tortoise-shell glasses with thick lenses that made her mildly protuberant eyes look even larger than they were.

Although she came upstairs to use the toilet, make her breakfast, and join us for our evening meal, she spent most of her day downstairs watching TV. After she went two weeks without bathing or changing her clothes, I made an appointment for her to see a psychiatrist I had worked with at Eastside Mental Health. Steven gave her a prescription for the antidepressant doxepin. She took it a few days, stopped it because it made her dizzy, and never went back.

At some level I knew she was extremely disappointed to discover that Naomi and I offered nothing more than a place to stay. I sensed her relationship with her son's family had broken down, that one of the main reasons she accepted my offer was to join in a family routine that didn't exist in our home. The reality was that Naomi and I spent very little time at home. Now that my practice was full, I either spent my evenings and weekends in my office typing, filing, bookkeeping and filling in insurance forms, or at political meetings—while Naomi went to her friends' homes to play.

I clearly recognized Edna's unmet emotional needs were a major factor in her depression. However, I myself was caught up in urgent political and professional decisions of my own that spring. There seemed little I could do about my guest's unhappiness without compromising existing commitments to daughter and my patients.

■

In April 1992, Catherine and I, along with the rest of the Speakers Committee, resigned from Health Care for All. The mass resignation was triggered by a vote in the Steering Committee—which I lost—for Health Care for All to cosponsor a legislative initiative launched by former representative Dennis Braddock. The Braddock initiative, like the proposal Clinton would launch in 1994, required all Washington state employers to enroll their workers in state-approved insurance plans run on a managed-care model. Rather than outlawing private insurance in favor of publicly sponsored health care, the Braddock initiative committed millions of taxpayer dollars to subsidize the private insurance industry that PNHP—and theoretically Health Care for All—sought to abolish.

My political activism assumed a new urgency after Oscar's murder. Thus after leaving Health Care for All, I felt a pressing inner drive to find other grassroots issues to engage in. I began by re-connecting with Earl and joining the half-dozen Central Area business owners who accompanied him to hearings in front of the school board and meetings with the deputy mayor. By 1992 Seattle had an African American mayor, Norm Rice, and Earl was engaged in complex negotiations with his office to obtain legal title to the old Coleman School. Earl himself was living with a girlfriend in south Seattle. However, he maintained the "occupation" by enlisting friends to live there when they lost their jobs or broke up with girlfriends and had nowhere to stay.

With Earl's encouragement I also joined Mothers Against Police Harassment, founded in early 1991 by Jolinda Stephens and a black woman named Harriett Walden. As a Mothers hotline volunteer, my duties consisted of retrieving all the messages that came in between 8:00 a.m. Thursday and 8:00 a.m. Friday, and assisting callers in filing formal complaints with the chief of police. Most victims were African American males and teenage boys of all races, though I took several calls from females after cops ripped their clothes or fondled them. The police misconduct I documented ran the gamut—from officers swearing and making racist insults, to hitting and kicking teenagers stopped at random on the street, pulling guns on routine traffic stops, or asking drivers to drop their pants, forced entry to African American homes without warrants, often accompanied by theft or destruction of personal property, and dozens of arrests in which excessive use of force resulted in severe bruising, dislocations, and other soft-tissue injuries.

Earl and I both joined the Coalition to Oppose Weed and Seed, a joint federal-city program to beef up local law enforcement. The "Seed" package bribed cities to participate by re-funding critical social programs Reagan eliminated during the 1980s. In return, cities committed to implement the "Weed" package—a range of draconian, blatantly unconstitutional police initiatives to lock up more African American offenders for longer sentences. One provision authorized police to take everyone on the street into custody in so-called "high density" drug areas—and placed the burden on detainees to prove their innocence. Another allowed the city to seize the homes and cars of any resident where police found evidence of illicit drug use—with no due process for property or vehicles to be returned if the owners themselves were acquitted of any wrongdoing.

Earl believed gentrification, which involved remodeling and re-selling highly inflated inner-city real estate to upper middle-class whites, was the primary driver behind these measures. "It offends our white neighbors to see more than one teenager at a time on a corner," he said. "Especially if they have faces that can't be seen at night."

■

The professional crisis I faced was financial—a novel situation in which I was suddenly earning too much money. Owing to a big jump in my gross earnings, I had until December to massively increase my overhead or risk, once my net income exceeded $90,000, turning over 43 percent of my income to the federal government. I had wrestled most of my working life with what, on one hand, I viewed as an ethical responsibility to pay my fair share of taxes—and, on the other, the utter unfairness of a scheme in which tax loopholes enabled major corporations to pay little if any federal income tax. And which forced small business owners to pay 30 to 40 percent of their income to finance a gigantic nuclear arsenal and continual wars of aggression in the Third World.

The most obvious solution, to hire office staff, filled me with enormous trepidation. After years of fending off the pseudo-patients and pseudo-activists who tried to insinuate themselves into my life, I faced an enormous risk in allowing any stranger access to my accounts and patient files. After several months of telephone negotiation, in early June I persuaded my oldest friend to consider working for me. Tony, a full-service bookkeeper stuck in a dead-end minimum-wage job in rural Ohio, flew to Seattle the first weekend in June. Together we went over my accounts receivable for 1991 and 1992. After satisfying himself, I could afford an adequate salary to cover his moving costs and the higher rent he would pay on the West Coast, we drew up a contract for him to design a Word Perfect macro to computerize my insurance, Medicare, and Medicaid claim forms. He would use the macro to complete my June and July billing from his home computer in Ohio. If it streamlined my billing process enough to justify paying him a twenty dollar hourly wage, he would relocate to Seattle on September 1 to become my part-time office manager.

■

My second, perfectly legal, tax-avoidance strategy was to form a limited liability partnership with Earl to purchase the old SeaVac building on Twenty-first and Union. In 1992 this particular corner had the highest density of crack dealers in metropolitan Seattle. With the Museum stalled, my African American friend was preparing to launch a second front by opening a youth activity center. For obvious reasons, the "night riders," as he and his friends called them, preferred to operate in boarded-up areas where there was no foot traffic to observe their activities.

His initial plan was to simply rent the lobby and the adjoining kitchen. At the end of April I fronted him $20,000, which covered a deposit, three months rent, and complete rewiring, replastering, and repainting of both the lobby and the kitchen. Five weeks later he had just completed the renovations when he learned his landlord was facing foreclosure for failing to make mortgage payments. A new owner had no obligation to honor Earl's lease. We stood to lose everything.

He laughed when he phoned to tell me all this, obviously pleased with himself. "The bank has offered to sell me the building. For a $36,000 down payment, they will hold a $149,000 note at 8.5-percent interest." Aware that my mother made her living from the market, he wanted me to ask her to loan him the down payment. "If I borrow it from people around here, they will skin me alive." With no credit history, Earl would pay 15-percent interest, which was at least double the amount he could recoup from rental income.

My mother was a scrupulously frugal woman who disapproved of lending money except for phone calls and bus fare. It came as no surprise when she declined to loan Earl the money. I nearly fell out of my chair when she suggested I do so myself. My mother and I were estranged when the harassment started. She knew Earl persuaded me to reconcile with her. I suspect this was her way of repaying him.

She went on to explain exactly how to raise the money. "You will easily qualify for a margin loan on the stocks your grandfather left you. You should get at least $11,000. You can raise the rest through an equity loan on your house."

■

My motives for backing Earl were complex. I had decided early in my career to use my disposable income for social and political ends. Earl, who had practically nothing to start with, had sacrificed his fourplex and real estate career to create an African American Museum. Without making a comparable financial commitment of my own, I was just playing at being a radical. Moreover, at the time, I mistakenly believed I could use my contribution to the partnership to reduce my 1992 tax liability.

The week that followed was one of the most hectic of my life. In between patients I had to see my broker at Merrill Lynch and the loan officer at Washington Mutual—twice. Earl and I had three appointments with the African American accountant in his late sixties who helped Earl set up his real estate business. Stallworth was an imposing man of nearly six feet with a tidy gray afro. He dressed in three-piece designer suits with exquisite Persian blue or mauve shirts. It was his suggestion to create a limited partnership to shield me from any liability beyond my $56,000 investment. Using a template he kept on his hard drive, he printed out a five-page partnership agreement for Earl and me to sign and file with Washington's Secretary of State.

On June 11 I went home during my lunch hour to look for my 1990 and 1991 tax returns and found a three-page letter from Edna, along with her house key, on my kitchen table. The letter informed me she had "blown" my cover:

"I now have proof. On the basis of several blatantly contradictory statements, I know you are working for the CIA and passing them confidential information about my psychiatric treatment." In the next sentence she alluded to "friends" in Ohio who informed her my future office manager was also a known CIA "asset." Edna had never met Tony. However, she obviously overheard me tell Naomi our friend was leaving Ohio and returning to Seattle to work for me.

The "contradictions" she referred to related to the shower and toilet she wanted me to build in the basement. Edna hated coming upstairs, especially at night, and had difficulty getting in and out of my bathtub. She had been pressuring me for weeks, stressing it was an investment and would improve the value of my home. I always ended the discussions by telling her I couldn't afford it.

"This was an obvious lie," she wrote. "You also say your family is well-off and would always help you in a crisis. If they were as supportive as you claim, surely they would lend you $7,000 to build a shower and toilet."

"I also know you and Tony Young had a secret meeting in Carnation, on the pretense of going strawberry picking." This was equally ludicrous. There was nothing secret about our trip to Carnation because I invited Edna to accompany us. Moreover, my future office manager and I had no need to drive seventy-five miles into the country to hold a private conversation.

"I have purchased a ticket and am flying to London this afternoon to apply for political asylum. I hereby revoke any prior permission to include any personal details about me or my life, even under a fictitious name, in your novel." Edna knew I had completed the manuscript and that an agent in Ithaca, New York, was submitting *Men, Women and Spies* to publishers. "I am prepared to file an injunction to block the book's publication."

This sudden blossoming of delusional thinking was a crushing blow. I still believed the prank calls, break-ins, and stalking Edna first complained about in 1984 were genuine. The pattern was too similar to the harassment Oscar, Dean, and I experienced, as well as that described by Cointelpro victims in the Black Panther Party and American Indian Movement. As these groundbreaking published accounts wouldn't appear for another five years, I saw no way she could describe the prank calls, break-ins, and intrusive stalking by street people so convincingly unless these events actually occurred.

Sadly, over time, the years of unrelenting persecution and intimidation took their toll. At some point, like many other victims of psychological harassment, Edna lost the ability to distinguish between deliberate harassment and random misfortune. As a consequence she attributed every slight and misunderstanding to a vast conspiracy—and in her own mind continued to be pursued, long after the government had lost interest.

CHAPTER 19

On August 21, 1992, one month after Earl and I took possession of the old SeaVac building, the Rhode Island Bank we bought it from went into receivership. As of that date, a federal agency called the Resolution Trust Corporation (RTC) assumed our note. Bush the elder created the RTC in 1989 to take over the 1,300 banks and savings and loans that went bankrupt between 1984 and 1988. Its official role was to investigate banks and thrifts that failed due to fraudulent activities, liquidate viable assets, and work with the Federal Deposit Insurance Corporation to restore depositors' lost savings. However, by then it was clear to much of the left, mainly based on Pete Brewton's *Houston Post* expose, that the RTC's real function was to orchestrate a cover-up concealing that U.S. intelligence was directly implicated in at least twenty-nine savings and loan failures.

The Bush family had links with the CIA that extended back long before Bush the elder became CIA director in 1975. This cozy relationship continued after he became president in 1988. In fact, two of his sons were personally responsible for two savings and loan failures—Jeb Bush helped bring about the collapse of Broward Saving in Florida by defaulting on a 4.56 million dollar loan, while Neil Bush, as a director of Silverado Savings and Loan in Colorado, was responsible for 1.3 billion dollars of loan defaults.

Earl first learned of the demise of Old Stone Bank from an attorney at Eisenhower and Carlson. This was the local law firm Old Stone hired to evict three hostile tenants we inherited when we bought the building. Earl had a clause inserted in our escrow agreement making the bank responsible for removing a draftsman, a real estate agent, and a homeless man who refused to sign rental agreements. On August 28, 1992, Earl called Eisenhower and Carlson to complain that none of our squatters had received eviction notices. The lawyer he talked to informed him that the RTC had taken over our note and that a "Mr. Black" in the Baltimore RTC office had instructed them not to proceed with the evictions.

Over the next six weeks Earl wrote Black three letters and placed a dozen calls to his office and got no response. On October 1, he used the balance owing on the down payment to hire our own attorney to file the evictions. He also applied to Evergreen Bank, Seattle's sole black-owned bank, to refinance the property. We had no legal means, short of suing them, to force the RTC to honor the sales contract they assumed when they took over our mortgage. A quicker and far less expensive option was to refinance and end our relationship with these federal crooks by repaying the note in full.

Two days after signing our loan agreement, Evergreen also filed for bankruptcy. A week later they agreed to let Key Bank buy them out, after the latter signed a Memorandum of Understanding (MOU) to honor Evergreen's outstanding commitments to Central Area patrons. Two weeks after that, Key Bank's senior loan officer informed us that the MOU didn't extend to our refinance loan. Earl and I never uncovered concrete evidence of a conspiracy between the RTC, Key Bank, and the Seattle developers who coveted our property. However, the unannounced visit that the senior loan officer paid to my office in early November suggested that there was some discussion, at least, between the bank and local real estate interests that the last undeveloped property in the Central Area was too valuable to indulge Earl's vision for it. After explaining how the bank "lost" money on small borrowers like Earl, he offered me a four million dollar loan to replace Earl as general partner, demolish our building, and replace it with a high-end retail outlet.

I told Earl about the visit, and he obtained a legal opinion from the lawyer who handled our evictions: our legal rights under the escrow agreement and the MOU weren't legally enforceable except by suing the RTC and Key Bank. A lawsuit against either one would cost us three times as much in legal fees as our original investment.

As there was still no response from Black, I asked Congressman Jim McDermott's office to intercede with the RTC on our behalf. I also phoned Pete Brewton at the *Houston Post*. Partly in the vain hope he might be willing to cover our problems with the RTC in his series—as well as to enquire what he knew about Old Stone. If I could prove the bank's demise was in any way linked to fraudulent loans, off-shore bank accounts, or shell corporations associated with the Nicaraguan Contras or other covert CIA operations, I was prepared to hire an attorney and spend the hundred thousand dollars it would cost to file suit.

The reporter answered his own phone. I briefly explained the problems we were having. I was disappointed but not surprised to learn Brewton was leaving the *Post* to pursue a law degree. The corporate media comes down hard on mainstream journalists who report on government crimes.

"Sorry," he said. "I've never heard of Old Stone. I know very little about the RTC, either. However, I have two friends who have done excellent exposes on some of their multi-million dollar scams. One of them was published in *Penthouse* two years ago. I don't have a copy, but I know where you can get one." He gave me a phone number in Santa Barbara.

■

The number was for Prevailing Winds. I called it and learned they were a non-profit corporation that archived academic and journalistic research that mainstream newspapers and news magazines refused to publish. The man who answered said they had seven articles on the RTC and suggested I send him two dollars for a catalogue. What I got back was a sixty three-page *Catalogue Reader* that listed a little over one hundred books, reprints, audiotapes, and videotapes. The titles ran the gamut from published exposes by investigative reporters and intelligence alumni, *On the Trail of the Assassins*, and other bestsellers on the ballistics and other physical evidence from John Kennedy's murder, to rare and out of print books, audiotapes, and videos by academics who researched more recent political assassinations and intelligence scams. The articles under the topic heading "The Savings and Loan and Bank Rip-Off" included five articles from Brewton's *Houston Post* series and a 1992 *Playboy* article entitled, "The Scandal at RTC," as well as the 1990 *Penthouse* series to which Brewton referred.

Under a section entitled "Intelligence Drug Cartels," there were three articles on CIA and Contra involvement in cocaine smuggling, a fourth entitled, "Air America," about a similar operation that smuggled heroin from Southeast Asia during the Vietnam War, and a fifth by Dan Sheehan of the Christic Institute regarding Governor Bill Clinton's obstruction of an Internal Revenue investigation into cocaine smuggling at the Mena airport in Arkansas.

Another section entitled "AIDS and Medical Fraud" featured seven articles, most by medical doctors, alleging the Pentagon had played a role in the creation of HIV. There had been rumors on the far left since 1990 of a so-called AIDS conspiracy. In recent months,

Tony, who was gay and HIV-positive, had been downloading and printing similar articles off the Internet. They were all technically dense treatises I had no hope of comprehending without a rudimentary knowledge of virology and molecular genetics—fields which barely existed when I attended medical school in the late sixties. I abandoned the effort altogether when I discovered one of the authors, a lawyer named Ted Strecker, was actually a right-wing conspiracy freak who blamed the AIDS epidemic on a UN-Soviet conspiracy to destroy the free world.

The largest section, entitled "Assassination Politics," consisted of an extensive body of scholarly research on the John Kennedy, Robert Kennedy, and Martin Luther King assassinations. The authors included professional journalists like Jim Mars and Jim DiEugenio, academics like Peter Dale Scott at the University of California-Berkeley, and even a U.N. research analyst named Sylvia Meagher. One article by William Turner, entitled "Farewell America," concerned an out-of-print book that two French intelligence operatives published in 1968. According to Turner, the French were the first to "crack" Kennedy's murder. They did so by tracing the money used to finance the assassination to a Swiss shell corporation called Permindex—intelligence they subsequently passed to Garrison for use in his grand jury investigation. French intelligence was already investigating Permindex for four assassination attempts against French President Charles DeGaulle in 1961 and 1962. In fact, Turner cites an interview with the French paper *Les Echos*, in which DeGaulle details his reason for expelling NATO from French soil in 1966—namely discovering that Permindex was operating out of NATO headquarters in Brussels.

■

Prior to the Internet, the archival services Prevailing Winds provided was a unique resource for academics and journalists determined to preserve a factual historical record independent of the "official" history the power elite concocts to preserve their own interests. After my five-year, largely unsuccessful crusade to connect names and faces to an invisible Shadow Government which nearly destroyed my career, I felt like a child in a candy store.

My first order cost me a little more than one hundred dollars. A week later I received a large manila envelope, containing the seven articles on the RTC, the Turner reprint on *Farewell America*, and *Nomenclature of an Assassination Cabal*. The 1992 *Catalogue Reader* indicates a member of Lyndon Johnson's inner-circle wrote *Nomenclature of an Assassination Cabal* in 1970—which purports to identify by name all the key individuals involved in the Kennedy assassination conspiracy. The catalogue entry also reveals the 1970 document was based entirely on publicly available sources—the twenty-six volumes of testimony taken by the Warren Commission that Johnson appointed to investigate Kennedy's murder—and the proceedings of District Attorney Jim Garrison's 1967 grand jury investigation.

Despite the pressing financial concerns that had led me, via Pete Brewton, to Prevailing Winds, I couldn't resist opening *Nomenclature of an Assassination Cabal*. My intention was to skip to the page that listed the names of the co-conspirators—I had been waiting four years for this moment—and then to read the seven documents which I hoped would form the basis of a lawsuit against the RTC. This proved impossible, as *Nomenclature of an Assassination Cabal* is essentially fifty-nine pages of lists—mainly of obscure federal agencies and the officials who ran them, and the corporate boards of prominent oil companies and defense contractors.

It took an hour of reading and re-reading the first five pages to ascertain the handful of men that David Copeland, who published *Nomenclature of an Assassination Cabal* under the pseudonym William Torbitt, identifies as the principal architects of the Kennedy assassination. According to Copeland, FBI Director J. Edgar Hoover,

Hoover's close personal friend Vice President Lyndon Johnson, and the Joint Chiefs of Staff initiated and oversaw the conspiracy. However, they turned over the operational details to a top-secret intelligence and counterespionage agency called the Defense Industrial Security Command (DISC). Like Turner, Copeland traces the financing to Permindex. He cites corporate records District Attorney Jim Garrison subpoenaed during the grand jury investigation regarding Permindex's principal shareholders. In 1963, the year Kennedy was killed, they included all the major U.S. oil companies; Brown and Root, the most highly paid defense contractor in Vietnam, and which happens to perform a similar function in Iraq as the Halliburton subsidiary Kellogg, Brown and Root; Bell Helicopter, run out of Dallas by the former Nazi war criminal Walter Dohrnberger; and numerous other munitions-makers and National Aeronautics and Space Administration contractors.

DISC's use of multiple layers and supposedly independent agencies and front groups was a deliberate strategy to conceal the identity of the twenty or so men who oversaw the conspiracy. It took me four readings to get them all straight. The first front group was an ultra-right wing white Russian exile group called the Solidarists. Its members fled the Bolshevik Revolution in the twenties with immense fortunes they invested in Texas oil, armaments, gun-running to anti-Castro Cubans, and Lyndon Johnson's Senate and Vice-Presidential campaigns.

The second, the American Council of Churches, was actually a top-secret division of the FBI, which Hoover created in 1941 to place agents posing as ministers and missionaries in Latin America and on a ranch in northern Mexico. It was here that the gunmen U.S. intelligence used to assassinate "unfriendly" foreign leaders were trained and housed.

The third group was the Free Cuba Committee, a small army of ultra right-wing anti-Castro Cubans the CIA kept on retainer after the failed Bay of Pigs invasion. At the behest of the CIA, these Cuban exiles also engaged in more than thirty assassination attempts against Cuban president Fidel Castro.

The fourth group, the Syndicate, had close ties with a Mafia family headed by Joseph Bonnano. In the early sixties the Bonnano family owned a controlling interest in a number of companies manufacturing munitions and supplies for the Department of Defense, NASA, the Atomic Energy Commission, and the U.S. Information Agency. The Syndicate was run by Johnson's close political crony Bobby Baker and Baker's business partner, Clifford Jones—ex-lieutenant governor of Nevada and partner in pre-revolution Havana casinos with Dallas nightclub owner Jack Ruby. Ruby's role in the conspiracy was to ensure that Oswald's intelligence background didn't come out at his murder trial by shooting him in the basement of the Dallas jail, while millions of TV viewers watched.

The fifth group, the Security Division of NASA, was a subsidiary of military intelligence and headed by Werner von Braun, Hitler's most highly decorated rocket scientist. Von Braun was a close friend to both Hoover and Major Clay Shaw, the co-conspirator Garrison indicted. As a former army intelligence and Office of Strategic Services operative, Shaw directly facilitated the secret entry of 127 Nazi scientists into the U.S. Von Braun's assigned role in the assassination was as immediate supervisor of John Osborne, the American Council of Churches "missionary" who ran the ranch in northern Mexico—and Ferenc Nagy, the exiled prime minister of fascist Hungary. According to Copeland, Nagy was clearly identified in fifty-nine Dealey Plaza photos as the tall, thin man who signaled the gunmen with his umbrella.

Like Garrison, Copeland believes there were seven snipers in Dealey Plaza, though the New Orleans District Attorney only positively identified three of them. The evidence Garrison compiled for the grand jury indicates that Emilion Santana fired the shot that hit Texas Governor John Connally as he rode in the front seat of Kennedy's limousine—from the DalTex Building, which was directly across from the School Book Depository. It reveals that William Seymour, who widely impersonated Oswald using the alias Leon Oswald, fired two shots from the sixth floor of the School Book Depository. Finally, it identifies the gunman who fired the fatal shot that blew off Kennedy's skull, from the grassy knoll in front of the motorcade, as Manuel Gonzalez. Copeland quotes directly from Garrison's interrogation of Santana, in which the sharpshooter confirms all this.

■

At 1:00 a.m., after reading *Nomenclature of an Assassination Conspiracy* for the fourth time, I got undressed and got into bed. It was pointless even trying to sleep. World fascism hadn't died in 1945, as we were led to believe. It was certainly alive and well as of November 1963. There was also every reason to believe its intimate relationship with U.S. intelligence had survived to the present day. After thirty years, many of the original Kennedy co-conspirators were dead. However, based on firsthand accounts from police and intelligence defectors like Phillip Agee, Sandy Gonzalez, and Michael Rupert, it was clear the children and grandchildren of these right-wing terrorists continued to engage in covert assassinations, illegal wars, narcotics trafficking, torture, and Third World death squad activity, all in violation of the Constitution and the laws enacted by our democratically elected representatives.

Nevertheless what I found most distressing was that the truth about Kennedy's real killers had been in the public domain for nearly thirty years. It was obvious the conspiracy's extreme complexity was instrumental in the success of the massive cover-up that followed. I wanted Americans to be outraged that their own government murdered a popular, democratically elected president—and got away with it. Yet it was hard to feel outrage over sixty-plus co-conspirators with unrecognizable names who worked for powerful groups and agencies that were carefully hidden from public view.

Even for intellectuals, it would take a college-level course to understand the complex interrelationships between Johnson, Hoover, and Nazi war criminals like Von Braun and Dornberger, and the powerful oil, munitions, and aerospace companies that financed the assignation. The close friendship between Hoover, Shaw, and Nazi war criminals like Von Braun and Dornberger only became plausible with a prior understanding of the secret CIA and FBI operations to smuggle ex-Nazis into the U.S. after World War II. Likewise, the notion of a secret branch of the FBI enlisting a Mob syndicate to carry out political murders was inconceivable without prior knowledge of the longstanding reliance of both the FBI and the CIA on the Mafia to carry out high-profile criminal activities—such as beating up and murdering striking Longshoremen in New York and San Francisco during World War II, as well as communists in Italy and Marseille in the early fifties.

The vast majority of Americans have no knowledge of the executive order—National Security Action Memorandum 263—that Kennedy issued in October 1963 to begin the withdrawal of U.S. "military advisors" from Vietnam. Nor that Johnson secretly reversed it—with National Security Action Memorandum 273—within two weeks of assuming office. Within months, Kennedy's replacement escalated the Vietnam "police action" into a full-scale war that lasted twelve years. And which translated into billions of dollars of profits for Brown and Root, Bell Helicopter, and other defense contractors who owned shares in Permindex.

There had to be some way to bring all this to public attention. Edna's threat to file an injunction became a non-issue after my agent returned my manuscript. Three publishers had rejected it as unmarketable—the plot and characters of *Men, Women and Spies* didn't engage the reader. I had already ruled out all the avenues Edna herself had pursued. Civil action was a non-starter, as I still had no concrete evidence linking any specific agency or group to the phone harassment or attempts on my life. Both Edna and Wil Clow had already tried the strategy of blanketing every member of the Senate and House and every mainstream media outlet with letters and e-mails. It led nowhere. For an hour or so I played with the idea of a new novel, based on a totally new premise unrelated to confidential information that my activist and whistleblower patients revealed to me. A new book would take at least five years to write and possibly even longer to publish.

As often happened, the answer came to me just as it started to get light: if people needed a college course to understand the Kennedy assassination, there was no reason not to teach one. No academic qualifications were needed to run courses through the University of Washington Experimental College. The Experimental College was first started by hippies in the early seventies to teach courses such as macramé, folk dancing, reflexology, massage, astrology, jewelry-making, organic gardening, woodworking, plumbing and rewiring, that weren't covered in the formal university curriculum. As a Washington state resident I was eligible to offer any class I could entice students to sign up for.

I called the Experimental College Monday morning for an application. After answering two general questions about my reasons for offering the course and the age and interest group I expected to appeal to, I was asked to provide a complete syllabus and course outline. On the basis of reading two books, I knew who paid for the assassination. However, my factual knowledge of the logistics was quite limited. Obviously, it would take months of research before I could consider myself an expert. In the end I decided on a syllabus consisting of four two-hour classes one week apart. The first would cover the extensive physical evidence compiled by the 1978 House

Committee on Assassinations. Unbeknownst to most Americans, the 1978 House Committee concluded there had to be at least two gunmen in Dealey Plaza. The second would focus on Permindex and the interconnections between the oil and defense contractors who financed the assassination and each of the five front groups that reported to the Defense Industrial Security Command. The third would concentrate on the evidence implicating Hoover and Johnson as principal architects of the conspiracy. The last would examine research linking DISC to the assassination of Martin Luther King, Robert Kennedy, and other major political figures.

CHAPTER 20

As I anticipated, the Prevailing Winds articles regarding the RTC documented a systematic pattern of corruption and cronyism. In forming the RTC in 1984, Bush appointed directors of major Wall Street firms to oversee the agency's operations. During their tenure these managers remained intensely loyal to the brokerage firms Bush recruited them from, companies that ultimately rehired them when the federal agency closed down in 1995. In the meantime, they sold their former employers billions of dollars' worth of real estate they acquired from failed banks and savings and loan associations—at prices well below market value. This meant it was up to taxpayers, who were ultimately responsible for reimbursing depositors for billions of dollars of lost savings, to pick up the difference. While it was very enlightening to have factual evidence of the RTC's criminal conduct, there was nothing in the articles related to the specific situation Earl and I faced.

Although the HIV studies Prevailing Winds had archived had nothing to do with the RTC or the Kennedy assassination, it was intriguing to find everything Tony had downloaded in the catalogue—particularly in light of the high standard of documentation they required. The "AIDS and Medical Fraud" catalogue entry that most interested me was a 1988 *Chicago Tribune* article Tony hadn't given me. It concerned the sudden death of an Illinois lawmaker named Douglas Huff who was helping attorney Ted Strecker promote his brother's research regarding a possible Department of Defense role in the creation of HIV. The article revealed that Huff, who shared Strecker's right-wing political perspective, had died of an alleged heroin and cocaine overdose. Given the minuscule odds of a right-wing conservative developing a heroin and cocaine habit, it was an obvious anomaly suggesting foul play—compounded by the additional details that Strecker himself was killed a month earlier by a .22-caliber rifle wound to the head. The Springfield, Missouri, police classified Strecker's death a suicide, despite a sworn statement by his brother Robert that Ted was in good spirits and looking forward to his next TV interview.

I had previously dismissed Ted Strecker as a right-wing conspiracy freak. I had second thoughts about jumping to this conclusion after learning of the circumstances of his death—and that his brother, Dr. Robert Strecker, was a prominent gastroenterologist and biomedical researcher. The *Catalogue Reader* went on to reveal that the Strecker brothers stumbled across evidence that HIV originated in the laboratory purely by accident. In 1973 they were assembling epidemiological and cost data on behalf of Security Pacific Bank, for a new for-profit Health Maintenance Organization similar to Kaiser Permanente. In a perverse way, any evidence suggesting researchers, witnesses, or whistleblowers were surreptitiously murdered for trying to publicize embarrassing government secrets automatically enhanced the credibility of their claims.

More ominous still was that both Strecker and Huff were killed during the period that I myself experienced six attempts on my own life—after receiving two credible warnings about my AIDS research being extremely dangerous. Obviously, I needed a clearer understanding of the scientific basis of Strecker's claims to ascertain whether U.S. intelligence was possibly linked to his and Huff's deaths. Furthermore, pinpointing who might have murdered them might also help me identify the people who wanted me killed.

Altogether, it took a little over twenty hours to get my head around what Strecker and the other AIDS researchers were saying and whether it had any scientific validity. Over the Christmas 1992 break, I took the eight-inch stack of documents Tony gave me to the UW medical library. After verifying all the sources listed in the original studies and consulting a dozen textbooks on microbiology, genetics, and immunology, I came to the following conclusions: first, that HIV had a unique genetic structure that couldn't possibly occur on the basis of random mutation—that it could only be the result of a recombination experiment; second, that the only lab that carried out this type of genetic modification in the early seventies was the old biological warfare laboratory at Fort Detrick, Maryland; third, that the "official" hypothesis that AIDS originated spontaneously in Africa was most likely a hoax and part of an elaborate cover-up of illegal biological warfare research; and, fourth, that I was most likely targeted by mistake.

■

The papers Tony printed included a four-page brochure describing a video made by Dr. Robert Strecker in 1990 called the *Strecker Memorandum*; sixteen pages of references that Strecker used in producing it; a paper called "AIDS is a U.S. Homemade Evil," by an East German microbiologist named Jakob Segal; a 1986 *Omni* article entitled, "Was There an AIDS Contract?" and numerous e-mails by Segal's American translator Michael Morrissey; and excerpts from the book *Queer Blood* by dermatologist and cancer researcher Dr. Alan Cantwell. Despite having no knowledge of Segal's work and pursuing a totally different line of inquiry, the American doctors who investigated the epidemiology of HIV for Security Pacific Bank came to the identical conclusion Segal did—namely that it could only have originated in a laboratory.

After tracing the Segals', the Streckers', and Cantwell's original sources, what I ascertained myself was that the so-called official theory that HIV originated spontaneously in the jungles of Africa was first promulgated by biomedical researcher Dr. Robert Gallo in 1984. Curiously, Gallo also claims to have discovered HIV that same year. However, the rest of the scientific community agrees it was actually Dr. Luc Montagnier of the Pasteur Institute who first identified the retrovirus a year earlier. Gallo's "green monkey" theory maintains that human HIV infection first came about when mutated Simian Retrovirus (SIV) spread to a human being through a green monkey bite.

Major problems with his green monkey hypothesis forced Gallo to discard it in 1990. In the first place, it fails to explain the rapid spread of HIV, despite the slow rate of transmission typical of an infection transmitted only via secretions and blood products. It doesn't explain how thousands of new cases could appear simultaneously in the U.S., Brazil, and Haiti, within months of the first African case. Secondly, SIV doesn't cause infection in green monkeys even when they are injected with it. Thirdly, AIDS wasn't identified in Africa until 1982, three years after the first case appeared in New York

What I found even more surprising was that the hypothesis that HIV was created in a laboratory predated Gallo's green monkey theory by at least six months. In early 1984, microbiologist John Coffin published genetic sequencing data suggesting that HIV, which prior to 1983 was known as HTLVIII/LAV/ARV, was an artificially manufactured mutant of sheep Visna Virus. Visna, which causes an AIDS-like illness in sheep, only occurs in remote areas of Iceland, although immunology and cancer researchers began propagating it in the lab in the early seventies. Despite its close genetic resemblance to Visna, HIV also possesses a three hundred-nucleotide envelope that in 1983 was almost identical to that of Human T-cell Leukemia Virus (HTLV-1). Although HIV itself has mutated drastically in the last twenty-five years, it was statistically impossible for Visna to acquire this specific nucleotide envelope via mutation. An HTLV-1 segment could only attach to Visna by recombination, a process whereby viruses exchange DNA segments. Moreover, this specific recombination couldn't occur in nature, as HTLV-1 and Visna don't infect the same animal populations in the wild.

In "AIDS USA Home-Made Evil," Jakob and Lili trace the origin of HIV, aka HTLVIII/LAV/ARV, to gene-splicing experiments in a Department of Defense Biological Warfare Program at Fort Detrick. They go on to describe the ferocious counterattack Coffin's paper provoked from Gallo, the controversial American virologist who, coincidentally, headed the biological warfare program at Fort Detrick from 1967 to 1974.

The Segals never identify their source, which their translator Michael Morrissey speculates was East German intelligence, for their claim that HIV entered the human population through a 1976 prison experiment in Queens. According to the Segals, inmates were offered early release if they agreed to be injected with the novel retrovirus HTLVIII/LAV/ARV. Unaware the resulting infection would take as long as five years to manifest symptoms, researchers monitored their subjects for six months. When none of them showed any evidence of ill health, they were released to the community.

The *Strecker Memorandum* brochure also traces the origin of HIV to genetic recombination experiments at Fort Detrick. Dr. Robert Strecker's sixteen pages of references provide evidence from two entirely different sources—the *Bulletin of the World Health Organization* and the 1972-73 WHO *Federation Proceedings* that the Agency for Cancer Research was experimenting in central Africa with retroviruses created at Fort Detrick. He concludes that some time between 1974 and 1977 HTLVIII/LAV/ARV found its way into World Health Organization smallpox vaccine. In his brochure he reproduces two maps. The regions in central Africa, Haiti, and Brazil in which WHO administered vaccines between 1974 and 1977 coincide almost exactly to the areas in which thousands of new AIDS cases developed simultaneously in the early eighties.

In the excerpt from *Queer Blood*, Dr. Alan Cantwell provides similar epidemiological evidence that an experimental hepatitis B vaccine given to thousands of American homosexuals in 1978 and 1979 was contaminated with HIV. This, in his view, explains its rapid spread within the US.

In 1990, Gallo was forced to admit he had yet to infect a single green monkey with SIV and advanced a new theory—that HIV developed from mutated SIV spread by the consumption of infected chimpanzee meat. A hypothesis that was equally implausible. Unlike green monkeys, lab chimpanzees can develop SIV infection if they are injected with it. However, eighteen years later there has yet to be a single case of SIV infection in wild chimpanzees.

■

Clearly, the preponderance of evidence supports the theory that HIV was created artificially, via genetic modification of sheep Visnu virus—whereas there is no data whatsoever to support Gallo's hypothesis that HIV developed in human beings after they ate chimpanzees infected with SIV. The notion was preposterous that the virus entered the human population via a UN-Soviet conspiracy to destroy the free world. Nevertheless Ted Stecker's paranoid beliefs in no way alter the genetic structure of the retrovirus.

More importantly, if, as Morrissey and others believe, genetic research linking HIV and Visna was deliberately suppressed, I finally had a plausible explanation why the U.S. government spent two years trying to kill me—only to suddenly lose interest in July 1989.

Presumably the police and/or FBI began tapping my phone in 1987 following the UW sit-in. They learned I was treating the ex-wife of a biological warfare researcher while simultaneously making numerous calls to local newspapers. Someone drew the erroneous conclusion that Jane discussed her ex-husband's work during our sessions and that I was trying to pass the information to reporters. My anonymous minders, in turn, informed military intelligence. Only a Department of Defense Agency would have detailed knowledge of the top-secret experiments that took place at Fort Detrick. Or access to chemical warfare agents, such as the cholinesterase inhibitor released in my basement.

After the Gay Men's Health Center presented the results of my Tagomet study at the 1989 International AIDS conference, the people trying to kill me realized I was only interested in treating AIDS. Once they realized I possessed no damaging information regarding the origin of AIDS virus, there was no longer any need to get rid of me. It was all a big misunderstanding.

Twenty years later there is no need to kill anyone to suppress the truth about where HIV originated. Thanks to Internet technology that permits wide, instantaneous transmission of limitless factual information, there are now thousands of doctors and scientists who understand the significance of the genetic experiments at Fort Detrick. In the new millennium, U.S. intelligence is so skilled in controlling the media and public consciousness that Americans remain passive and docile in the face of the most brutal and sadistic government crimes. Thus, it no longer matters how many people know.

Part IV –
Our Enemies Are All Under Us

A dozen make a demonstration.
A hundred fill a hall.
A thousand have solidarity and your own newsletter;
ten thousand, power and your own paper;
a hundred thousand, your own media;
ten million, your own country.
from *The Low Road* by Marge Piercy

CHAPTER 21

The Experimental College approved my proposal to teach "Exploring the JFK Assassination" starting summer quarter 1993. I received formal notification of my classroom assignment on May 1—along with a reminder that it was my responsibility to promote the course to potential students. The first year I taught the class, I publicized it by taking out an ad in the *Free Press*—a twelve-page monthly tabloid published once a month by two Generation X activists. I also put up fliers in all the neighborhood libraries and University District and Fremont cafes and coffee houses. Frank Zucker, who ran a local anti-CIA group called Citizens for Overt Action, took a stack of fifty fliers for a table he set up outside the Seven Gables, which was showing the Noam Chomsky documentary, *Manufacturing Consent*.

When Edward called on June 11, for the first time in over a year, I assumed one of his intelligence cronies had seen the fliers. He began the conversation by reiterating, in his unconvincing singsong, what an amazing woman I was and how he would always love me. He followed these initial declarations with an update on his "community work." Edward still liked to make out that he was a community activist because he went to regular meetings with the Seattle police as the Neighborhood Watch coordinator for his street.

"Right now I'm assisting some anti-apartheid activists escape from South Africa," he boasted. "I pick them up from SeaTac and drive them across the Canadian border."

"Are you sure they were working against apartheid?" I asked. In 1993, Mandela and the African American Congress were positioning themselves to take power. What Edward described sounded more like a rescue operation for police and CIA informants. I assumed the activity was classified and I was very surprised he would even mention it. "They sound more like government informants to me. When Mandela takes power the ANC will round them up and shoot them all."

"Oh, I wouldn't know about that." Edward's voice became strained and chirpy. I expected him to terminate the conversation, as he usually did when caught in a lie. Instead, he changed the subject and hurried on.

"Do you still hear from Earl?" he asked. "I wonder do he still sleep at the Museum or do other people stay there?"

"As far as I know different people take turns sleeping there," I answered. What Edward was really asking was whether we were still romantically involved. However, I had no intention of answering either the stated or unstated question.

Edward seemed satisfied by my answer and hung up. I immediately called Earl, worried that the police might be planning another raid. Earl, who shared the view that my ex-lover was most likely a federal agent, said he had to see me right away.

We agreed to meet at the International House of Pancakes on Madison. Thirty minutes later a waiter showed us to a booth. I saw Earl was wearing a plastic Harborview ID band on his wrist and asked about it. To his credit he came straight to the point.

"That's what I had to tell you. My girlfriend and I have a new baby daughter. I kept meaning to tell you. But I hate to hurt you."

■

Obviously, it hurt far more to find out this way. I suspected Earl hadn't intended to tell me at all—that he most likely would never have told me if Edward hadn't forced the issue. Earl understood the exact meaning of my ex-lover's question: did I know that Earl had left the abandoned school to move in with his girlfriend? Faced with the likelihood that either my former lover or one of our other monitors was about to inform me about Kamilah's birth, he no longer had any choice.

Simultaneously stunned and furious with him, I burst into tears. By the time I finally composed myself and dried my eyes on a paper napkin, the garden vegetable soup I ordered was cold and inedible. My relationship with Earl was very complex. When I rejoined the Support Committee in 1992, he was just breaking up with Yvonne and we resumed our on-off affair until January 1993. It was clear now this was the month he moved Susan from L.A. to Seattle. There was no formal break-up in a relationship that Earl never regarded as an affair. It was now painfully clear that he only had problems "being domestic" with white women.

Far more distressing was a growing suspicion that my friend deliberately manipulated me into investing $56,000 in a risky commercial venture, while concealing he was simultaneously starting a family, a major financial undertaking in itself. Earl always maintained I was his best friend and up until then had given me no reason to doubt him. He was the first and only man to respect and rely on my intelligence instead of punishing me for it—and the only person of either sex to share my conviction that real change will only occur when activists make it the primary focus of their lives. Yet owing to his failure to front-up about Susan and the baby, I could never fully trust him again. I would never be certain that the flirtatious and seductive behavior—and even the sex—weren't part of a deliberate ploy to entice me into buying the building for him.

■

As I dried my eyes, I reasserted my dignity by gesturing to our waiter to take my soup away. "Well, Earl," I said. "I suppose this is as good a time as any to bring up your obligations under our partnership agreement." We had been arguing for seven months over his refusal to keep a written record of his expenses or even let me pay Tony to do so. For me to claim a write-off on my personal income tax, D.E. and B. Limited Partnership had to file a partnership return documenting our loss. In early May we reached a temporary truce when he agreed to turn over his canceled checks and receipts for my tax accountant to prepare a K-2 return. I was still waiting. It was hard to suppress my growing apprehension that he hadn't bothered to save them.

Earl gave me a shamefaced grin and shrugged. "Touché. You would choose this moment to bring this up. You've caught me in a very vulnerable position."

I was in no mood to be trifled with. "I'm serious, Earl. I will give you five more days to bring me your receipts. After that I will take legal action to remove you as general partner."

It wasn't the first time I threatened to fire him. Earl had already breeched our partnership agreement by registering our title under the name of his renovation and real estate business. Fortunately this was easy to remedy by filing a lien against the property. The last thing I needed was the responsibility of managing a commercial building on top of a full-time medical practice. Earl knew this and never took any of my prior threats seriously.

This time he took me at my word. Earl collaborated almost exclusively with women, both in political and business ventures. I was fully aware of his deeply engrained, almost superstitious, belief that sexual jealously made females dangerous and irrational. The morning of June 15, he appeared at my office with a shoebox full of canceled checks, which Tony needed to create a spreadsheet of our partnership expenses. It turned into an enormously complicated and time-consuming ordeal. Not only had Earl written personal and business checks on the same account, but it was impossible to tell what three hundred of the individual checks were for without going through them individually with Earl.

The partnership agreement Stallworth drew up allowed Earl to draw a salary as general partner. After a lengthy discussion with my accountant, Tony recorded these personal expenses—such as rent for Earl's and Susan's apartment, groceries, and flute lessons for Susan's oldest daughter—in a final "Salary" column totaling $15,000.

■

My distress over Earl's duplicity was short-lived, as I immersed myself in exhaustive preparations for my course on the Kennedy assassination. I had applied to the Experimental College on a lark after reading two books. I now had seven weeks to transform myself into an expert. Apart from the initial injury to my self-respect, I found I had little emotional investment in whom Earl loved or slept with. Somehow, the intense longing which dominated my twenties and thirties—not to be loved so much as to be spared loneliness—had mysteriously vanished. My political work provided meaning in my life that I never found with men. To the contrary, the immense time and energy consumed by romantic relationships had the perverse effect of cutting me off from the political and creative activity that had come to define me. If my fear of being alone was my sole reason for seeking out men, the price I paid in stress and boredom was no longer worth it.

In preparing to teach Exploring the JFK Assassination, I relied mainly on the Prevailing Winds archives for the compiled publications and audiotapes of radio journalist and assassination researcher Mae Brussell—and the Seattle Public Library. Brussell, who died of breast cancer in 1988, was a housewife in November 1963. She became so troubled after witnessing Oswald's murder on national television that she dedicated the rest of her life to unraveling the assassination conspiracy. At the time of her death she read fifteen newspapers a day and subscribed to and cross-referenced 150 periodicals. She also broadcast a weekly radio program on intelligence abuses for seventeen years in Carmel, California.

The items I checked out of the library included the twenty six-volume *Warren Commission Hearings*; six books by pre-war journalist and historian George Seldes, one of Brussell's primary sources; Charles Higham's 1982 *Trading with the Enemy*; and the memoirs of two retired spooks who linked up with Oswald in Japan and the Soviet Union.

Ironically the Warren Commission Hearings provide the most detailed and credible evidence that Oswald worked for both the CIA and FBI. The compiled witness testimony supports Brussell's contention that David Ferrie, the bizarre homosexual pilot who was murdered before Jim Garrison could subpoena him, recruited Oswald for the CIA when he was still in high school. As a teenager Oswald enrolled in the junior Civil Air Patrol squadron Ferrie ran at Arlington Heights High School in Fort Worth. The young agent subsequently enlisted in the Marine Corps, via a process known as "sheep dipping"—whereby the CIA assigns agents to enter the military under "deep cover." Oswald's superiors and fellow Marines testified that in 1957 he was stationed in Japan as a radar specialist. In that capacity he held the highest security clearance possible and monitored over-flights of the top-secret U2 spy plane. Oswald clearly learned Russian in the Marine Corps, as he spoke it fluently when he was granted a hardship discharge in 1959. His discharge papers reveal he was released to look after his mother after a box fell on her. However, less than a month after leaving the Marines, Oswald was in Moscow trying to renounce his U.S. citizenship.

Brussell believes the elaborate subterfuge around Oswald's so-called defection to the Soviet Union suggests the CIA intended for the USSR to recruit him as a double agent. When the KGB failed to fall for this ruse, the State Department repatriated Oswald and his Russian wife. Between 1961 and 1963 U.S. intelligence moved him back and forth between Dallas and New Orleans, where FBI pay slips suggest he was assigned to infiltrate the pro-Cuban and leftist organizations he was identified with after the assassinations.

In addition to being the first journalist to publicly out Oswald as an undercover intelligence agent, Brussell was also the first to link Nazi war criminals, like Werner von Braun and Walter Dornberger, to the assassination conspiracy. American links to international fascism went back much further than I imagined. Brussell was the first to uncover, via declassified sources, that the CIA expropriated Hitler's entire spy network for Eastern Europe. In doing so, they illegally smuggled dozens of Nazi operatives into the U.S. to set up the Operations Division of the CIA. This was in addition to hundreds of Nazi aerospace and munitions experts the FBI secretly brought to the U.S. to provide technical expertise and corporate leadership for the growing U.S. military industrial complex. She also tracked the careers of dozens of Nazi war criminals the CIA helped to emigrate to South America where, according to Brussell, they were instrumental in setting up brutal dictatorships, death squads, and cocaine networks.

George Seldes, who died in 1995 at the age of 104, published his main work between 1945 and 1964. *Trading with the Enemy*, which Charles Higham published in 1983, picks up where Seldes left off. Both men meticulously document the corporate alliance, spearheaded by Henry Ford, William Randolph Hearst, President Herbert Hoover, Allen Dulles, and the Wall Street firms he represented, that openly financed Adolph Hitler's rise to power and the rearmament of Germany after World War I.

■

I also ordered the article Brussell wrote in 1976, entitled "Operation Chaos," when I realized it concerned the mysterious and untimely deaths of more than twenty rock stars, including John Lennon, Jimi Hendrix, Janis Joplin, Jim Morrison, Phil Oakes, and Bob Marley. According to Brussell, Operation Chaos was a top-secret program CIA director William Colby launched in the early seventies to "neutralize" hippies, rock musicians, and anti-war protestors. Although it had nothing to do with the Kennedy assassination, the subject was personally intriguing, in light of the psychic insight regarding Lennon's murder I experienced during my session with Ruth.

In studying the background Brussell provides on both Lennon and his killer Mark Chapman, I was very surprised to learn the ex-Beatle was also a left-wing activist and, like many U.S. leftists, subject to intensive surveillance and harassment by the FBI. This was a crucial facet of his persona that the mainstream media concealed during his lifetime. I now learned that Lennon financed the publication of Brussell's first article on Watergate, which exposed the CIA's involvement in the break-in six months prior to the *Washington Post* expose.

Although she admits her evidence is purely circumstantial, Brussell believes Lennon's killer Mark Chapman, like Lee Harvey Oswald, had links to U.S. intelligence. Like James Earl Ray, Martin Luther King's alleged assassin, Chapman pleaded guilty under pressure from his court-appointed attorney, despite having no recollection of aiming or pulling the trigger. In both cases, the guilty pleas precluded a homicide investigation and trial, in which forensic evidence and both men's likely intelligence connections could be fully explored.

Brussell could find no other reasonable explanation for many apparently "coincidental" occurrences leading up to the assassination. Including a six-month trip Chapman took to war-torn Lebanon—a known center in the early seventies for the training of CIA assassins—financed by a "security guard" he met while attending community college. As well as his subsequent decision to work in a World Vision refugee camp at Fort Chaffee, Arkansas, a military base with strong CIA ties. And his stay, following a suicide attempt, at Hawaii's Castle Memorial Hospital. Castle Memorial was infamous for its MK-ULTRA mind control experimentation, which is significant in view of Chapman's bizarre behavior immediately following the shooting. The police found him seated on the curb in front of Lennon's hotel reading a paperback copy of *Catcher in the Rye*. Noting the alleged killer's confusion and disorientation, a New York homicide detective was the first to speculate that Chapman was "programmed," via hypnosis, to kill the rock star.

Brussell raises other perplexing questions, such as where Chapman, an unemployed security guard, obtained the funds to travel around the world in 1978, to purchase $12,000 worth of Salvador Dali and Norman Rockwell originals and to stay at the Waldorf Astoria in the days prior to killing Lennon.

■

During his twenty seven-year stay in Attica Prison, Chapman, now 53, has yet to manifest any signs or symptoms of mental illness. Brussell and other assassination researchers cite his spontaneous "recovery" in making the case that he was programmed under hypnosis to kill Lennon. This allegation of hypnotic programming troubled me, as it totally contradicted one hundred years of research into the phenomenon of trance formation. No hypnotist in any controlled experimental setting has ever compelled a subject to commit acts they would find morally repugnant in a waking state.

In the end what I found, after tracing each of Brussell's sources and sources for her sources, were major discrepancies in the physical evidence. As with the murders of John and Bobby Kennedy and

Martin Luther King, the wounds were on the wrong side of Lennon's body—showing he was shot from inside the Dakota Hotel. My research also led me to a publication by Princeton psychologist Mark Hooper regarding CIA's "Model Psychosis" experiments. Hooper, also troubled by the miraculous recovery of Lennon's alleged killer, found references to this top-secret project in declassified documents he obtained through the Freedom of Information Act. In his paper Hooper reveals the "Model Psychosis" project was based on the finding that high doses of stimulant medication increase a hypnotic subject's compliance by overwhelming their voluntary control. The experimental procedure involves dosing subjects with either amphetamine or designer stimulants like ecstasy and then exposing them to a hierarchy of hypnotic suggestions.

I felt a sick, sinking feeling in my stomach as it dawned on me that I might have been the unwitting subject of a similar experiment. In my own case I was inadvertently self-administering the stimulants. Edward knew that I was taking Nardil, which produces an amphetamine-like metabolite called phenylethylamine. Most trance inductions involve a series of increasingly irrational suggestions—for example that a subject's skin is numb to a pinprick or that he or she only sees two fingers when you hold up three. I suddenly realized there was nothing random about the bizarre cues that sent me wandering around Capital Hill. These were actually hierarchical commands aimed at increasing my compliance.

No one poisoned my peaches. This was merely a hypnotic suggestion. I was supposed to believe they would kill me and eat one anyway. Thus further surrendering control to my invisible enemies.

It all made sense now, including the pressing interest in my mental state following the terrifying episode at the Harvard Exit movie theater—from the over-friendly patient on Ward Six, the psychologist on the train, the inquisitive African American who was my first patient on my return to my office, and, finally, the ubiquitous informant Mark Watson. They couldn't care less whether I was psychotic or not. They wanted to know if I consciously recalled and understood what they did to me. And more importantly, why the experiment failed—why I followed all their other cues but not the one to kill myself.

CHAPTER 22

Naomi, now 12, took a watercolor class through the Experimental College the same night I taught my first class. After escorting her to a small classroom in the basement of the School of Architecture, I gave her four quarters, showed her the nearest pay phone, and told her to call Gloria or Earl if I wasn't there waiting for her when she finished. It seemed prudent to expect some form of retaliation for revealing hidden government crimes that had already caused the death of more than eighty witnesses. In 1991, while making a movie version of *On the Trail of the Assassins*, director Oliver Stone received death threats too numerous to count.

All my precautions proved unnecessary. Aside from two middle-aged informants who enrolled fall and winter quarter, the powers that be showed no interest in my activities at the Experimental College. The spooks stood out clearly from the real students because they overdressed and asked a barrage of trivial questions that betrayed their disinterest in the ominous political ramifications of Kennedy's murder.

Twenty-seven students signed up for my first class, all men and, except for two University of Washington sophomores, all my age or a little older. I gave each of them a course packet consisting of a diagram from *Farewell America*, designating the location of the four main shooters, a copy of the *Torbitt Document*, biographical sketches of each of the fifty-seven known co-conspirators, and an Excel flow sheet that Tony designed outlining the interconnections between the men with supervisory and working assignments and the federal agencies and front groups that worked under the umbrella of the Defense Industrial Security Command. I also gave them a chronology that researcher Jim Marrs created listing all the assassination witnesses who were murdered or died under suspicious circumstances. The list runs the gamut of friends and employees of Oswald's assassin Jack Ruby, as well as a lawyer and a judge involved in his trial and appeal, private investigators, low-level and upper-echelon FBI and CIA operatives, reporters, Dallas cops, and miscellaneous strangers who came in contact with Oswald during the last year of his life.

After twenty years in the male-dominated field of medicine, I prepared myself for the standard accusations of making quantum leaps and other real or imagined logical errors. I was unprepared for the reaction I got—the dead silence of horrified attention—as I walked the class through the flow sheet. There was only one interruption when a younger student asked a question about Vietnam. Most of them had seen Oliver Stone's movie *JFK* and already believed the government killed Kennedy. However, up until now they had no inkling of the mountain of evidence pointing to the real killers. Nor that most of it had been in the public domain for nearly thirty years. I didn't have to tell the older students what this meant. The current U.S. government had no need to suppress the truth about the JFK assassination because they were immune to the rule of law—a cardinal feature of despotism and totalitarianism.

■

The letdown was profound when my first four-week course ended.

Thus, in August 1993, following a total change in leadership, I rejoined Health Care for All. The growing health-care crisis was the number-one voter concern in the 1992 elections, and Clinton won the presidency by promising to create a national universal health-care system. I had no illusions about effecting political change by offering a college-level course to a hundred intellectuals a year. Removing the crooks who controlled our government would require a mass movement of a million or more Americans. It was very unlikely a thirty-year old assassination had the potential to generate a movement of that size. On the other hand, fighting for a basic right people enjoyed in every other industrialized country clearly did.

It was actually our own representative Jim McDermott and Minnesota senator Paul Wellstone who introduced the first and only legislation, in June 1993, creating a publicly run health-care system for all Americans. Despite his election promises, the bill that Clinton launched in January 1994 didn't guarantee universal coverage, mainly because it didn't abolish private insurance. Physicians for a National Health Program opposed the Clinton plan. His proposal required all employers to enroll their workers in federally approved "managed care" plans. Not only did it substantially increase health-care costs—by introducing a whole new layer of regulatory bureaucracy—it also failed to cover millions of Americans. Workers in small businesses with fewer than fifty employees and self-employed business owners like me didn't qualify for Clinton's plan.

In February, PNHP, together with Gray Panthers, National Council of Senior Citizens, United Church of Christ, and other progressive churches, Oil, Chemical and Atomic Workers, and International Longshore and Warehouse Union, formed a coalition called Single Payer Across the Nation (SPAN) to lobby for the McDermott-Wellstone bill. In Seattle, Gray Panther vice president Paul Zilsel, a retired Austrian émigré and former communist, was single-handedly responsible for forming the Washington state chapter of SPAN. Altogether, forty-plus representatives of senior organizations, unions, and church social-action committees attended the first meeting he called at University Unitarian Church to form Washington Single Payer Action Network (WaSPAN).

In April 2004, buoyed by the surge in grassroots support for single-payer health care, Health Care for All organized our first and only protest demonstration. Wearing white coats and stethoscopes, twenty-five of us stood in front of the King County Blue Shield building on Minor Avenue holding large signs and banners calling on private insurance companies to stop ripping off the health-care system.

A week later I was at home with what I thought was the stomach flu when Paul Zilsel phoned me in a highly agitated state. "I am asking you to make immediate notification to the Health Care for All Steering Committee." Paul, who had an elegant Viennese accent, spoke the stilted English of a non-native speaker. "As you are no doubt aware, the WaSPAN board has stipulated that only the physicians and nurses in Health Care for All will make public presentations on behalf of the Coalition. Scott Hancock has been doing so without board authorization."

I had never attended a WaSPAN meeting personally. However, I was aware the coalition had elected a board of directors and registered as a non-profit corporation—and that one of the board's first official acts was to make the Health Care for All Speakers Committee responsible for all public speaking. The morning of Paul's phone call I had been up for three nights in a row with diarrhea and was headed for the walk-in clinic at CHEC Medical Center. In my brain-dead state, the significance of what he was trying to say was totally lost on me. Because the Gray Panthers vice president was known for his obsessive preoccupation with organizational protocol, I decided he was making a big fuss over nothing. It was a fatal error.

Of course, I had no idea at the time that Paul had worked with Scott previously in the Anti-Gulf War Coalition and the Seattle chapter of Democratic Socialists of America. It would be more than a year before I learned the self-employed carpenter had muscled himself into the leadership of both groups and that both folded within months after he took them over.

■

The doctor I saw at CHEC refused to prescribe anti-diarrhea medication because I was running a fever. Instead he took stool cultures and gave me a prescription for vibromycin. When he learned the diarrhea and a stabbing pain in my upper abdomen had been present for more than three months, he also referred me to a gastroenterologist at the Polyclinic.

I stopped the antibiotic after two days because it only made the diarrhea worse. When there was still no improvement after ten days of eating nothing but toast and taking the maximum recommended dose, simultaneously, of Imodium, Pepto-Bismol, and Kaopectate, I made an appointment with one of the GI specialists at the Polyclinic—knowing full well my insurance wouldn't cover it. After our premiums doubled in January 1993, I enrolled myself and Naomi in a catastrophic policy that only covered surgery and emergency-room care. Because I still wasn't sleeping, I also stopped accepting referrals and reduced my office hours to four half-days a week.

The gastroenterologist, a tall blonde woman in her early thirties with a hyphenated name, ordered more blood tests and stool cultures, a barium swallow, and a flexible sigmoidoscopy. Altogether, the visits and tests set me back a little over $1,000. At a follow-up visit she informed me I had a slight diverticulum on my stomach, an extremely rare finding of no clinical significance.

"Because you're uninsured," she explained, "I wouldn't recommend any more tests. Your condition most likely represents irritable bowel syndrome, which is natural considering the stress you must be under." Many non-psychiatrists view IBS, which afflicts approximately 20 percent of Americans, as a psychosomatic condition. However, despite receiving numerous referrals from GPs and internists, I had yet to encounter a single IBS patient who responded to psychiatric intervention of any kind.

"In many patients," she continued, "irritable bowel responds to antidepressants. I'm happy to write a prescription if you like."

I declined, politely, finding it incredibly presumptuous this woman felt qualified to offer me psychiatric treatment. "Antidepressants are contraindicated in people with a history of becoming manic on them," I replied. "I believe that I indicated I had an adverse reaction on my history form."

She, in turn, refused my request for prescription diarrhea medication. Instead, she gave me samples to dissolve under my tongue for the pain, which were useless. The stabbing pains continued to keep me awake all night nearly every night for the next three months. I was too sick to notice the single-payer movement was collapsing around me. For the first five months of 1994, Clinton's Health Security Act was the lead headline on the network news and in the major dailies. In June, the health-care issue vanished from the mainstream media after O.J. Simpson was charged with the murder of his wife, Nicole. By the time the media circus died down and networks and major dailies resumed normal news coverage, Clinton's bill had died in committee. With the result being that the health-care crisis simply evaporated from the mainstream media—and public consciousness. Many of us believed the corporate media deliberately buried the health-care issue with the massive dose of reality TV they bombarded us with during O.J. Simpson's arrest and trial.

■

I still had a thirteen-year-old daughter to support and spent most of that summer and fall investigating a variety of alternative treatments. In June 1993 I consulted an acupuncturist who successfully treated me for chronic sinusitis five years earlier. When six weeks of acupuncture failed to relieve the diarrhea and pain, Dr. Chan referred me to a naturopath who performed delayed food sensitivity testing. This controversial blood test, which measures antibody levels to ninety-six different food antigens, is based on the premise that the inability to digest certain foods inflames the intestinal lining. This, in turn, causes it to "leak" large, irritating peptide molecules into the bloodstream. According to Dr. Houghton, I was "sensitive" to 75 percent of the foods for which I was tested.

She was very alarmed by these results, which in her view were inconsistent with irritable bowel syndrome. She believed my intolerance to so many foods, along with the chronic ulcerations at the corners of my mouth, were indicative of a much more serious condition—namely the severe malabsorption of a potentially fatal inflammatory bowel disease, such as Crohn's Disease or ulcerative colitis. She strongly recommended I consult a new gastroenterologist for a second opinion. I refused. I still had no health insurance, virtually no income, and less than nine hundred dollars in savings.

Over time I would realize that my financial worries, which were real, were less of a deterrent than a nagging suspicion that the people targeting me caused my illness, either through the chemical they released in my basement or by slipping something into my food during one of the break-ins. If my condition resulted from a rare chemical- or biological-warfare agent, it was unlikely to be detected on routine medical tests. I could easily spend two or three thousand dollars, only to be told the problem was in my head. Unwilling to give my invisible enemies the power to make me ill, I simply refused to think about it.

■

By the July 1994 meeting, only two of us remained on the Health Care for All Steering Committee. Our sole item of business was for Reid, the Harborview nurse who chaired the Steering Committee, to announce that he, too, was resigning. In spite of my illness, shutting the organization down wasn't an option. It was mainly my own fundraising efforts that were responsible for the $2,700 in our account—money that the IRS would make me donate to another non-profit if we disbanded.

There was no legal requirement for Health Care for All to hold meetings. Thus, Reid and I agreed I would take over his duties of collecting the mail, putting out a quarterly newsletter, and attending WaSPAN meetings as the Health Care for All representative. In this way I could legally spend our hard-earned money to support the work of the single-payer coalition.

■

By the time I attended my first WaSPAN meeting, at St. Joseph's Church in the Central Area, Scott Hancock had taken over as president and the active membership had shrunk from more than fifty to fifteen. Because of my illness, I was oblivious to the upheaval that led to the mass exodus of the group's founding members. It would be more than a year before I learned of the vicious letter-writing campaign that Scott launched, after seizing control of the database, against WaSPAN's first president, Mildred Johnson. I was also unaware that one of his first acts as president was to take over all three of the coalition's committees, effectively disbanding them. The possibility of a covert agent taking over a thriving grassroots organization and running it into the ground never occurred to me. I had always viewed health-care reform as a "safe" issue, seeing no possible reason for the FBI or any other spy agency to feel threatened by the reorganization of health-care delivery.

The remaining WaSPAN membership met the third Saturday of every month around two folding tables in the center of St. Joe's massive community room. Except for Scott, myself, and a woman in her late forties with end-stage diabetes, there were no other members under sixty-five. My own back and abdominal pain were still so severe I could just manage a two-hour meeting by gripping the table edge with both hands to hold myself up. Yet, aside from Scott, Paul Zilsel and I were the only active members. Every month I made reminder calls to the thirty-five people on the "activist" printout that Scott gave me. Our president did everything else. In addition to managing the 2,500-name database of individual and group contacts, he wrote, designed, and delivered the monthly newsletter to AAA mailing service; he collected the mail and voice-mail messages; deposited the checks, paid the bills, and prepared a financial statement and agenda for each of the monthly meetings.

In October, over Scott's strenuous objections, Paul organized a protest at the Group Health Annual meeting. Before security removed them, the aging radical and four friends unfurled an enormous banner demanding Group Health's board of directors endorse the McDermott-Wellstone bill. Otherwise, we went through the same tedious agenda every month—a financial report, an update on a California citizen's initiative to establish a state-based single-payer system and long rambling monologues about Scott's meetings with Democratic legislators and union officials. According to Scott, they all believed the timing and political climate were all wrong for single-payer health care. They were only willing to support more moderate, incremental improvements to the health-care system. Scott never gave any specifics what some of these moderate, incremental reforms might be. After Clinton's managed-care bill died in committee, he and the Democratic leadership continued to support steady incremental cutbacks in Medicare and Medicaid and welfare entitlements, as Reagan and Bush had.

■

In October 1994, Earl also invited me to join the newly formed board of the African American Heritage Museum and Cultural Center. A year earlier he signed a tripartite agreement with Seattle Public Schools and Seattle's first African American mayor to end his eight-year occupation of the old Coleman School. The contract included a purchase agreement for the African American Heritage Museum and Cultural Center to buy the building from the school district for $417,000—and a commitment from the city to place the $417,000 purchase price in escrow, pending the Museum's recognition by the Internal Revenue as a 501(c)3 non-profit corporation.

The other board members included five of the original occupiers, a social studies teacher from Rainier Beach High School, an events planner for the UW Health Policy Program, an unemployed woman with a master's degree in public administration, and five "business" representatives appointed by Mayor Norm Rice, a former banker. Three of them, a Microsoft software engineer, an administrator with the Washington State Department of Transportation, and a grants coordinator for the Bullitt Foundation's environmental justice program, were African American. Two were Asian, a retired banker and an attorney in her late thirties who was executive director of the International District Public Development Authority. Earl's longtime friend Danny Piecora, who ran a pizza restaurant on Eighteenth and Madison, was the only other Caucasian.

By September I managed to stop the diarrhea by avoiding all dairy products, wheat, corn, and eggs, and drinking two bottles of Kaopectate a day. However, even on this very strict diet, I experienced no improvement whatsoever in the pain or my sleeplessness. The chronic sleep deprivation left me with a wooden flu-like feeling that made all thought, speech, and movement a grinding effort. The Museum board elected Earl as president. As I was still only working sixteen hours a week, I agreed to serve as secretary.

I was taking on far more than I imagined. In effect, it fell to me to compose, as well as type, all Museum correspondence, brochures, fliers, and leaflets. A stroke Earl suffered in December 1993 left him with a severe aphasia and a slight weakness in his right leg. With private health insurance, he would have received a range of rehabilitative treatments, including speech therapy, cognitive rehabilitation, smoking cessation, and regular blood-pressure monitoring. He received none of these services until he suffered a third, "mother of all strokes" in 2005 that left him unable to walk.

It was the first time we had worked together in seven years. Thus I had no idea how severe his deficits were, in both spoken and written communication, until he asked me to type some letters for him. Earl, like many stroke victims, was adamant there was nothing wrong with him. Because he could no longer write out a draft in longhand, he had to dictate what he wanted me to type. On a bad day he could only throw out random incoherent sentence fragments—and would explode with anger if I didn't immediately understand. This meant the chore of producing a two-page letter often took five hours or longer.

■

Earl also appointed me fundraising coordinator. It therefore became my responsibility to prepare a first draft of our 501(c)3 application. Rice had "volunteered" a junior partner at Preston, Gates and Ellis, the law firm co-founded by Bill Gates senior which the city hired to write all the bond measures for Seattle's capital projects, to finalize and submit the document on our behalf. Once the IRS approved our non-profit status, my next major project was to raise $2,500 to repair the roof and gutters at the old Coleman School to prevent further water damage. This was on top of my weekly shift on the Mothers hotline, the monthly WaSPAN meetings, and the JFK assassination course I taught every three months.

In essence, I became a full time activist that fall, devoting more than forty hours a week to grassroots organizing, in addition to my parental duties and the sixteen hours I spent in my office. Prior to my illness, I viewed workaholics with disdain, attributing their constant activity as a defense against self-awareness. In my own case it was the only effective distraction from the knife-like pain and mind-deadening sleep deprivation.

I was conscious even then of patterning my life after Earl, who devoted every waking moment to social change. I was always frankly envious of the focus and meaning his activism gave his life. My friend had a clear visceral response to deliberate Reagan-Bush policies to reverse decades of black economic development in their eagerness to hand over America's urban centers to white developers who stood to gain immense profits via the burgeoning "gentrification" industry. In Seattle this translated into the wholesale bulldozing of Central Area and Rainier Valley businesses and draconian Weed and Seed law enforcement policies resulting in the wholesale incarceration of a generation of African American men.

In many of his friends this came out in soul-destroying despair or violent rage. In Earl it came out in frenetic political activity, as if only total dedication and sacrifice could defeat such a monstrous evil.

CHAPTER 23

Despite trying to distract myself with constant activity, I was unable to suppress a growing angst that my condition was permanent; that there was no treatment for the diarrhea, pain, and chronic sleeplessness. This, of course, raised the specter of permanent disability, losing my practice, and being unable to provide for Naomi. In October 1994 I consulted a new acupuncturist, one who specialized in gastrointestinal diseases and treated Tony for HIV. Dr. Huang spoke better English than Dr. Chan. He blamed my symptoms on a "weak spleen," a condition that in Chinese medicine stems from excessive "cold" and "damp." He put me on a new diet that emphasized "warming foods," such as meat, chicken, and white rice, and eliminated "cold" foods, such as fruit, soy, cold drinks, and raw vegetables.

After a week on the new diet I no longer needed to take Kaopectate. Moreover, the pain, which had been constant, became sporadic, occurring mainly between 2:00 a.m. and 3:00 a.m. By going to bed at nine, I got in a good five to six hours of sleep before the pain awoke me. I discovered early menopause, another complication of my illness, had greatly reduced my sleep requirement. Thus, by

December I was waking up every morning refreshed, clear-headed, and confident of my ability to care for patients.

■

In January 1995 I resumed full-time practice. Although I continued to serve as Museum secretary, I abandoned my fundraising role. The Museum board had no need for funds, as the Department of Neighborhoods had locked us out of the old Coleman School and had erected a tall chain-link fence denying us access to the property. The board itself was on the verge of disintegration. Earl and I attempted to follow the same strategy in redeveloping the old Coleman School that he employed to rehabilitate the old SeaVac building. Our original plan was to repair the gutters and roof and then remodel one room and add one exhibit or program at a time–until we attained sufficient credibility to attract major government and foundation grants. I think Earl fully understood the powerful forces arrayed against us. I myself had no idea how controversial this incremental approach was with the developers who were seeking to gentrify the newly prosperous Interstate 90 corridor. Nor their vehement opposition to Earl's and Jabari's vision of incorporating a Cultural Center for "at-risk" youths in the Museum complex. For Seattle's white developers, this conjured up anxiety-provoking images of dark-skinned teenagers with boom boxes and low-rider jeans, which was in serious conflict with their plans to market new Central Area condos and remodeled Victorian-style bungalows to white yuppies.

I think Earl was fully aware that Norm Rice, the Department of Neighborhoods, and their developer friends were doing everything possible to sabotage our community-controlled board. Unfortunately, owing to his aphasia, he had no way to convey this to the rest of us. The justification the Department of Neighborhoods used for locking us out of the building was that one of their engineers had discovered asbestos in the heating pipes. They told us it was our responsibility to pay $35,000 to have it removed, which was untrue. The school district still owned the property. Even if they demolished the building, they were legally required to remove the asbestos first.

The city's next move was to pressure the board, over Earl's and my objections, to agree to a two million dollar timeline. We both knew this was impossible to fulfill without turning the entire project over to professional developers and project managers.

Even with all this high-powered interference, prior to his stroke Earl would have had no difficulty unifying the rest of the board against the half-time administrator the Department of Neighborhoods assigned us and the architect who replaced him after Earl got David fired. The sad irony was that with health insurance Earl would have received speech therapy for his aphasia. Together, in good health, we were a formidable team. With the ability to resolve our major health problems, nothing would have stopped us from creating a community-controlled African American Heritage Museum—and Cultural Center. Or, for that matter, establishing the first state-based universal health care system in the U.S.

Sadly, owing to Earl's basic inability to communicate, none of us, including me, understood the exact terms of the contract he signed with the city and school district in 1993. The only specific requirement for releasing the $417,000 to complete the title transfer was that the board obtain 501(c)3 status and raise $50,000 for a deposit. Even with no help from other board members, Earl and I could easily have raised this amount ourselves from the Central Area businesses that supported him. And taken possession—legally—of the old school within three months of acquiring non-profit status.

■

It didn't help that Earl's stammer and inability to complete sentences made him incapable of maintaining order at meetings. I tried to be diplomatic in relaying the complaints I got from other board members who were afraid to approach him directly. In addition to frustration about his failure to exert any authority as chair, they were openly angry about his habit of arriving twenty minutes late for meetings.

"They see it as disrespectful, Earl," I told him. I also recommended a solution, which was to share the responsibility of chairing with other board members. This infuriated Earl, who continued to deny there was anything wrong with him. In his mind, it was the ultimate disloyalty to even suggest such a thing.

The problem came to a head in April 1995, when Jabari returned from a six-month trip to Ghana, where he advised one of the regional kings on sustainable development. Earl wisely anticipated that Jabari would be a disruptive influence at board meetings, which is why he asked me to pay for his eight hundred dollar plane ticket. Earl believed that during Jabari's six-month absence the board would coalesce around a focused work program his friend would find difficult to derail. I found Earl's resolve to accommodate to his friend's so-called emotional instability—which, to me, looked increasingly like deliberate sabotage—difficult to understand. In hindsight I can see that Earl's perception of Jabari was colored by his philosophy that good organizing depended on "playing" the idiosyncrasies of other activists. In other words, his own vanity blinded him to a pattern of sabotage that was becoming too predictable to blame on emotional problems.

Jabari dominated the entire April meeting with a long harangue in which he accused me of embezzling Museum funds for Earl's and my own personal benefit. Obviously, this wasn't the first time Jabari accused his best friend of mismanaging funds. However, he hadn't previously raised the issue in such a public forum nor used it to prevent any other business from taking place. He could only make accusations in a very general way because our treasurer, Sue Taoka, prepared monthly statements revealing there was zero activity on our checking account.

If Earl had the verbal capacity to do so, he could have shut the discussion down in a matter of minutes. All he had to do was to point out that only Sue Taoka had signing authority on the account and demand that Jabari identify the specific financial discrepancies he was referring to. Unfortunately, Earl no longer had the ability to express something this complex.

When no one else spoke in my defense, I tried to make the point myself that neither Earl nor I had access to the Museum account. For reasons I never fully understood, Earl cut me off. He gestured with both hands to indicate his intention to speak but could not find the words. So Jabari continued.

"What you need to understand about Earl and Stuart is where their real interests lie," he said. "Who they talk to, in other words, when they're not here at our board meetings." There was an audible gasp from several board members as he said this. After a brief pause, he launched into a lengthy dissertation linking the local developers with the corporate elites who conspired to keep black people enslaved by denying them access to their true history. He didn't make specific reference to my white skin, but he didn't have to. The point he was making came across loud and clear—that I was no different from any of the other unscrupulous Europeans who had been exploiting Africans for four hundred years.

Once again, I tried to point out that Earl and I did not have signing authority on the bank account. Again, Earl refused to let me speak. When no one, not even Sue Taoka, rose to my defense, I walked out of the meeting.

■

The following morning I took my car to work and slipped my letter of resignation through the mail slot of the old SeaVac building. Although Jabari's vicious racist attack was both painful and humiliating, it forced me to confront that I had absolutely nothing to show for the hundreds of hours I had devoted to the African

American Museum and Cultural Center. Not only were we no closer to having an operational Museum than when the board formed in October 1994, but I had no support whatsoever from the other board members, who clearly didn't want me there.

Earl called my office, livid, the moment he opened the letter. He was surprisingly coherent when he was angry. "I thought you understood what I'm trying to do. But it's just personal infatuation, isn't it?" This was an accusation that I was trying to sexualize our relationship. I said nothing, and he began yelling into the phone. "Can't you see I have enough trouble without this?" He slammed the receiver down.

Two minutes letter he phoned back, a common pattern after his stroke. "All right, then. I'll tell them about my stroke. I will let someone else run the meetings. That's what you want, isn't it?"

■

Earl remained true to his word. Following a month of negotiations with the mayor's office, he brought a proposal to the June meeting to appoint one of the mayor's banking associates as an unpaid executive director. Bob Flowers, tall, lean light-skinned and in his early forties, was a vice president at Washington Mutual. It took the board four months to rewrite the bylaws to accommodate a new structure, in which the executive director chaired board meetings, based on an agenda developed by an executive committee, chaired by Earl. He believed, correctly, that Flowers shared Rice's desire to develop the old Coleman property. Without a strong executive committee, there was a substantial risk the Washington Mutual vice president would allow the city to renege on their 1993 agreement to site the Museum in the old school.

In November 1995 our new bylaws became operational, and with Flowers as chair, we had our first orderly meeting in over a year. The only major disruption occurred when Flowers floated a proposal to relinquish our claim to the school in favor of a smaller building on

Twenty-third and Yesler. Merciful Allah and Blessed Allah, two of Jabari's young protégés who joined the board the same night as Flowers, shouted him down.

At the December meeting Flowers ignored the new bylaws and brought his own agenda. In the midst of a heated debate whether to follow Flowers' or the executive committee's agenda, Harolyn Bobis, another of the mayor's appointees, made a motion to remove Earl from the presidency. I raised a point of order, reminding Flowers that our bylaws required two weeks written notice to remove officers or board members. He overruled me. Jabari, who controlled three votes now in addition to his own and Mosi's, seconded the motion.

I was never more aware of my deep affection for my friend as I watched the board unceremoniously dump him from a cause for which he sacrificed his real estate career, his Rainier valley fourplex, and ten years of his life. Four days later I paid a $5,000 retainer to engage a corporate attorney named Elizabeth Lewis to file an injunction to prevent Flowers from assuming the presidency. We now learned that Flowers wasn't merely in breach of our bylaws but also Washington State statute governing non-profit corporations. Earl and I spent five hours encapsulating Lewis's initial filing in a series of letters we sent out to individual board members, the mayor, the governor, the superintendent of schools, the school board, and both newspapers. The letters to board members alerted them to the illegality of Flowers' actions and potential criminal penalties they faced for conducting business under his leadership.

In direct response to these letters, Flowers and Jabari mustered their supporters to remove Earl and me from the Museum board.

■

Meanwhile, Earl and McDermott's congressional aid were working their way up the Resolution Trust Corporation hierarchy, in a frantic search for an official with the authority to sign off on the $100,000 settlement the RTC agreed to as a result of a March 1994 complaint Earl filed with the Federal Deposit Insurance Corporation. On December 7, 1995, three years after taking over Evergreen Bank, Key Bank notified us that our refinance package was complete. The bank reopened negotiations with us in July 1993, after Earl organized a group of brothers to picket their corporate office. All we needed to close escrow was an RTC signature confirming the balance we owed the federal agency. The woman who answered the phone at the Baltimore office, which still administered our note, informed us the elusive Mr. Black had resigned, and that the new director who replaced him had gone on leave for six weeks without designating anyone to act in his place.

When Clinton took office in January 1993, Earl and I, like the rest of the progressive community, assumed he would fire the crooks his Republican predecessor appointed to the CIA, as Kennedy and Carter had done, as well as prosecuting Neil and Jeb Bush and all the other CIA contractors who embezzled funds from savings and loan associations and the RTC. We also assumed he would deliver the Peace Dividend the Democrats promised us when the Soviet Union collapsed, that he would repeal Reagan's trade legislation enabling companies to relocate their factories to cheaper labor markets overseas and that he would restore the deep cuts that occurred under Reagan and Bush to Medicare, Medicaid, education, housing, and social services.

Of course, Bush's successor did none of these things. The noose Reagan and Bush placed around our necks—as they systematically dismantled the New Deal and Great Society programs inaugurated by Roosevelt, Kennedy, and Johnson—only tightened under Clinton. In the case of the RTC, Clinton himself was linked to a $39,000,000 loan default at the failed Arkansas thrift Madison Guaranty, as well as a fraudulent transfer of funds from Household Bank in Chicago to cover the default. In fact, the new president would richly reward Goldman Sachs, a major campaign donor, by appointing the firm's chief economist to oversee the RTC. He would also turn a blind eye when the RTC sold the Wall Street firm, at a sharp discount, billions of dollars of real estate the agency acquired from mortgage foreclosures.

Every RTC official McDermott's office contacted gave the same improbable answer: the only official authorized to sign the settlement was out of the country until January 1, the day after the RTC officially ceased operations. Earl and I both knew it was no coincidence our loan offer expired the same day the RTC ceased to exist.

Somehow, in my naiveté, I assumed the powerful white men who controlled the U.S. political apparatus would applaud my friend's repudiation of radical organizations like the Black Panther Party and the Black United Front to fight for African American economic development. That you didn't have to have black skin to recognize this was the only solution to the epidemic of illicit drug abuse in Seattle's African American community. The reality was that as "radicals," Earl and Jabari were extremely marginalized in the black community. Earl, like Harold Black, only became a serious threat with valuable commercial property under his control.

CHAPTER 24

By December 1995, when the board removed Earl from the museum presidency, WaSPAN was also defunct. The organization entered its death throes in July 1995, following a shouting match between Paul and Scott over the latter's refusal to call a board meeting. Somehow, perhaps due to Paul's history of bipolar disorder, Scott convinced the rest of us that Paul and his partner, Esther, were the villains. The fact remained that Paul's request to reconvene the board was perfectly legitimate. Scott's position, that we would only embarrass ourselves if no one showed up, was ridiculous.

There was nothing to meet about after Paul and Esther resigned. Only three people showed up for our August meeting—Scott, myself, and a disabled woman I drove to and from every meeting. After passing out copies of his most recent newsletter, he announced WaSPAN was officially dormant. "There is absolutely no point in holding any further meetings."

Although I made no objection at the time, I had no intention of accepting this pronouncement. By now there was a $3,000 balance in the Health Care for All account, mainly because Scott vetoed every proposal Paul or I made for WaSPAN to engage in specific outreach or education activities. The increasing acceptance of single-payer health care by the medical community also made me more resistant than ever to letting go of the one so-called "radical" issue I could openly lobby for in front of patients and colleagues. After ten years of relentless organizing by PNHP, even doctors who disputed the feasibility of single-payer health care had come to view it as a legitimate approach to reform.

When Earl realized I was approaching museum board members about serving on a second board, he offered to help me resurrect WaSPAN. This surprised me, as he had shown no prior interest in health-care reform. When Scott realized Earl and I were prepared to reconvene the board without him, he agreed to continue as president and to support Earl's proposal that WaSPAN organize a statewide conference on single-payer health care. Nevertheless, when the three of us were alone, Scott made no effort to disguise his antagonism towards my African American friend. At the first meeting of the WaSPAN executive committee, he and Earl got into a heated argument over the very first agenda item. My friend wanted to aim for a conference attendance of five hundred, while Scott was adamant that WaSPAN should only invite a core group of 150 activists. His inflexibility surprised me, as basic organizing principles called for continual expansion of a group's membership base.

Earl, in his own idiosyncratic idiom, pointed this out. "Why put yourself in a box like that? When it means the same work?"

Without warning, Scott flew into a rage. "You fucking bastard. I have invested more than two years in this organization. You think I don't know what you're doing?"

The anger seemed to come out of nowhere. It later occurred to me that Scott had inside information about the fisticuffs at the 1985 CAPDA meeting and thought he could goad Earl into hitting him. This was the one act that would guarantee his expulsion from a group of white liberals.

Earl, who privately referred to our president as "that silly punk," burst out laughing. Scott couldn't justify his position and had no choice but to back down.

A week later Scott woke me at midnight about a chapter-organizing kit that Earl and I, who co-chaired the Chapter Coordination Committee, had sent him for his approval. Before I could say a word he began yelling at me over the phone. "I know what you guys are doing. You two are the most fucking devious and manipulative people I know. Clearly you are only interested in undermining my leadership."

As a psychiatrist I knew there was no mental disorder that could account for such sudden irrational behavior. Panic-stricken that he was trying to drive Earl and me out of the organization, just as he had Paul, Esther, and the other founding members, I called and woke my friend.

"Someone has to be paying him, Earl," I said. At the time I assumed it was the government, but this was before I learned that corporations paid informants to infiltrate community groups that threatened their interests. "Remember, he's already shut the coalition down once. You have to help me expose him to the rest of the board before he can inflict any more damage."

Earl disagreed. "You are making a big mistake," he warned. "You won't be believed. Better to ask if he wants a job. Organizing the conference."

Earl couldn't explain, owing to the aphasia, why I should do this. However, as he anticipated, Scott leapt at the opportunity. At the March meeting the board approved a three-month contract paying him eight hundred dollars a month. And his prior antipathy towards Earl and me miraculously evaporated.

■

On June 6, 1996, 305 single-payer activists from across Washington state, as well as Oregon and California, attended

"Health Care at the Crossroads." The conference ended at 5:00 p.m.. Unwilling to relinquish the intoxicating collective energy, seventy-five of us piled into cars to head for an Italian restaurant in Queen Anne to celebrate our success. Earl spent the evening next to Susan Cieutat, an attorney from Berkeley and a key organizer in the Prop 186 campaign. By the end of the night they had hatched an ambitious scheme to launch simultaneous single-payer ballot initiatives in the strong liberal states of Washington, Oregon, and California.

Because Earl couldn't articulate his strategy, it only became clear as it unfolded. Having your organization taken over by an agent provocateur is like an inoperable brain tumor. Surgery is out of the question owing to the delicacy of the tissues that surround it. In Earl's mind the only way to counter Scott's pernicious influence was to outflank him, by creating more independent organizational structures than he could sabotage. My friend's first move was to pressure him into organizing a massive statewide conference, while simultaneously creating as many local chapters as possible. His next would be to pull in other states by forming a regional coalition. A three-state campaign was likely to draw national media attention. It would also force the powerful insurance lobby, which gutted Prop 186 through its negative attack ads, to divide its resources between three separate media markets.

At the same time, the mammoth effort Scott invested into Health Care at the Crossroads confused me. It made me wonder if I had misjudged him in deciding he was a federal agent. Fortunately, a third violent outburst in the middle of the June WaSPAN meeting totally dispelled any uncertainty. Thanks to the phenomenal success of the conference, the meeting drew forty new members in addition to the twenty regular attendees. Earl had just proposed we build on our successful conference by organizing a Central Area candidate forum during the fall primary. With no warning, Scott went ballistic, displaying to everyone present one of the vicious tirades Earl and I experienced in private.

"Absolutely not!" he argued. "No candidates will come to a forum on single-payer health care. The political climate is all wrong. We will all end up with egg on our face."

Only one person, a congressional aide from McDermott's office, sided with Scott. After Earl allowed me to amend his motion, the group voted to create a committee to "explore" holding a Central Area candidate forum.

To my surprise, Scott didn't oppose my own motion for WaSPAN to send representatives to a meeting in Portland between Washington, California, and Oregon single-payer groups. As president, he headed the Washington delegation to the first Pacific Rim Single Payer Summit the first Saturday in August.

On August 6, three days after returning from Portland, Scott, Earl, and I held our fourth—and final—executive meeting via conference call. By now the committee "exploring" a possible candidate forum had a tentative venue, Langston Hughes Community Center, and commitments from all the Central Area candidates running in the primary and eight co-sponsors. Scott was unconvinced. After a stream of obscenities he delivered an ultimatum: "If the WaSPAN board votes to proceed with the forum, I will resign as president!"

Unfazed, Earl made a motion the following Saturday for WaSPAN to co-sponsor a candidate forum with eight other Central Area groups who had agreed to help organize it. In response, Scott rehashed the same tired arguments about political climate and timing and getting egg on our face. The racist connotations of opposing an event organized by our sole African American member wasn't lost on the rest of the board. While not mentioning the "R" word, Forbes Bottomly, a former school superintendent and founding member of the original WaSPAN board, reminded us how hard it was to recruit minorities to the single-payer movement.

Only one person voted with Scott to oppose Earl's motion. Making good on his threat, Scott announced he was stepping down from the presidency due to health problems.

It was the only occasion in our fifteen-year friendship that I ever heard Earl accuse a white person of racism, in his view the root cause of our president's downfall. "I gave that punk health problems all right. His racism was so strong he choked on it."

■

Although Earl and I won the vote, the damage Scott inflicted was substantial and took years to repair. Over the next eighteen months I devoted more than twenty hours a week to holding together a deeply wounded organization. Scott's outburst at the July meeting destroyed all the new momentum we created with our statewide conference. Three other board members, including our secretary and treasurer, resigned, disillusioned by the apparent in-fighting. Aside from this stigma, Scott left WaSPAN with a $2,000 debt. Until we paid this off, I had no hope of persuading the remaining board members to approve any new organizing activities.

Washington's delegation to the second tri-state meeting in November consisted of Earl, myself, Dr. Hal Stockbridge from Olympia, and two elderly board members who rode to Portland in the back seat of my car. Although Health Care for All-California declined to send a delegation, the Washington and Oregon delegates reached an agreement to use an Alaskan single-payer bill, which state senator James Duncan flew down from Anchorage to present, as a template for a November 1998 initiative in both states. The vote was unanimous, except for the WaSPAN board member who represented Olympia. He phoned Scott that night to inform him WaSPAN was being pressured into launching an initiative campaign. Our former president seized the opportunity to dispatch a barrage of derogatory e-mails and letters to the entire WaSPAN membership and much of the wider progressive community.

Based on all the calls and e-mails I received, I estimated Scott sent out approximately five hundred letters and e-mails accusing me of being a "megalomaniac" who was about to destroy the single-payer movement by launching a foolhardy initiative campaign. He appeared to have sent one to each of our 305 conference participants and to every individual and organization who ever donated to WaSPAN. When Paul Zilsel phoned, I learned for the first time about Scott's letter-writing campaign against Mildred Johnson, as well as his role in the demise of Democrat Socialists of America and the Anti-Gulf War Coalition. It was pointless to share this information with the rest of the board. Or that our former president had shut down WaSPAN once before and fought Earl and me at every turn in our efforts to resurrect it. Thanks to Scott's stellar performance in organizing the conference, the other board members blamed his e-mails and letters on a personality conflict between the two of us. They took the position that it was our responsibility to work it out.

On Earl's advice I called an emergency board meeting to force Scott to air his grievances in an open forum. Our former president said nothing we hadn't heard before. He began by reiterating that "everyone" in organized labor felt the timing was wrong for single-payer. He went on to repeat the personal attacks in his e-mails and concluded with a few new ones: "No serious activists want to work with Stuart because she is reckless and inexperienced and deliberately misrepresents their political views."

The example he gave, that I named the Labor Party as a co-sponsor of our single-payer initiative without their permission, was a deliberate lie. However, as Earl coached me prior to the meeting, I refrained from denying any of Scott's accusations. Instead, I focused on my plans for WaSPAN to continue the momentum we created with the conference, the candidate forum, and the regional coalition.

When I finished, Earl asked Scott to outline his own vision for WaSPAN's future work. "Seeing as you don't agree with an initiative."

Our ex-president had no answer and simply repeated his phony mantra about timing and political climate. Earl then moved a straw poll of board members who agreed with "exploring the possibility" of a single-payer initiative. When only one person voted with Scott, he announced he was resigning his WaSPAN membership.

CHAPTER 25

Scott was merely the first of a dozen informants to infiltrate Washington's single-payer movement. I wasn't nearly as astute in spotting them as I liked to think. Ironically, three were staff I hired to assist with the initiative campaign. The new board WaSPAN elected in January 1997 gave tentative approval to a joint initiative campaign with Oregon—with one very onerous condition. The campaign coalition would have to raise $60,000 by January 1, 1998, the opening date for filing ballot language. This was one third of the $180,000 budget we needed for a successful petition campaign.

Professional fundraising was an arena Earl and I blundered into totally blind, making us easy prey for a series of "political consultants" who seemed to operate as freelance informants. None of them gave the appearance of being on any regular payroll. They floated in and out of different political campaigns and progressive organizations, as well as spending significant periods working at legitimate non-political jobs. They seemed to be constantly on the look out for a position of trust in one of these groups. At which point I assumed they went looking for some FBI, police, or private security official willing to purchase the information they gleaned.

We hired our first fundraising "consultant" in August 1997. After raising only $10,000 in eight months, I was desperate. A month earlier Phillip Bellamy, a graduate student and part-time fundraiser for the Washington State Democrats, approached me at the first meeting of the Bellingham chapter. He wanted to sell me a database of 10,000 liberal and progressive donors for five hundred dollars. The database ultimately set WaSPAN back $1,250, after I made the impulsive and foolhardy decision to offer him a job. This is what it cost us to get out of our contract

At thirty-five dollars an hour, we could only afford three hours a week of Phillip's time. The contract the board approved was for him to assist Earl, who we paid twelve dollars an hour as a part-time executive director, in soliciting $500 to $1,000 donations from the top fifty donors in Phillip's database. The two men had one two-hour meeting together. The next morning, two cops knocked on the front door of the old SeaVac building and demanded Earl hand over a second-hand laptop he purchased from a friend. Unbeknownst to Earl, who had never owned or operated a computer, it was stolen. Phillip was outraged when I accused him of contacting the police. However, except for me and the brother Earl bought it from, no one else knew the laptop existed.

■

I came across our second fundraiser in October 1997, after jazz singer Ernestine Anderson agreed to do a benefit concert for our single-payer initiative. This, in turn, led to a frantic search for an events coordinator to organize it. I began by contacting Blair Butterworth's FDR Services, Seattle's pre-eminent liberal political consultants. The junior associate I spoke to gave me three names. The second woman I called referred me to Cumberland Associates, the consulting firm run by husband and wife Peter Knight and Elaine Scofield.

Peter and Elaine attended our first meeting in my office together. Despite his snow-white hair, Peter's face was unlined and he could have been anywhere between forty and fifty-five. A little over six feet, he carried about fifty pounds excess weight, mostly at the waist and in a prominent beer belly. He had an uncanny resemblance to the stylized case officers Robert Redford portrays in his spy movies. He wore the same tortoise-shell glasses and high-end sports jackets over casual gabardine or khaki slacks and had the same artfully tousled hair. Elaine was younger, around forty, and heavier. She was also better dressed, in a stylishly cut skirt suit, nylons, and low heels. Following the initial interview, she was scrupulous in avoiding any further interaction with me. Their business number rang at home. Whenever I called, she hurried to put her husband on the phone the moment I identified myself.

Peter immediately took over the interview, as if they were screening me instead of vice versa. His shrewd grasp of interpersonal dynamics was obvious from the questions he asked about the history and membership of WaSPAN, Health Care for All, and the other organizations in the campaign coalition. He made detailed notes of my answers on a yellow legal pad. I recognized the ploy. I used it myself in my clinical work and believed I was immune to the intoxicating sense of importance it conveyed on the interviewee. I was also aware of a growing chemistry between us, but believed I was immune to this, as well.

■

From the outset Earl opposed my decision to hire a second fundraising consultant. He was incapable, as ever, of articulating his concerns. However, I assumed Peter's resume rang the same alarm bells for Earl as it did for me—the ones suggesting possible intelligence connections. Peter had run Congressman Mike Lowry's Seattle office in the late eighties, during the same period one of Lowry's staff helped to orchestrate phony demonstrations at the South African Consulate and just before Lowry became governor and was set up for a sexual harassment charge. Peter had also consulted on two of Barbara Boxer's campaigns at the time the California senator underwent a 180-degree reversal in her politics—from the left wing of the Democratic Party to the ultra-Wall Street corporate wing the Clintons championed.

I hired him anyway, one of the rare occasions I ignored Earl's advice. The rest of the WaSPAN board loved Peter. He oozed charm, in addition to being highly intelligent and politically sophisticated. More importantly he was the first mainstream political consultant to even consider working for a cause that the board members themselves regarded as a marginalized fringe issue. As for myself, I had three months left to build a viable campaign infrastructure and had run out of options. Without a workable strategy to raise $60,000, the campaign was over. Despite the board's nominal support of a single-payer initiative, I had yet to inspire any of them to commit major time to either outreach or fundraising. Even Earl. Owing to his language difficulties and lack of computer skills, my friend was incapable of offering either the fundraising or administrative support I provided when he ran the museum board.

There was also a grandiose part of me that saw an opportunity to get inside the anonymous forces that targeted me ten years earlier. After ten years of shadow boxing with anonymous strangers, I had a live person in front of me who, unlike Edward, Mark Watson, Scott, or the low-level operatives who posed as patients, was intelligent, well-read, and self-possessed.

"I will make you regret this." I formed the words mentally as I made out a check for a $750 deposit on Peter's $3,500 monthly fee. I told myself I could outwit him. I could extract the fundraising assistance I needed and get rid of Peter before he inflicted any serious damage. I sensed an underlying loneliness and alienation in his ironic witticisms and knew he was genuinely attracted to me. "If necessary," I told myself, "I can make him fall in love with me and break his heart." I was playing with fire.

■

Ten days later, on November 4, I drove a car full of people to Vancouver, Washington for the sixth meeting of the Pacific Rim Single Payer Summit. Peter insisted on riding in the front to plug his cell phone into my cigarette lighter—for an urgent call that never came. His real agenda was to barrage me with personal questions about my background, my family, my training and work, my hobbies, and the books I liked to read. These were interspersed with random anti-technology, anti-government, and anti-police comments. He made a joking comment in which he accused me of being a Luddite because I couldn't work the advanced acoustic features on my car stereo. He also made a bizarre statement about blowing up cell phone towers. After ten years of visits from pseudo patients, I was well familiar with the pattern. He was fishing for some idiosyncratic belief system I would feel irresistibly compelled to discuss with him. He himself had no interest in blowing up cell phone towers, but thought I might.

Determined not to personalize our relationship, I declined to answer all but three of his most innocuous questions. I told him I moved to Seattle in 1983 and owned my own home, and that my daughter attended Garfield High School. He immediately turned my cautiousness into a game, mimicking my terse answers with an exaggerated precision of his own. I played along with the banter, genuinely surprised to encounter a white man with a mental and verbal agility comparable to Earl's prior to his stroke. When Earl played "the dozens" with his friends, the joking insults took the form of good-natured verbal sparring. However, in some neighborhoods it could lead to violence

"So you don't want to tell me where you were born?" he asked. "I can see that would be hard to share. How about the name of your medical school? Is that a safe topic?"

"Actually, I went to two of them."

"That raises all kinds of stability questions, doesn't it? How about the name of your elementary school? Kids rarely turn dangerous before the age of twelve."

"That's where you're wrong. What if they have family problems and keep changing schools?"

The game continued all the way to Vancouver and resumed on the trip back. I knew it was obvious I was attracted to him, but this didn't bother me. I had spent thirty years flirting with male workmates and told myself verbal banter was harmless. It was the lingering looks and awkward silences that were dangerous.

On Monday he called my office to tell me how much he enjoyed the drive to Vancouver. "Perhaps we can take another road trip together some time," he suggested.

I heard this as a clear invitation to proposition him, panicked, and ended the conversation. I also called Earl and told him about Peter's seductive behavior, the best way I knew to ensure nothing would happen. Acting on my feelings meant instant disgrace. If I, as president of a non-profit corporation, had sex with an employee, I could kiss the campaign goodbye, as well as Washington's single-payer movement and possibly my medical license.

■

Peter's contract stipulated WaSPAN would conduct a $12,500 poll on voter attitudes towards single-payer health care to use in developing our fundraising strategy. He proposed to pay for the voter survey and his first month's salary by asking three of our physician supporters for $5,000 donations. I had read enough about professional fundraising to know it was up to me to ask for the money—that Peter would merely advise me how to go about it. My first target was Harborview medical director Dr. James LoGerfo, who had endorsed single-payer health care at a College of Physicians conference. After sending him one of Peter's shiny blue information packets, I made an appointment with his secretary. Sensing my extreme nervousness as I tried to convince him to give me a check for $5,000, he burst out laughing. A month later he, like the majority of the doctors I approached, gave us a hundred dollar donation.

Washington State had no other PNHP members at LoGerfo's income level. This left me no alternative but to fall back on small donor strategies I used in fundraising for CISPES, the Museum and Health Care for All. I got the PNHP office in Chicago to fax me the names and contact details for all their Washington members. Peter composed the "ask" letter I used. He made it clear it was up to me to type it and, using the mail-merge function Tony taught me, print 250 copies and address 250 envelopes. I mailed the letters in batches of twenty-five. I had to make sure I called each doctor exactly two days after their letter arrived.

Peter set a fundraising threshold of $8,000 before engaging a pollster. We met our goal the last week in November. He made all the arrangements for Paul Goodwin, a Los Angeles pollster who did the polling for both of Oregon's Death with Dignity initiatives, to fly to Seattle to meet with Peter, myself, and another part-time staff person named Chris Daw. I had hired Chris, who had a master's degree in public health, to perform a cost analysis of our proposed initiative.

The poll itself, consisting of an eleven-minute phone interview of three hundred randomly selected Washington voters, took three days. It took another three to run the stats and cross tabs. The results, comparable to national polls, revealed that 60 percent of Washington voters supported the creation of a state-run system of health-care financing. The bad news, revealed in the voting frequency cross tabs, was that we would only receive 50 percent or more of the vote in a presidential year. We couldn't win without the "yes" vote of low-income residents who only turned out to vote for president. This left us no choice but to wait two years and file in January 2000.

I was devastated. Except for Peter and Chris, I was still running the coalition entirely on my own. Scott and his friends had already killed off Washington state's single-payer movement once. Only the promise of a 1998 tri-state initiative campaign revived it. With the loss of that concrete goal, I was skeptical WaSPAN would stay together another two years.

■

I assumed Peter would use the six weeks remaining on his contract to approach potential co-sponsors, such as the Washington State Medical Association, Washington State Hospital Association, Washington Education Association, Washington Federation of State Employees and Trial Lawyers Association with our cost study and our $12,500 voter survey—and to help me construct the massive donor base we needed to finance a $180,000 petition campaign. This was a false assumption, as our high-priced fundraising consultant clearly had no intention of doing any fundraising. We continued to have weekly meetings. However, instead of discussing the campaign, he continued to sidetrack our sessions with questions about my personal life and observations about the shortcomings and idiosyncrasies of other board members.

Now that I was spending all my leisure time phoning doctors in order to pay his salary, I was very tired of this game. I confronted him the week after we got our poll results. "This is not what we're paying you for," I told him. "I can't see how my personal life has any relevance to raising money for an initiative campaign."

"Stuart," he said, "if I don't ask personal questions how will I ever get to know you?" Instead of waiting for an answer, he returned to one of his favorite topics—his view that the WaSPAN board was totally dysfunctional. "If you had a functioning board, you wouldn't have to rely on paid staff."

He was absolutely right, of course. However, I was determined not to let him isolate me from the rest of my organization, which I knew from my reading was a common Cointelpro tactic. "All left-wing organizations fall apart eventually," he went on. "Because they only attract unhappy, dysfunctional people. There are exceptions, of course." He gave me a significant look. I was different. In a last-ditch effort to personalize the relationship, he confessed he had a background in intelligence. "Does that trouble you?"

I told him no and changed the subject. The offer to talk about his intelligence work was tempting. At the same time I sensed it was just another ploy to personalize our relationship. I was skeptical he would reveal anything of substance, at least not at the level of detail I was after. He was unlikely to tell me exactly who in the U.S. government made the decision to run me down with a car and try to destroy my career. Or who ordered postal workers killed if they filed workers compensation claims.

Determined to divert our meeting away from his fundraising responsibilities, he launched into a more or less one-sided discussion of all the socialists and anarchists he knew who ended up in Congress and the state legislature. "Frank Chopp, for example. He was a socialist before running for the Forty-third District. I bet you didn't know that, did you?" He proceeded to mention several other names I never heard of.

After he left, the thought flashed through my mind that Peter and his superiors had illusions of grooming me to run for office, like Boxer, and Lowry, and then using me, unwittingly, for their own ends. The extensive personal attention I was getting made no sense if Peter, like Scott, had the sole objective of scuttling the single-payer movement. According to his resume, this was how Peter made his living after leaving Lowry's office—by grooming relative unknowns to become credible candidates for state and national office. If this was how U.S. intelligence exerted control over our elected representatives, it was an ingenious strategy. Members of Congress were totally dependent on their staff to read and analyze legislation and to write all their letters, speeches, and press releases.

At our second to last session he fell silent, which was rare for Peter, as I talked about a former CISPES member and organizer for the United Farm Workers who ended our friendship following my hospitalization. There was no question this was what he wanted me to talk about. After all these years he seemed to be on the same mission as the psychologist on the train, Mark Watson, and the sophisticated black "patient" who greeted me on my return to my office. He wanted to know what I recalled and understood about the government's role in my so-called psychotic episode.

■

In the end my relationship with Peter boiled down to a mammoth struggle of wills. He was determined for me to see him as uniquely intelligent and sensitive. I was equally determined to maintain my view of Peter as a crass manipulator who hated what I stood for and who, like Scott, had most likely sabotaged other progressive organizations and the career of at least one progressive politician. What I found most baffling was that I found his appearance physical repulsive. I found the mental image of making love to his ponderous, flaccid body almost as ludicrous as the pretense that he found me— with my mannish, unstyled gray hair, double chins and marionette lines—fascinating enough to jeopardize his marriage.

In December 1997, the *Stranger* carried a front-page article on Natalie Heard's death. It was a wake-up call, as I couldn't escape the parallels between her relationship with Ted and mine with Peter. I knew all about the pseudo intimacy that male case officers create to recruit their informants – who in most cases are also male. Despite knowing exactly what was happening, I seemed helpless to prevent it. The erotic attraction was as intense as ever, continually fed by Peter's witty insight into human idiosyncrasies and my sense of our shared loneliness and alienation. I wanted so badly for it to be real. Peter was the first and only man I ever met who was my intellectual equal. At fifty, I knew he would be the last.

Natalie, who first came to me in 1992 for post-traumatic stress disorder, was the first female and one of the first African Americans to become a professional race-car driver. In July 1997 the police found her body floating under the Aurora Bridge. During the five years I treated her, I learned how she ran afoul of the Drug Enforcement Agency, who in the late eighties had their own race car, and who, according to Natalie, were using the race circuit to launder drug monies. Following the defection of Sandy Gonzales and other legitimate agents from the DEA, it became common knowledge on the left that the federal agency responsible for fighting the drug trade, like the CIA, derived income from narcotics sales and money laundering.

Natalie also blamed the DEA for engineering the near fatal rollover that ended her racing career, after they learned she planned to disclose what she knew in a monthly newsletter she sent out to professional drivers. Despite her permanent disability, the harassment continued, in the form of anonymous calls, malicious damage to her home by neighbors, and a terrifying home invasion and rape. In the last year of her life she kept a detailed log of every call and each encounter with the disheveled males who wandered onto her property and into the bridal shop her family owned in Pioneer Square. She mailed a copy to all her friends after someone cut the fuel bladder in her father's van, which should have exploded when she started the engine.

"If anything happens to me," she wrote on a yellow post-it she attached to the log, "it is not suicide."

The police ruled her fall from the Aurora Bridge a suicide, notwithstanding the bridge's three-foot retaining wall, which Natalie couldn't have climbed without assistance due to her hip and knee injuries. They were largely influenced by her ex-boyfriend, an organizer for the Revolutionary Communist Party. Mike went to them of his own initiative following her death and told them she was acutely suicidal. During our last appointment two weeks before her death, Natalie told me about the strange mind games he played after they moved in together.

"Mike continually berates me for my weight and my lisp and the fact that I waddle when I walk." Natalie still had a marked limp from old racing injuries. "He has started going out at night for sexual encounters. One night he brought a woman home with him. I was sleeping on the floor because of my back and they woke me up to make fun of me."

Owing to its reputation for inciting violence at peaceful demonstrations, many Seattle activists believed the Revolutionary Communist Party was actually a pseudo-party created by U.S. intelligence. Mae Brussell was the first to expose the governmental origin of many so-called "underground" groups, including the Weathermen and the Symbianese Liberation Army, the group who kidnapped Patty Hurst. Without having any idea how she might react, I felt I had to warn Natalie of my concerns.

"I hate to bring this up," I cautioned. "Please tell me if you feel I'm out of line. Has it ever occurred to you that Mike might be a federal agent?"

She nodded, totally nonplussed. "It has. I've already made a deposit on a new apartment. I'm just waiting for my father to move my things."

■

On January 4, 1998, at our first meeting after the Christmas break, I informed Peter that I wouldn't be renewing his contract. I had no choice. My brief affair with Edward had nearly ended my career. My continuing involvement with our so-called fundraising consultant jeopardized not only the initiative campaign and Washington's single-payer movement, but my medical license, career, and possibly my life. After ten and a half years, it was unlikely I would ever get a clear explanation for the bizarre events that preceded my hospitalization. It was time to resign myself to this reality.

Peter seemed stunned at first but recovered quickly. "Is it the money?" Apparently, it only just occurred to him that I spent all my evenings and weekends fundraising to pay his fee. He didn't wait for an answer. "I'm happy to provide my services free, as a volunteer."

I shook my head. It was a waste of time to point out that he did no work for the campaign. He already knew this. I chose my words carefully. I wanted to convey that I knew what he was without being so specific he could deny it. It was possible he no longer worked for U.S. intelligence but for one of the private companies that did their dirty work for them.

"If I were not a deeply spiritual person I would try to hurt you," I finally told him. I had never thought of myself as spiritual before. However, after years of working with Earl, it seemed some of his boundless tolerance and willingness to forgive the most egregious personal injuries had rubbed off. Although I could never consider myself religious, the word "spiritual" was the only one that fit.

For the first time in our brief acquaintance, Peter's reply was spontaneous. "No, Stuart. You wouldn't want to do that."

I took it as an acknowledgement.

CHAPTER 26

A month later I stepped down from the WaSPAN presidency. As Peter repeatedly pointed out, I had yet to persuade any other board members to help me run WaSPAN, much less assist with the major outreach and fundraising necessary to form a statewide coalition campaign. I had no hope of running a $180,000 petition campaign by myself. The official justification I gave the board was that my practice was in financial difficulty. This was also true. I had just laid Tony off, thanks to Clinton's managed-care "revolution," which had cut my insurance reimbursements by more than $7,000. With no office manager, I was again spending all my evenings and weekends in my office doing my own billing, bookkeeping, typing, and filing.

I expected the group to fold when I stepped down. However, to my surprise, Chris Daw gave up her staff position to take my place as president. Despite the change in leadership, our board meetings continued to be disrupted by quirky strangers with a clear agenda of disrupting our work. Nelson Smithson, a tall, coarse-mouthed retired carpenter in his mid-sixties, made his first appearance at our March 1998 meeting. He dominated both the March and April meetings with belligerent tirades that made it impossible to accomplish any business. Instead of targeting Chris, who was chairing, he directed his accusations at me.

"This woman is deliberately misleading the public," he ranted. He was sitting across the table from me and jabbed the air in front of me angrily with his index finger. "She is deliberately misleading the public by claiming she is running an initiative campaign. However, there is no single-payer initiative and she refuses to write one."

He was partly right. On Peter's advice, Chris and I agreed to consolidate the campaign coalition—hopefully to include a number of health provider organizations and progressive unions—prior to writing our ballot language. None of these groups would support us if we included provisions that disadvantaged their members in some way.

In response to Smithson's constant bullying, Chris drafted ballot language herself. My reaction was to absent myself from the June and July meetings. I mistakenly believed I could thwart his disruptive behavior by removing myself as a target. However, in early August another board member notified me of an emergency meeting to ratify new initiative language Smithson supposedly co-wrote with a policy analyst from the Department of Social and Health Services. In my absence, he somehow persuaded Chris to substitute his ballot language for her own single-payer initiative.

I immediately recognized the document she faxed me as John Burbank's initiative to expand Washington's Basic Health Plan (BHP) by increasing the cigarette tax. With financial backing from the Washington State Labor Council, Burbank first circulated the measure in mid-1997. WaSPAN opposed the BHP initiative, in part owing to its failure to outlaw private health insurance. More importantly, we knew the presence of two health-care measures on the November 1998 ballot would split the vote and spell automatic defeat for both of them. Coincidentally, a month after we abandoned our 1998 campaign, Burbank also scrapped the BHP initiative. Then it mysteriously resurfaced in the hands of a belligerent stranger with an overt agenda of sabotaging our work.

■

We easily defeated Smithson's attempted coup and never saw him again. At our September meeting we had a new visitor, previously unknown in Seattle's progressive community. Al Norman was a heavy-set, openly seductive forty-something who introduced himself as a "liberal" activist with many years experience with both the Democratic Party and the Jewish Anti-Defamation League. Unlike Smithson, he was never openly disruptive. His approach was to beckon me into the corridor in the middle of meetings to complain about Chris.

In fact, this was how he introduced himself. "I have just moved out here from Chicago to Seattle to start a political consulting business," he told me. He handed me his card, as if he thought I might offer him a job. It seemed by now that I had a reputation for being vulnerable in this area. "You know as well as I do that you can't let her run the organization," he continued. "She is way too defensive. She can't compromise or build consensus. You will need a broad-based coalition to launch an effective health-care campaign. And there is no way someone that sectarian can run it."

"Sectarian" was a polite word for "leftist." My politics were far to the left of Chris's, which grew out of her Quaker background. However, I saw no point in telling Norman this. He wasn't a genuine activist and this wasn't a real conversation. Once again, it was extremely unorthodox for a total stranger to single me out instead of the official head of the organization. Besides, I was far less concerned about Chris's shortcomings than the key role the Anti-Defamation League played in helping the FBI spy on CISPES.

When he failed to engage me in a conspiracy to resume the leadership, Norman also disappeared. WaSPAN experienced no further visits from covert agents—at least none Earl or I recognized—until we filed our initiative language in February 2000. Over the next year, the main strategy our opponents pursued was to launch a parallel single-payer organization. Ironically, by 1999, it was clear that the Washington State Labor Council, rather than the insurance lobby, was our most dangerous adversary. In fact, all the evidence suggested it was actually organized labor, not the government or the insurance lobby, who secretly engaged Scott to take over WaSPAN and run it into the ground. In early 1999, the Labor Council openly hired Scott, much as they financed John Burbank's launch of a competing health-care initiative, to form a parallel single-payer organization for union staffers called Just Health Care.

Despite the strong support our single-payer initiative enjoyed from the Machinists Council and the public employees union, who between them controlled two-thirds of the votes on the Washington State Labor Council, it was obvious that the paid officials who ran the AFL-CIO and the State Labor Council opposed single-payer health care. On the surface this made no sense, given that skyrocketing employer health costs were the primary cause of all strikes in the 1990s, as well as a major cost factor driving U.S. companies to shut down and move overseas.

■

In June 1999, WaSPAN renamed itself Health Care 2000 and hired Cindi Laws, an activist with the Thirty-ninth District Democrats, as a part-time campaign manger. Her first task was to consolidate the campaign coalition and finalize the ballot language we would file with the Secretary of State in January 2000. Over the next six months she circulated Chris's draft initiative and successive revisions to the Washington State Medical Association, the Washington State Hospital Association, both nurses unions, and other progressive unions and health-related groups we hoped to recruit as co-sponsors. All but one, the Washington State Labor Council, identified sections that potentially affected their members and proposed new wording. The Labor Council lobbyist and their lawyer continued to stonewall Cindi, as they had Chris, despite both women's repeated requests to negotiate the treatment of Taft Hartley trusts under our proposed initiative. The collective bargaining agreements of Taft Hartley unions require their employers to pay health benefits directly to union-run trusts. Obviously, employers couldn't make contributions simultaneously to Taft Hartley trusts and the Washington Health Care Trust created by our initiative.

On December 1, Cindi e-mailed Labor Council president Rick Bender with draft language exempting members of Taft Hartley unions from payroll deductions unless they chose to participate in the Washington Health Care Trust. Over the next six weeks, she sent him six more e-mails reminding him of the resolution the Labor Council passed in October 1999 in support of our single-payer initiative. On January 27, four days before we filed with the Secretary of State, she received a fax from his assistant. It consisted of a printout of her e-mail with a short, handwritten note: "The Labor Council could support these provisions."

■

Two weeks later we were about to deliver a layout of our petition to the printer when the Washington Technical Alliance, one of our smaller coalition partners, faxed us a two-paragraph memo Bender had just issued to all state locals. It asserted the Taft Hartley provisions in Initiative 725 (I-725) were unworkable. Bender cited an obscure federal ruling that any state law making specific reference to either Taft Hartley law or Taft Hartley trusts automatically violates federal law. That afternoon, rather than going full-time as planned, Cindi resigned. Like Scott, she blamed health problems—migraines and peptic ulcer disease—which, in her case, were genuine. However, we both knew the real reason—without support from organized labor we had no hope of collecting the 180,000 signatures we needed by the July 7 deadline.

Because Dr. Hal Stockbridge and I assumed responsibility for fundraising after Cindi left, it became our decision to continue a losing campaign. As founding members of Health Care for All, we both fully appreciated the significance of sending hundreds of volunteers into the streets every weekend to collect signatures for single-payer health care. As there were no other applicants, we had no choice but to promote Jerry Adams, who Cindi hired as field manager, to campaign manager. Two and a half weeks later I made the embarrassing discovery that I had once again hired a covert agent to spy on us. Jerry was a long-haired thirty-something musician and neighborhood activist who had run the successful campaign to block the Seattle Commons. Initially, I blamed his youth and inexperience for his failure to turn up at the campaign office before 2:00 p.m. or to assist Mel, our student intern, with fundraising or recruiting signature gatherers. When Mel called me at home at eight o'clock one morning to inform me he had tampered with our database, I had no choice but to ask him to resign.

Our third campaign manager was Sally Soriano, a long-time activist and the lead Seattle organizer for the 1999 anti-WTO demonstrations. In this capacity she used friends in the King County Labor Council to outmaneuver both the State Labor Council and the AFL-CIO and win a hotly contested vote that would add 30,000 unionists to the protests. Older Health Care 2000 members who previously belonged to the Communist Party saw sinister motives for organized labor's staunch opposition to both the anti-WTO movement and single-payer health care. In the early sixties, former CIA operative Tom Braden openly bragged about the hundreds of AFL-CIO officials he put on the CIA payroll. None of us saw any reason to believe this practice had stopped. By the 1990s, unions were no longer the preeminent liberal institution driving liberal politics in Washington. This responsibility had shifted to so-called liberal "think tanks," such as the Equal Opportunity Institute, and non-union trade groups like the Washington Trial Lawyers Association. However, the unorthodox but surprisingly unanimous reaction from these groups to majority popular support for publicly sponsored health—that it was politically unfeasible—suggested U.S. intelligence also planted operatives among their leadership.

Sally, who knew we had no money to pay her, ran Health Care 2000 on a voluntary basis for seven months. In essence, we split the role of campaign manager, with Sally taking charge of our campaign office and volunteers, and me the responsibility for our fundraising and campaign budget.

Our opponents, who gave us thousands of dollars of free publicity by railing against us on the editorial pages and talk radio, appeared not to realize I-725 was doomed from the outset. Aside from the Labor Council's bait and switch and Jerry's feeble attempt to destroy our database, Scott Hancock engineered the most damaging sabotage. Just Health Care, the single-payer organization the Labor Council hired him to form, had no real agenda other than a bimonthly newsletter, which Scott wrote and devoted almost entirely to trashing I-725. When this failed to deter the scores of pro-single payer unionists who were circulating our petitions, Scott seized on a June 2000 email by our Olympia coordinator, who was most likely an informant himself. The email concerned a meeting between Sally and the Labor Council lobbyist over I-725's Taft Hartley provisions. It boasted the Council was about to make concessions they hadn't formally agreed to—one of the worst sins a community activist could commit in the eyes of many union staffers. Scott forwarded the e-mail to Bender, who wrote me a certified letter canceling all future meetings.

■

As Cindi, Hal, and I anticipated, Health Care 2000 reached the July 7 deadline with only 100,000 of the 180,000 signatures we needed. Sally and I immediately re-filed our petition, with minor modifications, as an initiative to the January 2001 legislature. Under Washington State Law Initiative 245 (I-245) was a new measure, which meant our signature count restarted at zero. However ,this time we would have a full six months, until December 31, to collect 180,000 signatures. As we now had five hundred volunteers submitting a weekly average of 150 signatures, this goal was well within reach.

Meanwhile, Hal and I, who knew there was no way we could finance a second campaign in our spare time on evenings and weekends, persuaded the board to hire a professional organizer named Ezra Basom to take charge of fundraising. Sally initially supported hiring Ezra—until she read a clause in his contract guaranteeing him a $40,000 annual salary. As a staunch ex-Communist she couldn't agree to pay any employee more than we paid our intern, newly promoted to Campaign Office Coordinator. When Sally reconvened the board and threatened to resign, they rescinded Ezra's contract. Without a dedicated fundraiser or fundraising strategy, our money ran out on October 1. This was the day we laid Mel off and shut the campaign office.

Part V –
The End of a Friendship

*It goes on one at a time,
it starts when you care
to act, it starts when you do
it again and they said no,
it starts when you say* **We**
*and know you who you mean, and each
day you mean one more.*
from *The Low Road* by Marge Piercy

CHAPTER 27

Two months later, on December 3, Health Care 2000 held its fourth annual meeting. For the first time in five years the group adjourned with three autonomous committees: a conference committee, a Help Line to assist uninsured Washington residents obtain medical care and medication in Canada, and a Legislative Committee to lobby the Senate Health and Long Term Care Committee to sponsor I-245 as a bill. Thanks to the initiative campaign, our paid membership had quadrupled. Yet, even a coalition of 5,000 members was far too small to have significant impact on the legislature. Although our senate bill garnered ten co-sponsors, including a Republican from Pierce County, the Democratic speaker blocked its introduction in the House. When the legislative session ended in April 2001, Washington state's first single-payer bill in ten years died in the Senate Rules Committee.

Had I failed in transferring the organization's leadership to the board and committee chairs, I would have allowed the coalition to fold, as Scott had done five years earlier. The massive grassroots movement I visualized when I first joined PNHP in 1988 never materialized. Owing to a complete blackout of the U.S. health care crisis by the mainstream media, the majority of Americans were totally unaware of the epidemic of bankruptcies among doctors, clinics, and hospitals, or that 20,000 children, seniors, and minimum-wage workers died of treatable conditions every year because they couldn't afford medical care. Americans are deeply conditioned to allow network TV to define their consciousness. Social problems only become real when they receive regular coverage on the nightly news. Everything else becomes a non-issue in the daily struggle to keep up with rent, mortgage, and credit card payments.

■

I had even less to show for the hundreds of hours and more than $100,000 I had invested in the African American community. After successfully unloading the leadership of Health Care 2000, I rejoined the Museum Support Committee in one last effort to pressure the city and school district to honor the agreement they signed with Earl when he ended his occupation in 1993. In early 2001, a strategic opportunity developed to block the Urban League, which was in the process of purchasing the old Coleman School to convert it into condominiums. A year earlier the police shooting of an unarmed, mentally retarded black man had generated a surge of activism in Seattle's Central Area. By June 2001, the Coalition for Police Accountability was drawing seventy-five to a hundred evenly divided white and African American activists to weekly marches and rallies.

The Museum board reinstated Earl in 1998, after Jabari and the Youth Action Committee learned that Bob Flowers was having an affair with the new Department of Neighborhoods staff person and that $300,000 of museum funds were unaccounted for. Two boards met for six months, one led by Earl, Jabari, and the Youth Action Committee, and the other by Flowers and his supporters.

The city-controlled board collapsed in January 2000, after Washington Mutual transferred Flowers to California to keep the sex scandal out of the local papers. It took Earl a little over three months to raise the $50,000 the city and school district required to complete the title transfer. Three months later, without explanation, the Superintendent of Schools returned the certified check. The next day, a front-page article in the *Seattle Times* revealed the school district had reneged on their 1993 purchase agreement by accepting an offer from the Urban League. The Urban League was a national organization whose Seattle board was run by Flowers, Rice, and other African American bankers and professionals. All but Rice lived in affluent eastside suburbs, where their children were well shielded from the drug and gang activity that surrounded Seattle's public schools.

The *Times* article also disclosed that the Urban League planned to transform the old Coleman school into "income generating" condominiums, except for 1,600 square feet on the first floor to be reserved for a Northwest African American Heritage Museum. They were financing the purchase with a $417,000 grant from the Department of Neighborhoods—the same $417,000 the city placed in escrow when Earl ended his occupation.

■

There were approximately fifty people in the sanctuary of New Hope Baptist Church when Earl stood up to address the June 2 meeting of the Coalition for Police Accountability. Despite his aphasia, he hadn't lost the ability to turn a meeting around with a single astute observation.

"This is a historic opportunity," he began. He paused and stuttered as he fumbled for words. "We make a mistake just fighting racism. We're talking about children and grandchildren. Who need something positive. Like the African American Heritage Museum. Which the city is doing its best to steal from us."

The young anarchists and environmentalists from the anti-globalization movement already knew Earl from the community meetings Sally organized in December 1999 as part of the Anti-WTO Days of Action. As the gathering broke up, a dozen of them followed Earl, Jabari, and me on a six-block march to the old Coleman School. At Earl's direction, we stationed ourselves on both sides of Twenty-third and handed out leaflets to protest the planned condominium conversion.

A week later, on June 9, twenty of us waited an hour on the corner of Twenty-third and Massachusetts for Jabari, who kept all the fliers, signs, and banners in his car, to arrive. I believed the tardiness was deliberate. After working with Jabari for thirteen years, I knew the pattern. The minor sabotage would escalate until he triggered some major upheaval that would throw both the new Museum Support Committee and the larger Coalition into total disarray. In 1987 I was too naïve to understand the significance of Jabari's call for mercenaries to fight in Mozambique. Fourteen years later I knew with absolute certainty that no leftist group—white or black—had the resources to pay mercenaries, unless they were on the CIA payroll. In addition I had just learned the museum board technically missed their March 1, 2000 deadline to pay their $50,000 deposit by ten days—because Jabari withdrew $15,000 from the bank account without authorization.

That night I shared my concerns with Earl. "Earl, I think he's a federal agent. All this sabotage. I know he's incredibly narcissistic and self-centered. But this is more than mental instability. The pattern is too predictable to be accidental."

I couldn't bring myself to use his best friend's name and "federal agent" in the same sentence. However Earl knew instantly who I was talking about. I reminded him of the virulent anti-Semitism blossoming among Jabari's protégés on the Youth Action Committee. Of the board meetings where Blessed and Merciful circulated the *Protocols of Zion*, as well as Henry Ford's essays and other overtly anti-Semitic propaganda. We both knew that fomenting racial paranoia was an old tactic that Cointelpro ran very effectively against the Black Panthers.

"I'm sure he's the one who gives them all that stuff," I continued. "They're too young to know it even exists much less where to look for it. Even if they don't get it from him, he knows they're doing it and does nothing to stop them."

Earl grumbled dismissively. It wasn't a topic that interested him.

"Earl, we both know it's just a matter of time. It's happened so many times before."

"Some people become agents inadvertently," he finally said. "For financial gain."

I tried to get him to clarify. "Are you saying someone is paying Jabari to sabotage the Museum? Or just that he benefits indirectly. For example, if the Urban League engages his construction business to develop the property?"

Earl's response, like much of his speech following his stroke, was unintelligible. Then he changed the subject.

■

Jabari's unreliability didn't deter our young supporters, who were almost reverent in their admiration for Earl's eight-year occupation. From then on they printed their own leaflets and made their own signs and banners. They also created an African American Heritage Museum website, using a scanner to upload fifteen years of news clippings and legal documents that Earl had saved from the beginning of the occupation.

Although the small group of radicals who picketed the Museum leveled out at thirty, by the last Tuesday in June the Coalition for Police Accountability was large enough that 250 of us shut down the intersection at Twenty-third and Union for two and a half hours.

Earl's mother underwent open-heart surgery the following week, and he canceled the first picket in July to spend the weekend in Portland. I was on a ladder repainting the trim on my dining room windows when I heard the news update on the local National Public Radio station. An unnamed protestor at a Unity Festival at Twenty-third and Union had struck Mayor Paul Schell with a megaphone. The blow fractured Schell's cheekbone and knocked him to the ground.

The city-sponsored "Festival" celebrated the opening of a new upscale shopping plaza, another milestone in the city's agenda to "gentrify" the Central Area and Rainier Valley. Snell's smugness about a program that systematically displaced their friends and neighbors infuriated the black businesses owners and residents who remained. Moreover, they all saw a clear link between David Walker's murder and the aggressive policing initiated under Weed and Seed and actively promoted by Schell. With the help of the Coalition for Police Accountability, twenty of them picketed the Unity Festival, demanding that the mayor appoint a civilian review board to investigate police misconduct.

I knew instantly who committed the assault and foresaw the chaos it would create. Jabari pleaded not guilty, despite statements from Schell's wife and a dozen activists and journalists who witnessed the attack. Alluding to a thirty-year history as a "non-violent resister" of North American apartheid, Earl's friend claimed the police were framing him——that he handed the megaphone to another protestor before going up to speak to the mayor. A woman whose name he didn't recall.

Following the account that appeared in Monday's *Post Intelligencer*, the Coalition for Police Accountability split into two factions. The Revolutionary Communist Party, representing the far left, proclaimed the black activist a political prisoner and demanded his immediate release. The more moderate church and peace and justice activists were not unified enough to make a public statement. Yet all of those I talked to excused the assault on the basis that Jabari was mentally unbalanced.

To my amazement, the entire progressive community swallowed the lie about Jabari's non-violent past. Earl's friend had ranted for twenty years, during multiple campaigns for school board, city council, and mayor, about retaliating "by any means necessary" against the "violence" that dominates African Americans' lives. In 1986 he knocked on the door of the South African Consulate with a handgun in his pocket. A year later he hit a campus cop with his briefcase and grabbed his gun away from him. Yet, somehow, this was forgotten or overlooked.

■

Jabari's arrest for hitting the mayor also spelled the end of my fourteen-year friendship with Earl. He called my office Monday afternoon when he returned from Portland.

"You need to call your people," he said. He was aware I made weekly reminder calls for the Coalition for Police Accountability and invited them to attend the museum picket after the weekly planning meetings. "The arraignment is tomorrow. We need a Legal Defense Committee."

"I can't, Earl," I said. "Two of them saw him hit the Mayor."

"Jabari called me from jail. He says he didn't do it."

"Earl, can't you see he set this up? Deliberately. It will tear the whole coalition apart."

Despite his repeated betrayals, Earl couldn't entertain that his friend might be lying. "I can't turn my back on a brother."

"Earl, you will have to do this on your own. I can't help you with this." I knew I was asking him to make a choice: between an African American male who sabotaged every grassroots campaign he and Earl worked on, and a white female who re-mortgaged her home to support the most important political endeavor of his life.

Conditioned by generations of racial oppression, he went for the black face. "I don't give a fuck what you think," he blurted, slamming the phone down.

My years of personal and financial sacrifice were of no consequence. I was the wrong race—and the wrong sex. In the end, the asexual nature of our relationship hadn't protected me. Earl couldn't conceive of a woman in any role other than assisting and supporting a man in his vision. I was deceiving myself to think otherwise.

■

By the end of September the hopelessly factionalized Coalition for Police Accountability had collapsed, as I, along with the majority of Seattle's activist community, regrouped to form the 9-11 Coalition to protest Bush's invasion of Afghanistan. In early 2002, in the absence of any community opposition, the school district quietly transferred the deed to the old Coleman property to the Urban League.

Earl and I didn't speak again for six months. The years of battle had taken their toll—over his refusal to keep books, file tax returns, acknowledge his speech impairment, or allow me input into the limited partnership or the museum board. By now he had also lost title to the old Sea Vac building. The Federal Deposit Insurance Corporation inherited our note from the Resolution Trust Corporation and promptly sold it to a bank in Oklahoma without acknowledging the $100,000 settlement the RTC agreed to in 1994. In December 1999, by some miracle, Earl located a small mortgage company in Tacoma willing to loan him $250,000 to cover the original loan, plus outstanding mortgage payments, interest, and penalties. To qualify, he had to buy me out of the partnership, a paper agreement to pay me thirty-six monthly installments of $1,000. My friend had an impeccable credit record, unlike DE and B Limited Partnership. Our limited partnership had operated at a loss for six years and filed no tax returns since 1995.

Earl had an appointment in September 2000 to sign the closing documents when Cascade Finance notified him they were rescinding the loan offer. The reasons they cited were unresolved questions about the property's zoning, and "neighborhood complaints" about noise and fumes from the auto repair business in the warehouse. He found the letter of complaint—signed by the same white couple who purchased the property at the October 2000 foreclosure auction—among the court documents he received with the surplus proceeds. Someone had leaked the name of our lender and the details of our refinance loan to a developer with a competing interest in the property, a felony offense under banking privacy regulations. However, no one in the Clinton administration was willing to enforce these laws. And once again we had no recourse other than filing suit and paying more than twice our original investment in attorney fees.

■

After losing my only child to college, it was a bad time to lose my only comrade. Despite the word's historic links with Soviet Communism, it's the only one I know to describe the intense intimacy resulting from activists jointly sacrificing their personal time, financial security, health, and even lives for a shared vision.

Owing to the sudden loss of this relationship, it also hit home how my twenty years as an activist had left me feeling lonelier and even more alienated than ever. I was first drawn into grassroots organizing in 1982 because of the connection I believed it offered with other human beings. Yet nearly all my work for both the museum and Health Care 2000—all the fundraising letters, fliers and newsletters, phone solicitation and reminder calls—I did alone at my desk.

The reality is that serious organizing in the U.S. is a solitary pursuit. Even among staunch leftists, it's rare to encounter individuals willing to commit to the sustained effort needed to achieve any substantial public presence. Except for the spies, of course. They remain as eager as ever to insert themselves into positions of trust.

Most of the activists who attended the 9-11 meetings at the

University Baptist Church were still more focused on the high-pressure jobs that paid for the thousands of dollars a year they spent on lattes, electronic toys, SUVs, and large, smartly furnished, energy guzzling homes. They still didn't fully appreciate that they owed all these luxuries to proxy dictatorships the U.S. had set up around the world to provide an unlimited supply of cheap oil and sweatshop labor.

Few of them shared my view that the U.S. wasn't merely headed towards fascism but had fully arrived—at least in Mussolini's sense of the word—of government under the total control of corporations. In fact, most still embraced the exceptionalist beliefs they learned in school: that despite major political flaws, the U.S. was the most democratic, productive, efficient, cleanest, healthiest, transparent, just and scientifically advanced nation in the world. It was none of these things, of course. It was merely the most ruthless.

Aware of the role personal hardship plays in radicalizing people, for a long time I attributed their naiveté to my sense that most of them led easier lives than I did. Most of them had private health insurance and could see a doctor when they were sick. Except for Catherine, a handful of African American activists and two gay activists with ACT-UP, none of them had to cope with vicious phone and personal harassment, nor the extrajudicial murder of people close to them.

I now saw this was only a tiny factor in the growing chasm between myself and other progressives. For some reason I still found it very difficult to accept that my working-class upbringing had endowed me with very different values from most of them. During the sad months of introspection that followed my falling out with Earl, I could no longer escape this reality. I hadn't found Earl by accident. I had gone out looking for him after CISPES and ISO collapsed in 1985, determined to connect with other leftists from blue-collar backgrounds.

The middle class continues to delude itself that American

affluence has done away with the class system in the U.S. Yet professionals and academics who grow up in the streets or in the care of siblings carry the hidden injuries of class into every aspect of their adult lives. Even when we fail to form the conscious thought, the knowledge is innate. We have suffered the elite classes our entire lives: their superficiality and lack of common sense, their avoidance of anger and conflict, their fickle sense of loyalty, their equivocation, and, above all, their obsession with guilt, "appropriateness," and political correctness.

At the same time I could no longer minimize the role my working-class origins played in the decision by U.S. intelligence to target me. Obviously, my income and medical credentials worried them. Both enhanced my credibility and theoretically my access to the mainstream media. Yet the other doctors in Health Care for All, who were either on salary or saw private fee-paying patients, earned two to three times as much as I did. No one harassed them. Obviously, the clientele I catered to added to the threat I posed. Even the mental health clinics, faced with relentless federal and state budget cuts, turned away the unemployed labor activists and whistleblowers who had their careers and lives ruined for their courage in speaking out.

However, after struggling for fourteen years to pinpoint the motives of my anonymous admirers, it was suddenly crystal clear that it was precisely my inability to let go and move on that made me so dangerous. Unlike my middle-class friends, I totally lacked the capacity for intellectualization, rationalization, obsessive undoing, or compartmentalization. This is all technical jargon for the ability to put unpleasant thoughts and feelings temporarily—or permanently—out of awareness.

It was something we never learned in my family. If something upsets us, we are right there in your face about it, even if it leads to violence. Professionals and academics from working-class backgrounds learn very early that we can never pass for middle-class. We will never think, speak, dress, decorate our homes, or handle our children like our professional colleagues, even the most liberal ones, no matter how much money or status we acquire.

CHAPTER 28

I never abandoned my dream of emigrating. I applied for my first overseas post after Bush the elder invaded Iraq in 1991. This was the same year that New Zealand began its drive to recruit overseas psychiatrists. I called Global Medical Staffing after seeing their ad in the *Psychiatric News* and submitted my resume. When the recruiter called and wanted me to commit to a date, I lost my nerve. I knew only too well the distress my daughter would feel at being wrenched away from the school friends who were so central to her young life. In a New Zealand school, Naomi would most likely be the only American. From twenty-five years of listening to the early histories of my clients, I knew how cruel children could be to classmates who are new and different. I also knew it left emotional scars that could last a lifetime.

By the time my daughter left home in 1999, I was in charge of a $200,000 initiative campaign. Two years later, when my fourteen-year relationship with Earl came to an abrupt end, the only remaining obstacle to working abroad was my health. I was still tied to a daily routine that focused around shopping and meal preparation. Any deviation from my menu, which was limited to rice, potatoes, and lean meat or fish, meant I couldn't sleep or work.

I made one appointment in 1998 with the gastroenterologist that Pam Houghton had recommended, only to cancel it. I knew I was looking at several thousand dollars for tests and procedures—money I didn't have, given the steady decline in my practice income. When Naomi turned sixteen, she obtained her own health insurance by taking a part-time job at Ballard Market. That was the year I turned fifty and learned the cheapest individual policy in my age bracket cost $7,000. Money that I simply didn't have. Through my efforts to build a single-payer caucus in the Washington State Medical Association, I encountered dozens of solo practitioners of all specialties in the same predicament: insurance companies paid them too little to purchase health insurance for themselves.

Obviously, there were group policies on the market back in 1998, with premiums that ran 40 percent less than individual policies. While the coverage they provided was quite limited, I'm sure I could have found one I could afford by making other financial sacrifices. In 1999 my practice income dropped so low that I was forced to move into the basement and rent out my bedroom to a boarder. There was no reason I couldn't have done this a year earlier and come up with $4,000 for a group health insurance policy.

The point is, I never even considered the possibility. I couldn't. Not without facing the lingering uncertainty I didn't want to face—that the people targeting me somehow caused my illness.

■

All this changed in October 2001 when I met Winslow. The thirty-something ex-GI and I linked up through a dating hotline that advertised in the *Stranger*. I was in my office Saturday night doing my September billing, and I dialed the hotline in a fit of boredom. I selected the fetish option and put the call on speakerphone. This left my hands free for data entry. I allowed Winslow to ramble on about exotic masturbation techniques, the Capitol Hill S&M club he attended Friday nights, and the dominatrix he hired twice a month to humiliate him. When I learned he had served in Iraq and had advanced training in biological, chemical, and radiological warfare agents, I gave him my home phone number.

I had only one "date" with Winslow, who lived in Puyallup and attended Pierce County Community College on the GI Bill. My interest in pain and humiliation faded quickly after I picked him up at the Greyhound Bus station. We ended up at Denny's, where I bought him breakfast.

Winslow continued to call at least once a month, to update me on the sex toys and instructional sex videos he ordered through the Internet. He was an active John Bircher with friends in Washington's right-wing militia. Some months we talked about NAFTA, the WTO, and the villainous Trilateral Commission, three issues on which the far left and far right agree. Our shared interest in alternative health remedies led to a discussion of my illness. I told him about the 1987 break-in and the sickly sweet smell that wafted up from my basement. He asked me to describe my symptoms. Then he assured me that as of 1991 when he was discharged, the U.S. military possessed no chemical or infectious agents capable of causing this type of illness.

■

Two months later, despite vigilant adherence to my diet, my illness worsened. By February 2002, I had lost ten pounds and was back to working a sixteen-hour week. With the help of the new Health Care 2000 Help Line, I located an insurance company in Tucson with a $3,500 group policy for small-business owners. The coverage it offered—reimbursing only 60 percent of "allowed" services, was extremely limited. However, mere possession of an insurance card entitled me to discounted "insured patient" fees for all doctors, hospital, and laboratory visits. All the major insurance companies forced doctors and hospitals to discount their fees by approximately 30 percent, forcing them to compensate by doubling the fees they charged uninsured patients.

On April 4, the day my coverage started, I was in Steven Wegley's office with my Polyclinic records in my lap. After taking a history and examining me, he scheduled an urgent upper endoscopy. One week later I awoke from "conscious sedation" to learn that I not only had a diagnosis but one that was fully treatable. The GI specialist had left an eight-by-five-and-a-half card on the bed tray in front of me. On it were six small round snapshots the color of raw meat. The so-called stomach "diverticulum" the Polyclinic diagnosed from my X-ray was actually a large peptic ulcer.

Next to the card was a prescription for omeprazole, a proton-pump inhibitor. These drugs work by blocking the production of stomach acid. Even half asleep, I was ecstatic. The last remaining obstacle to emigrating had been removed. There was nothing to block my escape from a lonely and politically fruitless life.

The pain disappeared within twelve hours of starting medication. Within days I was eating dozens of foods, eggs, corn, oatmeal, apples, and cooked vegetables I hadn't touched in more than five years. The diarrhea didn't improve. In mid-May, Steven performed a colonoscopy and small bowel biopsy, which were normal. I was disappointed not to find a cause for the diarrhea. At the same time I knew no country in the world would grant me a work visa with a debilitating illness, such as Crohn's Disease or Ulcerative Colitis. After about a year of Internet research, I discovered the diarrhea most likely stemmed from an organism called Mycobacterium Avian Paratuberculosis—that is carried by U.S. dairy herds and resists pasteurization. Yet even before Steven mailed me the biopsy results, I figured out on my own that I was totally symptom-free so long as I limited my fiber intake and avoided gluten and dairy products. It was a diet I could follow anywhere in the world.

By early June I was well enough to begin a job search. I compiled a list of vacancies from the New Zealand Ministry of Health website and e-mailed my resume to clinical directors and human resource managers in Auckland, Wellington, and Christchurch. Five mental health centers set up phone interviews. It was my first experience being interviewed via conference call, necessitated by the ten thousand miles that separated me from my potential employers. When I realized both Canterbury and Hutt Valley District Health Board were about to offer me a position, uncertainty set in.

I was awake for seventy-two hours straight as I contemplated the momentous decision that confronted me. There would be no turning back once I gave up private practice. I would be locked into working for someone else—potentially in a job I hated—until I became eligible for Social Security at age sixty-six. I had worked full-time in community mental health centers during the early years of my career, and detested it. The non-physician managers who ran them bullied and fired psychiatrists who refused to accept the misguided and often dangerous cost-saving measures they were hell-bent on enforcing. The main advantage of private practice was having near total control over the care that I offered patients. The only drawback was the financial uncertainty created by the steady decline in my third-party reimbursements.

I held out longer than most of my colleagues because of my willingness to accept Medicare and Medicaid, do my own clerical work, and rent my bedroom out to boarders. However, with Bush slashing Medicare and Medicaid to finance his permanent war on terrorism, I faced another five thousand dollar reduction in income for both 2002 and 2003. If the war in the Middle East didn't end by early 2004 I, too, would face bankruptcy and join dozens of my colleagues in early retirement or a non-medical career.

In my case it also raised the possibility of becoming a full-time activist. Surely this was more consistent with my values than traipsing halfway around the world to maintain the perks of a high-status profession. At the same time, I knew myself too well. A creature of habit, I was skeptical that I had the resilience to cope with such a drastic life change.

As I lay awake waiting for it to get light for the third morning in a row, I told myself it was a simple matter of identifying the reasons I became an activist—and whether they were still important enough to give up medicine. I had no interest whatsoever in politics until I became pregnant with Naomi and suddenly felt incredibly guilty for bringing a child into a totally fucked up world. From then on, the only way I could live with myself was to try to fix it.

Six years later I met Earl, he fell in love with someone else and I fulfilled my unmet needs through a non-sexual relationship based on nonstop political activity. These primitive longings had long since vanished. Yet the drive to participate in community organizing grew more intense than ever as I witnessed the catastrophe that unfolded in Eastern Europe in the 1990s. When the Soviet government collapsed in 1991, there were no independent unions, churches, or neighborhood organizations to distribute food and other essentials. The KGB had destroyed them all. American intelligence, the best-resourced security apparatus in history, was far more efficient than the Soviet secret police in infiltrating and crushing unions, community organizations, and even non-political church groups that showed an excessive interest in human rights.

There were unmistakable warning signs that the U.S. economy, which was deeply in debt and had lost its manufacturing base, was also on the verge of disintegration. Unless activists worked fast to rebuild the civic and community groups that U.S. intelligence had destroyed, Americans, like the Soviets, were doomed to decades of starvation, disease, and brutal poverty.

I was still left with the most obvious question—why become a full-time activist when I had so little to show for my fifteen years as a part-time organizer. And the critical dilemma of how I would support myself if I gave up medicine. My politics were far more radical than those of Citizen Action, Public Citizen, and the other non-profits that hired staff. This meant I could only work for my own political vision until my savings ran out–when I would have no choice but to work for someone else's.

Clearly there were too many unknowns, no matter which direction I took. Desperate to stop the noise in the back of my head, I resorted to my own idiosyncratic form of prayer. I still had no idea who or what I was praying to. However, I was happy to embrace Ruth's concept of a Sky Spirit—an invisible force that connects us to other living beings and to a vast impenetrable Universe.

"Please, if there is someone out there, help me not to make a decision that is willful or greedy, that will hurt other people or make my life worse than it already is."

■

The stabbing stomach pain returned as I listened to daily updates regarding the impending war on Iraq. If this was an answer, it was a disappointment. I had hoped for something more tangible. Yet, in this instance I saw a clear connection between the knots in my stomach and my emotional state. Once again, the government and mainstream media were feeding us outrageous lies. And once again, there wasn't a damned thing I or the growing anti-Iraq war movement could do about it.

The U.N. Security Council and everyone to the left of Dick Cheney, including moderate Republicans like Secretary of State Colin Powell and the President's own father, knew Bush was lying about Saddam Hussein's weapons of mass destruction. Thanks to the Internet, thousands of leftists also knew George W. Bush had stolen the 2000 election and that high-level members of his administration were linked in some way to the terrorist attack on the Twin

Towers. We knew about the forewarnings both the CIA and FBI received of the attacks; the insider trading in American and United Airlines stocks on September 10, 2001; the order for Air Force fighter jets not to intercept the hijacked airliners; and the cozy relationship between Bush senior and the Bin Laden family and between the CIA and Pakistani intelligence, which had wired $100,000 to the lead hijacker in early September 2001.

I also had no choice but to confront the reality that control over public consciousness by U.S. intelligence and the corporate elite was so complete it no longer mattered how many of us knew. Dan Rather, Tom Brokaw, and Robin McNeill told us all we needed to worry about was crime, dark-skinned people, and immigrants. Obligingly, the majority of Americans turned a blind eye to increasing evidence that the U.S. government was complicit in the deliberate slaughter of three thousand of our own citizens.

Without U.N. backing, the impending invasion became a war crime under international law. Suddenly it came to me: the only important decision was whether I wanted to share in the responsibility for Bush's illegal war of aggression. So long as I continued to work in the U.S. and pay taxes, I would be partly responsible. It made no sense to march up and down bemoaning Bush's criminal behavior so long as I contributed to the economy that supported it. I couldn't expect my daughter to take a stand unless I did.

■

The contract I signed with Canterbury District Health Board gave me an October 16 start date. This meant I had exactly seven weeks to refer all my patients and close my practice, sell my house, dispose of my furniture and small appliances, which were useless on New Zealand's 240-voltage electrical grid, and pack and ship everything I couldn't cram into two suitcases. I had no car to get rid of, having totaled my second-hand Saab in January 2000. Given the difficult choice between replacing it and paying Naomi's college tuition, I opted for the latter. I already used my bicycle to commute to work. With a minor adjustment in my routine, it became possible to use it for most errands, as well.

By now I was one of two private psychiatrists in King Country who still accepted Medicare and Medicaid patients. It took me more than three weeks to find new doctors, in our five mental health centers and six community clinics, for the 250 I was responsible for. The other major hurdle was finding someone to ship, or store, my patient files. Washington State law required me to retain medical records for seven years. A local freight-forwarding company wanted $15,000 to send them to Christchurch. I didn't have $15,000 or even an address in New Zealand to ship them to.

Ten days before my departure, I located a Bellevue start-up called Paperless Business Solutions. For $8,000 they agreed to scan my files onto two sets of eight CDs. I kept one set and mailed the other to Tony, who had moved back to Ohio. For a hundred dollars a month, he agreed to process all the records requests I received from former patients, as well as collecting outstanding accounts and paying my business taxes for 2002.

■

I left Seattle with a net worth of $500. Washington state officially entered recession the week I listed my home. In seven weeks I got only two offers, both well below my asking price. The one I accepted was contingent on the buyers selling a home in San Diego. As a result we were still in escrow when I left for Christchurch. On top of the $8,000 I paid Paperless Business Solutions, New Zealand immigration required I buy a round-trip ticket for $2,000 and my insurance company demanded $6,000 for a "tail" to continue my malpractice coverage.

The $600 that I made from a giant yard sale just covered the postage to send my winter clothes, business and tax records, and a dozen rare, out-of-print books to Christchurch via surface mail. I paid Ruth the $250 I got for the mahogany secretary my grandfather made to haul away the computer table, chair, bedding, and cooking utensils I used during my last nine days in Seattle. These items would end up in her backyard, along with the three cars, five washing machines, three barbecues, two couches, and countless small appliances and items of furniture—until the Universe put a worthy African American family in her Path.

To ease my "passage" to a new life, she spent my last night in Seattle in my spare bedroom. While I slept she was awake all but two hours, sifting through my garbage and recycling to ensure I discarded nothing of potential value. I awoke to find five items on the kitchen table she couldn't identify—two moxa sticks left over from my acupuncture treatment, a small vial of Chinese liniment, a screwdriver magnetizer, and a tiny bronze incense holder in the shape of an elephant.

Eleanor Owen, now eighty-one and the newly elected secretary of the newly renamed Health Care for All-Washington, gave me a ride to the airport in return for my office fax machine. It would turn out I left the leadership of the single-payer coalition in far stronger hands than I realized. Health Care for All-Washington continued to grow, though very slowly, after I left. However, along with PNHP and dozens of other state-based single-payer groups, it kept the vision of publicly sponsored health care alive until the economy officially collapsed in 2008. It was an economic crisis of this magnitude that spurred Western Europe to nationalize health care after World War II. It was also the catalyst that returned single-payer health care to the political landscape for the first time since Clinton's election in 1992.

I had paid Aurora Cycles twenty-five dollars to dismantle and box my bicycle. After three minutes of brute shoving, it barely fit, on the diagonal, in the back seat of Eleanor's vintage Cadillac. My bike would be my only transportation until my house sold. We left before

Ruth did. My final recollection of my Seattle home is of my five-foot-three African American friend hoisting my solid oak table on top of my futon, already lashed to the roof of her Honda Civic.

I had no regrets about leaving a house connected with so many painful memories. I received my final hang-up call only five days before my departure. Yet nothing the government did to me—including railroading me into the hospital, the attempts on my life, the break-ins, the incessant phone disruption and prank calls—came close to the agony of nine years of unrelenting abdominal pain and sleep deprivation, nor the heartache of sending my only child four thousand miles away to college.

■

Following 9-11 and enactment of the Patriot Act, I was required to check in at SeaTac airport three hours before my flight to Los Angeles. Under the scrutiny of the national guardsmen armed with machine guns, I waited ninety minutes in a line extending the length of the terminal to have my luggage and door-sized bicycle box X-rayed. Both suitcases and the box failed the X-ray and had to be opened and hand-searched before I could check them through to Auckland.

I waited another twenty minutes to pass through security. This involved walking through a metal detector while more security guards X-rayed my carry-on luggage—a backpack which contained my wallet, lip balm, hand cream, diarrhea and hay fever medication, and the novel I was reading. The flight to Los Angeles International took a little under two hours. It was a twenty-minute walk from the domestic to the international terminal, where I waited in a forty five-minute line to pass through security again.

I was too stunned to react when the Air New Zealand security guard pulled me out of the boarding line for a full-body search. I only burst into tears once she finished and sat me down to put my shoes on for me. I was still crying as she handed back my boarding pass and hurried me down the ramp to the waiting plane.

I had spent the last fifteen years on survival mode. Hunkered down in a virtual state of siege, I was continuously hyper-vigilant for any new assault on myself, my daughter, my patients, or the political groups I belonged to. I hadn't shed a single tear over the ostracism and bleak isolation that I endured after being labeled insane, nor the raw anxiety of providing for a child with no income, nor the grinding guilt and rage I felt over my powerlessness to identify and expose Oscar's and Natalie's murderers. It took this final humiliation, coming when I least expected it, to overwhelm my defenses.

The stewardess helped me find my seat and stow my backpack under the seat in front of me. The feeling of sadness lingered as I found myself reflecting over the circumstances of my patients' murders. Natalie's parents also refused to let me talk to reporters regarding the vicious harassment that preceded their daughter's death. In her case, as in Oscar's, all I could do was look on from the sidelines as her family grieved their enormous loss.

I tried to comfort myself that journalists and historians who were far more prominent than me had failed to expose the truth about extrajudicial murders—of John and Robert Kennedy, Malcolm X, and Martin Luther King—that were high-profile historical events. By now there had to be several thousand academics, researchers, and activists who knew the names of Kennedy's real murderers. The same scholars also knew that Martin Luther King's family won a lawsuit against the U.S. government in 1999, after establishing his real killers worked for the FBI and military intelligence.

Deep down I knew that recorded history would continue to blame these, and all the other major assassinations, on scapegoats like Lee Harvey Oswald and James Earl Ray. Unless the White House and mainstream media made the truth official by acknowledging it. I was skeptical this would ever happen, at least not while the U.S.

government subjugated all foreign and domestic policy to its ambitious agenda of global dominance. Most history books still make no mention of hundred-year-old conspiracies responsible for the murder of presidents Lincoln, McKinley, and Harding.

■

As the giant 747 took off and circled into the blackness of the Pacific, I felt a massive weight lift from my shoulders. In another twelve hours I would begin a new life in a small nation of four million people that had no pretensions about world military or economic domination. There would be no pressure there to champion New Zealand as the healthiest, most democratic, productive, and efficient—or most powerful—country in the world. For as long as I could remember, the only world I knew was overshadowed by an Enemy—first the Soviets, then Muslim terrorists—and by weapons and war. It was hard to imagine living in a culture free of the stranglehold the U.S. military and U.S. intelligence had over our economy, our elected government, and, most importantly, public information.

I no longer had any illusions about escaping the excesses of American consumerist culture. The U.S. public relations industry markets our insidious pseudo-culture to every cash economy on earth, supplanting unique local cultures with an insatiable desire for flashy cars, fast food, and designer sneakers, jeans, hairstyles, and bodies. At the same time, I was well aware of New Zealand's nuclear-free harbors, free public health care, and robust social services. I had every reason to believe New Zealanders could still make some choices based on genuine human values. I lay back in my seat, heady with the rush of wide-open possibility.